Praise for
We: A Manifesto for Women Everywhere

"*We*, which is written in a conversational, almost confiding tone—no pop-psychology babble here—is a fresh, smart look at how women can cut through the bull---- cluttering their lives and focus on the things that are truly important."

—*Entertainment Weekly*

"From longtime friends Jennifer Nadel and Gillian Anderson (yes, Dana Scully) comes a book that's part self-help, part social theory, centered in the idea that instead of having it 'all,' women can live happier, better lives by becoming more free. We all have the power to create change, one woman at a time."

—*Glamour*

"*We: A Manifesto for Women Everywhere* is a bracing, honest, uplifting manual for changing the world by owning your gifts, telling the truth, expressing gratitude, and living with joy. It's for every woman, everywhere on the planet. Open to any page. And there you will find a truth that can set you free. We're all in this together. And *We* is the GPS for the journey."

—Christiane Northrup, MD,
author of *Women's Bodies, Women's Wisdom*

"By focusing on the female experience and combining many well-known personal growth procedures, this guidebook offers a somewhat fresh perspective. Fans of Anderson and Nadel will be drawn to their accounts of striving toward self-actualization."

—*Library Journal*

"Inspiring and provocative, it challenges the annoying concept of women 'having it all,' and instead, using the authors' personal experiences and career trajectories, focuses on maximizing happiness and fulfillment. It's actionable and girl power-y—just the kind of book we need right now."

—PureWow

"Anderson and Nadel present nine principles for a life focused more on you, and less on keeping up with those (metaphorical) Joneses."

—*Coastal Living*

"Warm and easy to use as a reference . . . Readers will find both specific and more holistic advice, essential practices, affirmations, reflections, aphorisms, and mantras. The overall effect is a journey by small steps, which could be inspiring material for discussion groups."

—*Booklist*

GILLIAN ANDERSON

AND

JENNIFER NADEL

A MANIFESTO

FOR

WOMEN EVERYWHERE

ATRIA PAPERBACK

New York   London   Toronto   Sydney   New Delhi

ATRIA
PAPERBACK

An Imprint of Simon & Schuster, Inc.
1230 Avenue of the Americas
New York, NY 10020

First Atria Books Paperback edition March 2018

ATRIA PAPERBACK and colophon are trademarks of Simon & Schuster, Inc.

For information about special discounts for bulk purchases, please contact Simon & Schuster Special Sales at 1-866-506-1949 or business@simonandschuster.com.

The Simon & Schuster Speakers Bureau can bring authors to your live event. For more information or to book an event, contact the Simon & Schuster Speakers Bureau at 1-866-248-3049 or visit our website at www.simonspeakers.com.

Interior design by Amy Trombat

Manufactured in the United States of America

10 9 8 7 6 5 4 3 2 1

Library of Congress Cataloging-in-Publication Data has been applied for.

ISBN 978-1-5011-2627-7
ISBN 978-1-5011-2628-4 (pbk)
ISBN 978-1-5011-2629-1 (ebook)

This is a journey that begins and ends with love, so whatever has called you here, welcome.

AN INVITATION TO YOU

*Tell me, what is it you plan to do with your one wild and
precious life?*

—MARY OLIVER, American poet

At some point in our lives, most of us feel the gentle calling of our
soul. Sometimes it's so quiet we can barely hear it: a soft tapping,
no louder than a leaf falling from a tree.

We may imagine we didn't hear it. Or perhaps it is louder and
takes the form of a persistent ache; a nagging sense that there is
something missing. "Is this it?" we wonder when we wake in the dead
of night or find ourselves caught on the treadmill of our daily grind.

It may be a hint of loneliness that endures even in the company
of friends. Or a sense of injustice and a desire to change things that
feels urgent and necessary, but also hopeless before it even begins.

Perhaps our heart tells us there is a better way of living; that we
need to stop ignoring what really matters—the suffering of others
and our planet's future—but our head insists we're naïve and tells
us to knuckle down and get on with our lives as they are.

For others, the call may take the form of a crisis: a breakup or a
breakdown, a betrayal or a loss. Or perhaps it's addiction, depression, or another serious illness.

However it comes, it is an invitation to take a journey. You may resist. Many of us have resisted it for years, even decades. Ultimately it's your choice. But it will wait for you patiently, tapping daily or every so often in small and big ways to remind you that, in truth, you can't avoid it if you truly want to live a meaningful life.

If you've heard that call, this book is for you. It's for women who want happiness and meaning. It will guide you toward inner peace and provide the power to help transform the world in which we all live.

Contents

Foreword xi

The Journey xiii

Why Now? xv

How *WE* Works xvii

Why We Wrote *WE* xix

WE's Vision xxiii

PART 1
The Essentials 1

ESSENTIAL PRACTICE 1
Gratitude: A Mind-Altering Substance 5

ESSENTIAL PRACTICE 2
Gentleness: Changing the Messages We Give Ourselves 13

ESSENTIAL PRACTICE 3
Responsibility: Taking Care of Ourselves 21

ESSENTIAL PRACTICE 4
Meditation: Creating a Safe Space and
Making Way for the Sacred 39

PART 2
The 9 Principles 49

PRINCIPLE 1
Honesty: Getting Real 55

CONTENTS

PRINCIPLE 2

Acceptance: Making Friends with What Is 83

PRINCIPLE 3

Courage: Ending the Victim Trap 109

PRINCIPLE 4

Trust: Living Without Fear 135

PRINCIPLE 5

Humility: Unmasking Our Ego 157

PRINCIPLE 6

Peace: Ending the Conflict Within 181

PRINCIPLE 7

Love: Transforming Relationships 207

PRINCIPLE 8

Joy: Living Fully 243

PRINCIPLE 9

Kindness: Love in Action 267

PART 3

The Manifesto 293

A World in Need of Love 297

Appendixes 309

Resources 313

Further Reading 333

Endnotes 339

Index 351

FOREWORD

Since the first edition of this book was published the need for a different way to approach all areas of our lives has become even more evident and urgent.

In our own home countries, America and Britain, we've seen intolerance and bigotry endorsed at the ballot box. There has been an increase for many in levels of fear and uncertainty, not just for ourselves and our communities, but also for our world and the future of our planet.

There is another, better way of doing things. The principles and tools in this book lay out a blueprint for positive change—both for us as individuals and for the world that we all share.

Please read, enjoy, and share with other women. Together—joyfully, lovingly, and with compassion—we can make change happen.

THE JOURNEY

Take courage, join hands, stand beside us.

—CHRISTABEL PANKHURST

WE is a journey based on 9 Principles that have been taught by sages and saints throughout the ages. They have the power to transform your life and the world around you.

It isn't a lifestyle choice to be bolted onto our normal *me-centered* way of living; it's a path of radical transformation that puts compassion for the world at its core.

Use this book both as a guide and a source of inspiration. If you're hurting, it will help you heal. If you're lost, it will steer you home. If you're searching for a purpose, it will gently lead you toward fulfillment.

We arrive in this world without an instruction manual, and we grow up without an emotional tool kit. So it's easy to lose our way.

As we go through life, we amass emotional scar tissue from the knocks that we inevitably take. We become like electrical circuit boards that have gotten so clogged up by the sediment of life that we can no longer connect with ourselves and our core beliefs, let alone with the world beyond.

All of us start out in life with a strong internal value system: a sense of what's right and wrong and what's fair and what's unjust. But then life intervenes. In the cold light of reality, our ideals can quickly seem naïve, unrealistic, and untenable. However strong and heartfelt our intentions, it's hard to give effect to our beliefs when we're struggling, stressed, or in emotional pain.

Before long, we've abandoned those values in favor of the rules we're taught by the world. Succeed, compete, and accumulate. Deep down, we feel conflicted, but at the end of the day, we each have to get by, don't we?

A gulf emerges between the values we choose for our personal lives and those we live by in the world at large. In our homes and families, we believe in sharing and making sure everyone's okay. But once we step outside our front door, the rules change. The common good is replaced with the quest for personal success. Within seconds, *we* dissolves into *me*, and we're elbowing one another out of the way in the race to the finish line. Except, of course, there isn't one: just a horizon that moves farther away the closer we get.

The 9 Principles in this book have the power to heal our wounds and return us to our center. As you learn to apply them to your life one by one, you will be taken on a journey from *me* to *WE*. Loneliness will evaporate. You will discover a sense of purpose, and you will be freed—freed to live a life that is authentic, happy, and meaningful.

WHY NOW?

Politics hates a vacuum. If it isn't filled with hope someone will fill it with fear.

—NAOMI KLEIN

Our current way of doing things—the "me culture"—isn't working. And around the world there is hunger for change.

The world we all share is more divided and unequal than ever.

Rates of anxiety, depression, and self-harm among women are skyrocketing. And the hard-fought rights that we, as women, thought we'd already won are once again under renewed attack.

More than seven hundred million women live in hunger, and yet those with plenty battle obesity and depression.

Every minute, one woman dies needlessly in childbirth, while elsewhere in the world another woman spends thousands on cosmetic surgery because she isn't able to feel comfortable with how she's aging.

Violence against women is rising, yet at the same time, refuge services—especially for black and minority ethnic women—are being cut.[1]

The gap between rich and poor is widening, causing social

division and ill health,[2] but instead of investment and redistribution, we have cuts and austerity.

Large swaths of humanity are threatened by climate change, yet our governments fear tackling it lest they offend big business and consumers.

The list goes on and on, and every one of us knows that it's crazy and it's wrong.

Yet instead of joining together, we often find ourselves isolated and in competition. Trying to put a positive gloss on our lives to disguise the huge gap between how things look externally and how they feel inside. Not able to lift our eyes to the horizon and deal with the bigger issues because we each already have so much on our plate.

There is a different way of doing things. One that combines our own emotional and spiritual healing with active engagement with the world around us.

Our current political systems have failed us, but it's not possible to heal the divisions in our world without also healing the wounds which drive them. We can't heal our broken system by sitting in judgment. Within each of us lies the seeds of intolerance and hate. If we simply declare others wrong and ourselves right, we deepen the divide. But to remain silent is also not an option—it leaves us complicit.

WE is a movement for change; a manifesto for a female-led revolution: a quiet, peaceful about-face that doesn't require the consent of those in power. It just asks each of us, one woman at a time, to be the change and take the journey from *me* to *WE*.

HOW *WE* WORKS

*We must not wish for the disappearance of our troubles but for
the grace to transform them.*

—SIMONE WEIL (1909–1943), French philosopher and political activist

WE combines spirituality, politics, and psychology. We're often
taught to compartmentalize them, but they are intimately
connected.

Unless we work across all three disciplines, it's impossible to
achieve lasting, sustainable change. It's not possible to get happy
without getting kind, we can't be spiritually fulfilled without roll-
ing up our sleeves and helping others, and we can't help others
without healing ourselves.

This is not a self-help book to enable you to get more out of life
or a spiritual text to encourage you to float above your difficulties.
Nor is it a lecture on how to try harder! It is an intensely practical
guide to healing and activism from the heart.

Each of the 9 Principles in this book can be applied to your
own life and to the world at large. Their impact is cumulative. Once
you've completed the process, you'll have a set of tools that will
enable you to handle whatever life throws your way.

Most importantly, underpinning all *WE*'s Principles is an ancient rule that can be found in almost every ethical, spiritual, and religious tradition: the Golden Rule. (See page 225.)

At its simplest, the Golden Rule states that we should treat others as we would like to be treated ourselves—in other words, with love. It is a simple rule that has the power to change everything.

Our goal in taking this journey isn't individual happiness—though that comes as a welcome by-product. It is to live in a way that is true to our inner calling. A way that is kind and just. That leads to personal fulfillment and helps other women across the planet.

WHY WE WROTE *WE*

History has shown us that courage can be contagious and hope can take on a life of its own.

—MICHELLE OBAMA

This book doesn't come from lofty heights. It comes from two friends who have stumbled along together, trying, failing, crying, laughing, learning, and trying again.

It is about a set of principles that led us out of darkness, from a place where both of us were in despair, and into a way of life that has meaning and purpose.

We discovered the hard way that no amount of external success could fix how we felt on the inside. The more we had, the more we felt we needed to get. No matter what we achieved, it didn't make us happy. It made us feel guilty that even with the gifts and luck we'd been given, we couldn't seem to make life work.

In the end, we'd both become dependent on a whole host of unhealthy crutches: alcohol, drugs, work, food, abusive relationships—you name it, we tried it. And at the same time, we underwent therapy, did yoga, and tried to puzzle life out.

Our crises were severe enough that we had no option but to change. To start a process of complete rebuilding. Root and branch.

We're passionate about the 9 Principles in this book because they've transformed our lives. That doesn't mean we're happy all the time, or that we handle every situation perfectly, or that we're saints. Far from it—we are, like every one of us, perfectly imperfect. But when we're willing to use them, *WE*'s Principles give us access to a peace of mind and inner freedom that we'd never even dreamed was possible.

We aren't doctors or therapists or priests. Our principal qualification is that we handle emotional pain so badly that we've been forced to look for answers. For over twenty years, we've each searched for what works. The wisdom in this book isn't ours; it's distilled from a myriad of teachers far wiser. We are passing it on with gratitude and in the hope that others might gain comfort and meaning from it.

When both of us started walking this path about twenty years ago, we were cynical and resistant. But now, from our own experience, we know that transformation and happiness are possible and that miracles do actually happen. Hopefully you haven't hit as bleak a patch as we both did, but wherever your starting point, if you follow this path, you will experience profound changes.

I came to the journey that is contained in this book when I was a single mother of two boys working my dream job. I was a network news correspondent who got to tell the world about the issues I cared deeply about. Then one morning I woke up and realized I couldn't go on. I called the news desk and said I was very sorry, but I couldn't come in—not that day and, as it turned out, not ever. Unsurprisingly, my life fell apart. I was diagnosed with severe depression and burnout. Thus began the journey I'd been avoiding for the previous thirty-five years: the journey to meet myself and to find a way of life that corresponded to who I really was at my deepest level. I sought help and wisdom from numerous teachers, support groups, and professionals. I met friends who were seekers also, like Gillian. Today I am the same person, but I am so much happier. I have meaning, I have connection, I have people that I truly love in my life. Of course, I still hit patches of pain and difficulty, but I wake up each day excited to be alive.

The journey that these 9 Principles map out doesn't ever end. But it contains truth. Truth that I know from my own life has the power to guide us away from doubt, depression, and self-hatred, and for which I'm infinitely grateful.

—*JN*

I think I started searching for some kind of deeper meaning to my life when I was in high school, but I don't feel like I properly put solutions into practice until I was in college. By then, I had turned to so many outside sources for comfort to deal with my fear and uncertainty—my sense of loneliness, confusion, and feeling misunderstood about the world and my place in it—that when I started practicing some of these Principles, the effect was dramatic and life changing. I suddenly felt a sense of stability and grounding, personal power and purpose. And I am absolutely certain that had I not established that foundation when I then achieved what turned into international career success, I simply would not have been able to deal with it. That's not to say I haven't struggled or handled things appallingly or turned toward unhealthy ways of coping for long stretches, but what I learned in those initial years were tools for how to handle life's hardships better. And on a daily basis, I get to choose how my life plays out. How do I deal with this rejection, this grief, this fear? With these practices in my pocket, it's my choice.

—GA

You don't have to take our word for it. Treat this journey as if it were a scientific experiment. See what happens if you practice the Principles as they are laid out. If, at the end of this book, you don't feel better, you can always have your old life back.

The 9 Principles in this book work.

Change is possible.

There is no need to feel panic or overwhelmed. Nothing is asked of you now, other than that you read *WE* and give the Principles a try. This is not another thing to add to your to-do list. It is a gateway to an inner freedom and a peace of mind that you may not have known was possible.

You have nothing to lose but your unhappiness, and the world has everything to gain.

WE'S VISION

Like life, peace begins with women. We are the first to forge lines of alliance and collaboration across conflict divides.

—ZAINAB SALBI, Iraqi-born women's rights activist and author

Imagine a sisterhood—across all creeds and cultures—with an unspoken agreement that we, as women, will support and encourage one another. That we won't seek to take advantage of another's weakness, or sit in judgement of another's shortcomings. That we will remember we don't know what struggles each of us may be facing elsewhere in our lives, and so we'll assume that each of us is doing her best. That we will do the work to heal ourselves so that together we can create a more compassionate world.

PART 1

The Essentials

You change the world by changing yourself.

—YOKO ONO, artist, musician, peace activist

𝒴ou are at the start of a miraculous journey. The 9 Principles within these pages will change your life.

As with any expedition, before you set out, you need to prepare. The Essentials in this section are vital for your well-being and will ensure that you get the most out of *WE*'s Principles.

On this journey, you'll be engaged in emotional archaeology: digging down beneath layers of hurt and protection and confronting deep emotional truths in order to reconnect with your true self. You'll be dismantling the parts of yourself that no longer serve you and transforming your relationship with yourself and the world around you.

These Essential Practices will hold you steady as you do the work. The extraordinary thing about them is that they do far more than just provide you with support for the journey ahead. Each one is also a powerful agent for change in its own right.

Like the Principles that follow, these practices are a distillation of what works within innumerable traditions. When they're used together, you'll find that an alchemy takes place, producing astonishing changes. In fact, if all you feel ready to do right now is introduce these four healthy habits into your life, you will be amazed by the miracles that start to flow immediately.

Taking care of yourself emotionally, physically, and spiritually is a profoundly political act. As women, many of us have been conditioned to be caretakers and to measure our worth by how much we do for others. But when we sublimate our own needs, we risk ending up dependent on others and too vulnerable on many levels.

Martyrdom is for saints. Real women have needs, and real giving comes from a place of plenty, not a place of lack. Self-denial only sets us up for failure.

Self-care is even more crucial if you have children. When we harm ourselves or suppress our needs, we model that neglect and abuse are acceptable. If we want our daughters to think of themselves as worthy, we need to model self-worth. Similarly, if we want our sons to see women as strong, independent beings, we need to show them that is what we are.

Use the following four Essential Practices on a daily basis. They are the foundations for your new life and indispensable for the journey to come.

You'll be amazed at how great you feel when you start giving yourself the care you've longed for from others.

WE's Exercises

This is an experiential process. Each chapter contains exercises that will integrate what your mind is learning with what your heart already knows. These exercises are not optional extras; they are essential to the journey you are on, so please don't skip them. Knowing is not enough: you need to experience the Principles for them to achieve their full transformative power.

The more diligent you are in completing the exercises, the greater the results. It is better to do them hastily than not do them at all, so don't let perfectionism creep in. You'll find exercises throughout this book. They're designed to maximize the impact of the Principles. From time to time, you'll need to write things down, so a notebook or journal will be useful. You may also want to ensure that you have a quiet place where you can work on them without being disturbed. This is a sacred process that deserves a sacred space.

You can return to any of the exercises and repeat it once you have finished working through the Principles. Use them if you hit a bump in the path, or if you're feeling stuck. Each exercise works on an emotional, intellectual, and spiritual level, so take advantage of them. You will get out of this journey what you put in.

Center yourself before each exercise. Start by taking five deep breaths, in and out, allowing your outbreath to last a beat longer than your inbreath to calm your nervous system. If you have the time and space, light a candle to signify the sacred nature of the work you're undertaking. You're doing it for you and for many. Try not to sit on the sidelines, figuring out how to understand the journey by intellectualizing it—take the plunge, dive in, and experience it!

WE's Affirmations

At the end of each chapter you will also find affirmations. These are antidotes to the toxic messages we give ourselves on a daily basis. Use them to ward off negativity, as you would use a medicine to prevent infection. Repeat them to yourself as you go through the day, knowing that each time you say them, you are gradually moving away from self-harm and toward self-care and self-love.

Essential Practice 1

GRATITUDE:
A Mind-Altering Substance

When we focus on our gratitude, the tide of disappointment goes out and the tide of love rushes in.

—KRISTIN ARMSTRONG, Olympic gold medal cyclist

Gratitude has the power to transform everything: our perceptions, our experiences, and our state of mind.

A lot of us come to this journey with a mountain of disappointments and hurts. Feeling grateful may be the last thing you want when you're unhappy, when you're disappointed about all the things you haven't got, and all the things that have gone wrong. But however low, angry, or despondent you feel, you will start to experience the benefits of gratitude as soon as you allow this tool into your life.

A warning: like many of *WE*'s tools, "gratitude" may sound simple—way too simple and perhaps not quite complex enough for our sophisticated female brains. Don't be deceived. Remember those connect-the-dot books you had when you were little, where you joined numbered dots together, and a picture emerged? This is what we do every day of our lives: we link events and assign them meaning so that we can interpret the world.

The problem is that very often we connect the wrong dots. As we go through life, many of us notice all the things that seem to go wrong rather than the things that are going right. We focus on the times we haven't gotten what we wanted, when life has disappointed us, when we may have been ignored or slighted in some way. Like fortune-tellers, who are capable of foretelling only negative conclusions, we examine the tea leaves of our life and decide that life is unfair, that we're just not destined to be happy, that we don't have the good luck others seem to enjoy.

Not surprisingly, if you join up these dots, you end up with a depressing picture.

But stop right there. From this moment forward, you are going to try a different approach.

I don't have to chase extraordinary moments to find happiness— it's right in front of me if I'm paying attention and practicing gratitude.

—BRENÉ BROWN, researcher into emotions and personality traits such as vulnerability, courage, shame, and authenticity

Exercise: Daily Miracles

This exercise will begin a mind-altering process by showing you how to incorporate the practice of gratitude into your daily life. Make yourself comfortable and close your eyes. Breathe in and out five times, as described on page 4, until you feel centered and settled.

Take up your journal and write down ten things in your life right now that you're grateful for. They can be as small or as big as you like. Notice if your mind leaps in and lodges an objection. It may claim that it can't find anything at all to be thankful for, or it may want to remind you of all the disappointments, trials, and losses you are experiencing. Like a miner panning for gold, try to pick your way through the silt and mud that your mind kicks up and find the treasure that rests in its midst. Keep looking until you find something—anything at all—that you can be grateful for. Perhaps it's that you've got a roof over your head, or you have eyes to see your children with. Or perhaps it's that you started your day with a warm cup of tea and have something to eat in your cupboard. The items on your list don't need to be any more complicated than that. In fact, the most basic things are often the most powerful. Imagine what life would be like if you didn't have them.

Your list might also include some of the simple daily events that we so often overlook because we take them for granted—yet if they were to disappear suddenly, we'd be lost.

Keep writing until you've got ten. If you've got more than ten, that's great, too—you can keep writing until the flow stops naturally. Now read it back to yourself. Or, for maximum effect, read it aloud and say, "Thank you for . . ." each item on the list. It will likely feel awkward at the beginning, but the more often you do it, the easier it will get.

Gratitude lists will become a staple of your new life. We suggest writing a list daily while working through the remaining chapters. After that, it's up to you, but it's very possible that you won't want to stop.

What you'll discover is that as you list the many little things for which you're grateful, the picture you have of your life starts to change. Behind the gloom, a more positive image starts to emerge. One that is tender and full of wonder. One that existed the whole time, just beneath the surface. We're not deceiving ourselves; we're simply connecting a different set of dots.

Gratitude unlocks the fullness of life. It can turn a meal into a feast, a house into a home, a stranger into a friend.
—MELODY BEATTIE, author of *Codependent No More* and other self-help bestsellers

Gratitude is infectious. It creates its own virtuous circle. The more grateful you feel, the more you'll have to be grateful for. Knowing that you'll need to come up with a list of positive experiences each day means you'll start to become more aware of them. When you're on the lookout, miraculously they start to appear far more often.

It is as if your mind is a magnifying glass expanding whatever you choose to focus on. Suddenly you become aware of sources of gratitude that you've never noticed before. A fellow train passenger's smile; the friend who's agreed to mind your child for an hour to give you a much-needed break; the first shoots of spring pushing their way through the cold earth; the warmth of the bathwater we sink into at the end of a tiring day.

"Thank you" is the best prayer that anyone could say. I say that one a lot. Thank you expresses extreme gratitude, humility, understanding.
—ALICE WALKER, writer and activist

As the picture you paint of your life starts to change each day, miraculously so too does how you feel about life. The situations you find yourself in somehow no longer seem so bad. There is some good in almost everything you discover.

And before long, other people start to notice the difference in you, and in turn you'll find that they are warmer and friendlier to you. This is the magic multiplier effect.

When you practice gratitude, you exercise a spiritual muscle. Have you ever wondered why some people seem to be cheerful no matter what is happening around them? It's because of their attitude. Everything that you add to your list and every thank-you that you say silently or aloud changes your attitude. It has a profound impact on your mind-set and, consequently, on your life and the people in it.

Gratitude can also be used as a shield to ward off negativity— either your own or other people's. As you become more positive, those around you, whether they are colleagues, friends, or family, may become confused. They may be so used to you despairing or complaining about your lot that they don't know how to react to your new, more positive outlook. They may invite you to pick up your list of woes again. Try your very best to resist. Whatever you focus on grows, so keep your focus firmly on the good in your day.

Like any exercise, the more you practice, the easier it gets. Before long, you'll wonder how you ever managed without it.

TIP: *Keep a small notebook or space in your journal for your gratitude list. Experiment with what time of day you write it. Use it as a spiritual remedy to either kick-start your day or get a restful night's sleep. And you can always refer to it halfway through your day if you need an instant hit of positivity.*

I was very depressed when I first started this practice. I did it to people-please—someone had told me to—not because I thought it would work. To my cynical intellect, it seemed trite and insincere. For the first few days, I struggled to find anything I felt grateful for. But somehow each day it got easier, and now my list is so full of wonderful things that if I do it too late at night, it can keep me awake through excitement. The more good I see in my life, the more good seems to come.

—JN

I know it seems absolutely ludicrous with everything that I have that is good in my life, but I have a habit of complaining. I can't believe I'm admitting that, but it's true. I go through stages where I forbid myself to complain. The minute a negative thought is about to leave my lips, I force myself to say the opposite. "Thank you for getting me here safely," as opposed to "Oh my God, the traffic!" The difference it makes in my life is huge. And yet before long, there I am again finding ways to complain through humor or storytelling. Obviously, sometimes this has got to be okay—to find humor in the ridiculous—but I have to stay vigilant to make sure that it isn't just another excuse to talk about what's wrong as opposed to what's right in my life. The more I keep up my gratitude lists, the less likely I am to complain in a day; it's as simple as that.

—GA

Reflection

Joy is what happens to us when we allow ourselves to recognize how good things really are.

—MARIANNE WILLIAMSON, spiritual teacher-lecturer
and author of *A Return to Love*, among other books

It takes only a miniscule turn of the steering wheel to change the direction of an ocean liner. When I'm off-kilter or worrying about what I haven't got, I use gratitude to redirect myself. It usually takes only a moment of pausing and thinking of something we have to be thankful for to get back on track. Whatever we focus on grows, so we make sure that we keep our gaze on what is good so that I can open myself up to joy.

Action. Today I will notice all the nice things that happen, and I will say thank you.

Affirmation. I am lucky, and I am blessed. My life is full of wonder.

Essential
Practice
2

GENTLENESS:
Changing the Messages
We Give Ourselves

Peace begins with a smile.

—MOTHER TERESA (1909–1997), nun, missionary,
and canonized Saint Teresa of Calcutta

Imagine if every morning you woke up with a radio station blaring full volume inside your head. It would drive you crazy. In fact, that very tactic is used to torture prisoners into submission. And yet that is exactly how we all live: with voices inside our heads telling us crazy, negative, self-defeating messages.

Take a moment to think of some of the thoughts you may subject yourself to on a daily basis, without even realizing you're doing it. We all have our own individual ones, but here are a few favorites: "I don't fit in." "I'm too fat." "I'll never meet anyone." "I'm going to end up broke and alone." "I'm a failure." "I'll never get anywhere." "It's not fair." "She doesn't like me." "He's going to leave me."

Get the picture? Your voices may be slightly different, but they all come from the same place: a place of fear. Fear that there is not enough, that we are not enough, that anything good we may have will be lost, that things are ultimately not going to be okay.

It's as if each of us has an internal propaganda machine generating messages of fear and inadequacy, so that even when things are going well, the machine is at work warning us that it will never last or things will never be this good again.

We have been taught to believe that negative equals realistic and positive equals unrealistic.
—SUSAN JEFFERS (1938–2012), psychologist and author

To compound and complicate things, many of us have come to believe that the messages being broadcast by our negativity transmitter are in fact helpful. We tell ourselves that they protect us from disappointment and loss by ensuring that we are realistic. We mistakenly believe these messages are our friends—that they stop us from getting carried away and having dreams that will never be realized; that they keep us firmly on the ground.

In fact, the opposite is true. And there's a much better source from which to generate the messages we give ourselves: *love*. That may sound a little hippy-dippy, but think about it: Would you talk to your best friend or someone else you love—a child or a partner—the same way that you talk to yourself? You may be quite comfortable telling yourself that you're useless or stupid or a failure, but you probably wouldn't say it to someone you really cared about.

You cannot have a positive life and a negative mind.
—JOYCE MEYER, Charismatic Christian minister and author

14

Every time you say something cruel or unkind to yourself, you are wounding yourself, whether you are aware of it or not. Think how you feel when you receive a compliment. It's not always easy to let in positive messages, but think how good you feel when you do. Remember that burst of confidence. Now compare that with how you feel when you're criticized.

Just as you can't expect to lose weight if you live on a diet of fast food and sugar, you can't expect to live a peaceful and happy life if you're living on the mental equivalent of an unhealthy diet.

What's more, we often unwittingly pass on these internal messages to others—particularly our children (if we have any). So the abuse we give ourselves gets handed down through the generations—unless we make a conscious decision to intervene.

I love my children more than anything in the world. They are the most important part of my life, and when I'm with them, I am happiest—and yet I find parenting hard. I do my very best to carve out as much time as possible to be present and active with them, but I'm not entirely sure that my nerves are built for the noise, the intensity, and the constant requirements to be selfless and to remain calm. It takes everything in me not to nag them to quiet down and stop everything childish, which would obviously be devastating for their childhoods!

I see other mothers who seem to find it less of a struggle. Perhaps they have grown up in bigger families or have tougher nerve endings. I have worked extremely hard to practice patience and to pause when necessary before reacting, but, on the other hand, I also have to remember to forgive myself. So, for instance, even when I do the "right thing" and get down on the floor to play Legos, my kids can sense that it's not the easiest thing for me. I will do it, and I will stay there and engage, but somehow it's a struggle, even if I'm pretending it's not, and consequently they can tell. But it has taken me years and years not to feel guilty, to accept that I have limitations in that area, and that I really am doing the best that I can. When I accept and forgive my own weaknesses, then I can be lighter in the moment because I'm not trying too hard to be perfect, and in the end, my kids benefit too.

—*GA*

There is growing scientific evidence to suggest that negative attitudes can distort our experience of reality. Just as the placebo effect has been shown to produce improvements in patients' health, there's now evidence of a *nocebo* effect: patients who were told they would experience negative side effects from a treatment may experience them even if they were given nothing more than a sugar pill. An analysis of several patient studies found that when people were told that they would experience negative side effects from the powerful chemotherapy drugs, four in five complained of nausea and hair loss—even though in reality they'd been infused not with anticancer agents but with a harmless saline solution.[1]

It is often what we believe about a situation, rather than the truth, that influences our responses.

Exercise: A New Script

This exercise is to help you start reprogramming the propaganda machine in your head.

Pick one of the negative messages that you tell yourself. Write it down so you can see it for what it is: mean, unkind, negative, unhelpful. The problem is, your brain usually doesn't see it that way. Your brain thinks it is *protecting* you by conveying that message. So, one step at a time, you are going to have to retrain your brain. Later on, we'll work with specific tailor-made affirmations (see Exercise 1, "What's Your Story?," page 111), but for now, let's use a message as an antidote that fits almost every situation.

Underneath the sentence you have written, write this: "My name is [_____]. I am a good and kind person. I do not need to please everyone. I do enough. I am enough."[2]

Now cross out your original sentence, and then say out loud the new message you have given yourself. Every time you notice a negative thought coming into your head, repeat your new message until the negative thought has gone.

Each morning and each evening for the next fourteen days, when you brush your teeth, look in the mirror and say your message out loud to yourself three times. Look yourself in the eyes and say it tenderly, as you would to someone you care about. Are you cringing? If so, that's good: it means you're hitting a live nerve. Morning and night, eyeball to eyeball in the mirror, three times. Try it. You've nothing to lose but a bit of pride, and everything to gain!

How will you ever know whether there's a better way unless you try?

....

This technique for reprogramming our internal message machine can feel incredibly awkward when we begin. "What if someone hears me talking to myself?" It's ironic that so many of us have no problem with bombarding ourselves with negative messages but then feel embarrassed by the prospect of giving ourselves kind, positive, and encouraging ones.

You'll be amazed at how changing the way you talk to yourself will make a difference in your life. For a start, you'll begin to enjoy your own company more. After all, who wants to spend time alone with someone who's going to be mean or moan all the time? But more importantly, it starts to change how you actually feel about yourself. Having positive thoughts coursing through your mind can't help but lift your spirits—and your attitude.

And then, of course, the magic multiplying effect of this exercise starts to kick in. As you feel better about yourself, your perception of the world around you starts to shift, and your relationships start to improve miraculously. And this is just the beginning of the process. Please don't take our word for this: try it out for yourself. The changes may be almost imperceptible at first, but they will accumulate. So much more good is yet to come.

TIP: *Write your message on a Post-it note and, if you feel comfortable to, stick it on your bathroom mirror. Otherwise keep it somewhere you'll see it often to remind yourself that you are in the process of learning a vital, life-transforming new habit.*

I've found a great benefit in creating an internal intolerance toward self-criticism. Granted, it isn't foolproof and is a work in progress, but it works more often than not. The second a negative thought even reaches the periphery of my mind, I try to banish it—kind of like Dr. Evil's "Shhh" in the Austin Powers movies—humor really helps! If I were to let the thought develop, it might look like: "If only I looked like so-and-so" or "If only I was right for that job, but I'm not, so I'm just not going to try." It doesn't matter how big or small the thought: I let it go before it gets beyond "if." For me, just the act of refusing to let a negative thought into my consciousness is liberating.

I spent years doing the opposite and letting the negativity sit there and grow until it led to further self-deprecating thoughts and inaction. Suddenly I'd find that it was twenty minutes later, and I'd forgotten to wish my colleague happy birthday, follow up on something important, or sign up for a class or activity that would have been enjoyable or even life changing, because of self-obsessing and essentially self-harming.

—GA

One day my teenage son, who had exams fast approaching, came to me and said he felt ill. "Push through it," I told him. "Just get one more hour in." His face fell as he dragged himself back to his desk, and as he went, I realized I was passing on exactly the lesson I'd learned in childhood: "Don't stop, ever. Even if you're ill, you've got to keep working or you won't amount to anything."

I'd carried that same message into my working life as a journalist, and it had eventually resulted in my burning out. And yet here I was all those years later—despite having worked on myself—passing on exactly the same harmful message to my son.

I boiled the kettle, made him a mug of honey and hot lemon, and insisted he close his books and lie down on the sofa and relax instead. The relief and gratitude that swept across his poor, tired face reminded me that knowing how to be kind to himself would carry him further in life than any uplift in his grades that the extra hour's study might have given him.

—JN

Reflection

*Imagine how much happier we would be, how much freer to be
our true individual selves, if we didn't have the weight of gender
expectations.*

—CHIMAMANDA NGOZI ADICHIE, Nigerian writer

If I don't take care of myself, I can start thinking I am only my job
or someone's wife or mother. Or I can think I am my body weight,
my looks, or my brain. Before long, I'm telling myself I'm fat or
lazy or dumb or hopeless.

And then I remember the truth: that who I am is not dependent
on any things I own, have, or do. That I exist beneath and beyond the
facts of my life—that I'm a spiritual being on a human quest.

Action. Today I will be kind to myself.

Affirmation. This is who I am, and I feel glad to be me.

Essential
Practice
3

RESPONSIBILITY:
Taking Care of Ourselves

*When I was around eighteen, I looked in the mirror and said,
"You're either going to love yourself or hate yourself." And I
decided to love myself. That changed a lot of things.*

—QUEEN LATIFAH, rapper, actress, talk-show host

As women, we often find it far easier to give love than to receive it. Culturally, we're encouraged to be selfless, putting others' needs before our own. It can feel more comfortable to love our friends, partners, and children than ourselves. Being kind to yourself can even feel indulgent, greedy, and selfish. But it isn't. It's vital.

Our bodies need love just as much as our hearts and minds—and if they don't get it, they often start filling the deficit by looking for it elsewhere. Perhaps in a partner who's not good for us, in endless box sets, or tubs of Häagen-Dazs. Or maybe it'll play out at work, where we crave a disproportionate amount of recognition, or online, as we develop a low-level shopping addiction.

Ignoring our needs can become habitual. Sometimes we don't even realize we're doing it, and we may not even see it as a problem. Maybe we're comfortable living small—or, at least, we tell ourselves we are. We may give ourselves just enough to get by so there are no crises, but we never actually reach our full potential.

Some of us shove our wants and needs down deep inside so that we can be *nice*. Or maybe we call it being *realistic*. If we don't "want," we can't be disappointed when we don't "get," our subconscious reasoning goes. But our needs are still there, gnawing away at us from beneath layers of self-protection. The problem is, we risk sabotaging the good that awaits us if we don't attend to them.

Exercise: Befriend Yourself

This exercise will help you identify the things you may be missing in life.

Have your journal handy. Then take five breaths in and out to center yourself. Now imagine that a close female friend—someone you really love—is having a tough time. You invite her to stay over for a few days, and to prepare for her arrival, you make a list of things you could do to make her feel loved and cared for. Perhaps you'll run her a hot bubble bath at the end of each day to help her unwind. Maybe you'll take her to a movie, or walk through the park to your favorite coffee shop. Or perhaps you'll download a comedy that you know will make her laugh or create a special playlist for her to listen to.

Make your own list—put at least ten things on it. Notice what happens to your energy as you write each item. Let yourself imagine how happy and cared for she'll feel. Now circle the three things that you think would be most fun and uplifting for her to do.

Okay, here's your assignment: do those three things for *yourself*. Take out your diary and schedule them in. Notice any resistance—in particular the voice that tells you, "This is silly" or "You're too busy/tired/broke." From now on, you're going to cherish yourself as you would someone you love deeply. If you've got time to do more than three, then go for it. And don't forget to enjoy yourself—this exercise is about allowing yourself to have fun.

....

The list you've just made is a great resource. You can turn to it when the going gets tough. Add to it whenever you think of something else you'd enjoy, and use it whenever you feel needy or depleted. As a rule of thumb, schedule a minimum of one fun or nurturing experience every week. More if you're able.

As you do the work laid out in this book, one of your aims will be to treat yourself as if you were your own best friend. If you find yourself about to do something that might cause you harm, ask, "Would I do this to someone I love?" If you find you're berating yourself for a mistake, ask, "Would I talk like this to someone I loved?" If you find your "comfort" through eating or by spending money you haven't got, ask yourself, "Would I want someone I loved to do that to herself?" It takes time to establish new behaviors, but do your very best to be aware of and interrupt any negative habitual responses as often as you can.

Don't blame or shame yourself. Have compassion and use your list to come up with kinder ways of comforting yourself. Some may find this harder than others; some may even find it excruciating.

But it's really important that the love starts with you, and that you start embracing all aspects of yourself from here on out to the best of your ability. It may seem like a mountain to climb today, but we're all in this together, and there will be hundreds if not thousands of women on the same path to extend a helping hand.

Precious Vessels

Caring for myself is not self-indulgence, it is self-preservation, and that is an act of political warfare.

—AUDRE LORDE (1934–1992), writer and feminist

Our bodies house all that is vital to our existence, yet we judge them and abuse them, and allow others to as well. Eating disorders and rates of self-harm among women continue to escalate, and even those of us who stop short of obviously harmful behaviors often struggle with how we see ourselves.

Billions of dollars are spent each year trying to convince us that our lives would be better if we changed the way we looked. We may think of ourselves as independent-minded feminists, but, on average, we spend more time and money on trying to look good than ever before. Even the women's magazines that profess to elevate our independence and confidence frequently encourage us to compare and improve our bodies, boosting sales by stoking our fear that we're not good enough as we are.

It's not surprising that so many of us struggle with how we see ourselves and, by extension, how we treat ourselves.

Criticizing our physical form can also be a way of avoiding our real feelings. It can be easier to hate our bodies than to admit we're feeling sad or lonely or let down. Plus, if we can blame our body for our situation, we have an element of control—and a scapegoat. Our subconscious thinking goes, "My body is to blame. And there's something I can do about it: I can starve it or overexercise it or ignore it."

How we treat our bodies is an indicator of our emotional and spiritual state. If we're not comfortable in our own skin, it means we have internal work to do and emotional wounds to heal. Our ultimate goal is to inhabit our bodies and selves with ease, joy, and grace.

As a result of walking this path, we will come to see our bodies as unique and precious vessels rather than objects to criticize and compare. But for the Principles to work their magic, you first need to get some basics in place.

Think of what happens to a toddler who doesn't get enough food or sleep: tantrums. We may be older and more sophisticated, but our bodies have the same needs, and our emotions will be affected if those needs are not met.

It can be humbling to discover that quite often when our emotions are out of control it's not because of the complexity of the issues we're facing but because we've been ignoring a simple physical need, such as keeping our blood sugar level steady.

TIP: **HALT** *is an acronym for:*
Hungry
Angry
Lonely
Tired
Used widely in twelve-step fellowships, these are free groups set up to help people in addiction or affected by it. (See page 46.)

Whenever we're hungry, angry, lonely, or tired, we're in danger of our emotions getting out of control and tipping us off balance. So if you notice yourself feeling one or more of those four, HALT and attend to it, fast.

The Four Essentials to Self-Care

There are four essential areas that we often neglect or let slide when it comes to our physical well-being. If you want to get the benefit from all that *WE*'s Principles have to offer, commit to taking care of yourself in each of them in turn.

Food

It's only human to want to be desired, and so most of us at some point cave in to the toxic messages of the beauty and diet industries and play with our intake of food. The extent to which we do this will depend upon our self-esteem, our conditioning, and how addictive our personality is.

If you find it difficult to regulate your food intake, or if your weight tends to yo-yo, fuelling self-hatred, we recommend following an eating plan for the duration of this work.

Structure and boundaries around what we consume free us up to think about more important things and keep us from exacerbating the natural highs and lows of our emotional and hormonal circuits.

There's nothing faddish about it; it's boringly sensible, which is why it works. Three moderate-sized meals a day, eaten at regular intervals (between four to six hours apart), with one snack either midafternoon or before bed. If you're not sure what moderate means, ask someone else to serve your portion, and make sure it contains protein, which sustains your energy and doesn't give you the ups and downs that sugary foods and high-carbohydrate foods do.

Watch for resistance in the form of "But I'm not hungry," "I'm just not a breakfast person," or "One more muffin won't make a difference." Try your best to ignore those voices. Many of us have trained our bodies not to need or want what is actually healthy or to want much more than what is healthy. Try following this simple plan and you'll be amazed by the results.

If you're prone to binge eating, avoid foods that trigger cravings. For some, that will mean foods full of sugar or white flour; others have problems with dairy. All of us benefit—if our budgets allow—from cutting out processed foods that are laden with hidden sugars and additives. If your body-fat ratio is above or below the average range, you may need more concentrated help. Remember, your own assessment may be distorted. For more information on healthy body weight go to, https://www.cdc.gov/healthyweight/assessing/bmi/index.html.

When I went into treatment for depression, and health professionals told me to eat three meals a day, I thought they were trying to make me fat. I'd spent so many years avoiding breakfast to try to shrink my stomach for the rest of the day that I thought the act of consuming a bowl of oatmeal each morning would add another fourteen pounds to my weight. But after two weeks of eating three meals a day, I found that not only had I lost seven pounds but also ended the battle that had raged in my head since adolescence. I was liberated from the almost constant "Shall I eat this or not?" debate and free to think about things that mattered far more. Plus, I started to feel a lot more comfortable and at ease with my body.

—JN

For most of my life, I have vacillated between carefully watching what I eat and eating whatever I want. The periods where I stay away from sugar and wheat and cut down on or even remove caffeine, I am a calmer, more patient, and kinder human being. When I don't, I am moody, impatient, and grumpy. It's really that simple. And it's my choice.

—GA

Physical Exercise

When we don't feel comfortable in our bodies, we can view them as separate from ourselves and get stuck in our heads, thinking obsessively about whatever is preoccupying us from one moment to the next.

For many women, food and exercise have ceased to be forms of self-care and instead become two more levers we pull to try to change how we look. If we can't starve or eat ourselves into the right shape, then we can exercise our way to it.

Physical activity is, of course, an important aspect of healthy living. It not only gets our limbs moving but also sends vital oxygen to the brain, helps our organs to function properly and our muscles to stay supple, and maintains bone strength. We know we should do it, but often we either don't do it at all, or we exercise like crazy, or we swing between the extremes.

If you find it hard to exercise, starting small can sometimes be the only way in. Committing to just ten minutes a day is enough to make a real difference. Try a brisk morning walk, or, if you're short on time, get off the bus one stop early so that your exercise uses up time you'd be spending in transit anyway. There are also hundreds of miniworkouts online that you can download for free. It needn't cost you anything to feel better about your own body.

If you're at the other extreme and think you might be overexercising, try cutting back and notice what happens to your anxiety levels. If there's an increase in self-judgement and panic that you're going to put on weight, it's highly possible there are feelings underneath your regimen that you're suppressing. Again, start small by cutting down on the intensity of your workout or the hours you spend at it per week and see what comes up. This is a good place to start getting honest about what's really going on for you, because that's a big part of what this journey is all about.

Rest

We know we need rest, but the pressures of modern life often make it impossible to prioritize. It may simply be that we're working too many hours or nursing a waking baby, or we may resist rest because of our own internal resistance to self-care, but like nutrition and exercise, your brain needs rest to function effectively.

Do you have enough energy as you go through your day, or do you find yourself feeling sluggish or falling asleep? Do you push through exhaustion so that you're stuck in an adrenaline-fuelled cycle, or do you take breaks as needed? Do you keep your sleeping space safe from the stresses and strains of daily life? If you have trouble sleeping, is it because you're using your laptop or phone in bed? That alone can lead to stress and sleep disturbances.

Even when we know what's missing, it can still be hard to change our behavior around it. Try to imagine you have a daughter with the same sleep-related issues. What would your advice be? Really think about it. Don't take your phone or laptop to bed? Head on the pillow before midnight? No caffeine after four in the afternoon? Whatever your loving advice might be, follow it yourself.

It's also really important to take at least one break in the middle of the day. If you can't take a lunch hour, make sure you take a pause of some kind. Notice the sky, notice the temperature, breathe deeply, and center yourself before engaging in your next round with life.

Appreciation

How do you feel about your body?

Try asking yourself that question while standing naked in front of a full-length mirror. "What?!" you might ask. Once you've moved through the shock and the fear and are actually standing before your reflection, notice your reaction to what you see. Hopefully, you feel happy and fond of your physical form—that's certainly what we're working toward. But many of us are not only uncomfortable but also highly critical. We focus on the parts of our body that we don't think are perfect—like our thighs, our tummy, our breasts. We feel vulnerable and even ashamed. Our poor bodies endure some harsh judgements, whether we are naked or fully clothed.

Now take in your whole reflection again, but spend a moment centering yourself by breathing in and out deep into your belly. Instead of thinking about what your body looks like, think about what it does for you. This magnificent vessel before you enables you to live this life. Look at your legs, which carry you every day; your arms and hands, which perform so many tasks; your torso, which contains your vital organs: your heart, your lungs, your stomach.

This body houses you. It has grown with you. It sounds like an obvious statement, but so often we forget that it is the same body we came into this world with. Would we forgive it more if we remembered our newborn selves? Try to connect with the kindness you'd feel if it belonged to that baby or to someone else you love.

Run your hand over the parts that you find hardest to love. Breathe deeply, take your time, and consciously release each negative thought that crosses your mind.

This is a powerful experience. If you can, try to commit to doing it a couple of times a week until the habit of praise for what you have overrides the habit of shame. One day this body will be gone. The time you have with it is precious. From now on, commit to treating it with kindness and care.

For a large part of my life, I hated my body. Even when I was at my skinniest, which was really underweight, I thought I was fat. At the depths of my despair, I used to self-harm as a form of punishment for being what I thought was ugly. Now I'm deeply happy to be me. I'm older (of course!) and heavier than I've ever been, but I wouldn't be any other way. However, I still have to put in the right action on a daily basis: it takes only a missed meal or too many late nights, and my mental state starts to slide, and suddenly I'm looking in the mirror and checking my tummy to see how many inches I can pinch. Now, though, I know exactly how to get back on track. And I do. Fast.

—JN

So many of my living years have been spent engaging in one form of self-abuse or another. I've often wished and prayed that it wasn't so easy to escape. Denigrating oneself is a form of abuse and a way to hide because, in doing so, we refuse to see and acknowledge the beautiful being we are, just as we are. What if we could make a commitment to ourselves and to our daughters that we will stop abusing ourselves and our bodies in thought and in action? When we abuse ourselves, we teach others that we are worthy of being treated badly. We show our daughters that we think we deserve to be abused, and therefore they deserve it too—which is not true. Nobody deserves to be abused.

—GA

Beauty Really Is an Inside Job

A mother who radiates self-love and self-acceptance actually vaccinates her daughter against low self-esteem.

—NAOMI WOLF, author and journalist

Taking care of your body will make the work ahead infinitely easier and more pleasurable. When you write your gratitude list each day, find at least one thing you're grateful to your body for. And as you go through your day, find ways to say thank you to your body through your actions. Notice how your relationship with it starts to shift as a result. You may also start to feel more confident in the process, because you know that you are doing right by yourself. Self-assurance will come more naturally, and your relationships with others will change for the better. If we don't care for our body, how can we expect anyone else to?

A woman who is truly comfortable in her own skin radiates an inner beauty regardless of whether she conforms to cultural norms of beauty. When someone is genuinely joyful and at ease with herself, we gravitate toward her—and feel better about ourselves for being in her presence.

In my twenties, I was quite consistently in the public eye. I remember doing one particular photo shoot for the cover of a magazine and being completely focused on, and distracted by, the fact that I felt fat. It wasn't so much that things weren't fitting, which has happened, too, on many occasions—in fact, one time I ended up wearing a tarpaulin over my shoulders because nothing else was working—but on this day, I just felt unattractive in myself, and I remember turning inward and being uncommunicative and allowing my negative thoughts to essentially ruin my (and maybe, for all I know, other peoples') experience of that shoot. Now, the pictures that were created that day expose not a hint of my inner turmoil—many over the years have been more revealing. Today what I see when I look at those photographs is a very young, fresh-faced, beautiful, young woman who had no sense or appreciation of how lucky she was in so many ways.

—GA

Hormones

For many of us, the onset of puberty marked the beginning of a monthly hormonal roller coaster. Menstruation affects each of us differently, but mood swings, pain, and changes in weight and libido can leave us feeling scattered and crazy each month. In fact, half of all women's suicide attempts are made during either the four days prior to menstruation or the first four days of menstruation.

A few pioneering companies have introduced a "period policy," so that their employees can take sick leave if they need it, but most of us have learned to just "deal with it." This may mean going to work when we're in pain, rushing around doing chores rather than resting, or feeling guilty for being bad-tempered. During your next cycle, consider listening to your body more carefully and responding to yourself with more compassion and kindness.

Pregnancy, miscarriage, oral contraception, and fertility treatments can also create hormonal chaos in our lives. And then, as we get older, there is another journey that we all end up taking as women: the menopause.

The Menopause

It's astounding what a taboo topic the menopause—the cessation of periods—continues to be despite affecting 50 percent of the population. Women commonly enter the menopause between the ages of forty-eight and fifty-five. Each woman's experience will be unique, but common symptoms include hot flashes, night sweats, difficulty sleeping, reduced sex drive, memory and concentration problems, vaginal dryness and pain, itching or discomfort during sex, headaches, mood changes, palpitations, joint stiffness, reduced muscle mass, and recurrent urinary tract infections. The symptoms often arrive several months or years before the menopause itself, during the perimenopause, and can continue to affect women for up to twelve years after their last bleed.

For me, the perimenopause was a sudden inability to cope with anything when I had been seemingly used to coping with everything simultaneously for years without many hitches. It came in the form of sudden uncontrollable emotionality and hysteria, and feeling like someone else's brain had replaced mine. I honestly think I have been in gradual perimenopause since my thirties. When I finally identified and acknowledged what was going on for me—or, I guess, when it finally got so bad that I needed to seek out a solution: bioidentical hormones—I could not remember when my brain had felt that "normal." I started to realize how long I had been living with some of the symptoms.

When I began discussing it with my female friends, I was amazed by two things. One, how many women had been through it, but it had never been a part of our conversation. I felt like we were whispering in covens, discussing the best witch doctor to go to in order not to turn into a toad. And two, how many women had no idea it was coming or that some of their symptoms might be related to it. If someone had told me sooner—if the subject had been less taboo, and I had understood earlier what to expect and what lifestyle choices could make it worse—I might have saved myself years of emotional turmoil.

How great would it be if we as women didn't feel embarrassed talking about the menopause and perimenopause? If we embraced this transition as one of the natural rites of passage of being a woman? How wonderful would it be if we were able to immediately identify the signs because we had been educated about them, know that we're not alone, and could seek early help?

—*GA*

There are a range of natural remedies, dietary changes, and hormone replacement therapies out there, but unless we know we need help, we can't access them. Too many women suffer either in ignorance or shame.

We should no longer feel obliged to just "deal with it" or educate our daughters to do the same. If women started to speak about it more openly, we would embrace our hormonal experiences with curiosity and fearlessness as another example of what joins us together.

Reflection

When a woman becomes her own best friend, life is easier.
—DIANE VON FURSTENBERG, Belgian-born fashion designer

I used to think that it was selfish to take care of myself. I wanted others to love me, so I spent my time caring for them. I abandoned myself in pursuit of my quest for love and acceptance. Now I know that the relationship I need to foster, especially if I'm feeling low, is with myself. The longer I spend developing a relationship with myself, the more rewarding and fulfilling are the relationships I have with others. When I treat myself kindly, I'm able to relate to others from a place of wholeness rather than a place of need.

Action. I will notice my needs and attend to them.

Affirmation. I love and care for myself.

Essential
Practice
4

MEDITATION:
Creating a Safe Space and
Making Way for the Sacred

Making Way for the Sacred

*When you find peace within yourself, you become the kind of
person who can live at peace with others.*

—PEACE PILGRIM (born Mildred Lisette Norman,

1908–1981), spiritual teacher and peace activist

Many of us spend our lives searching for safety in one form or
another. Some of us have looked for it outside of ourselves: in
partners, in jobs, in families, in material possessions. Others have
tried to keep safe by putting up a barrier between ourselves and the
world around us.

But there is a genuinely safe place that each and every one of us
can access. It's a sacred space that we can enter at any point during

our day—regardless of what is happening around us. In that place we find peace and we find healing. We create this space through meditation.

Like the habit of gratitude, meditation creates a new "muscle group" that will enhance your emotional balance and intuition while cultivating the resilience to handle whatever life throws your way.

Most of us spend our lives rushing. If we're not physically racing around, our minds are full of mental hurry. We're thinking of what we ought to do, what we've done wrong, what we should have done better, what we're going to do, and so on and so on. Meditating provides a break from those thoughts. We create distance and the chance to connect with what lies underneath the bustle of our chattering minds and our ever-lengthening to-do lists.

I am not afraid of storms, for I am learning how to sail my ship.
—LOUISA MAY ALCOTT (1832–1888), author of *Little Women*

You may already have your own meditation technique, and if so, you know what we're talking about. But if you don't have one, or you're new to meditation, this section will get you started with a practice that you can use for the rest of your life.

For now, just think of meditation as a moment away from the rush of your day and the clutter of your mind. A moment of stillness.

Of course, stillness can't be forced, just as healing can't be made to happen. But what you can do is create an environment in which stillness and peace are fostered and can grow.

As your mind grows quieter and more spacious, you can begin to see self-defeating thought patterns for what they are and open up to other, more positive options.

—SHARON SALZBERG, Buddhist meditation teacher and author

When you get to *WE*'s 6th Principle, peace, you'll learn how to deepen and strengthen your meditation practice, while the 8th Principle, joy, will introduce you to prayer, which you can use whether you have a faith or not. But for now, all you have to do is decide to commit to taking a few minutes out of your busy life at the start of each day. And when we say a few minutes, we mean just that: two minutes a day. That's all you need to begin.

Even though all of us can manage to find two minutes, it's quite likely that at this point you'll experience resistance or even self-sabotage. You may start to find excuses before you've even read through this section. Perhaps your mind is defending how busy or tired you are. Or maybe you've just remembered that you took a meditation course once before, and it didn't work. Or that there's meditation at the end of your exercise class or yoga class, but you just fall asleep each time.

Be aware of all these rationalizations and do this exercise anyway.

Exercise: Daily Meditation Practice

This exercise is to help you establish your own daily meditation practice. Two minutes, that's all. You can download one of many free meditation timer apps or use the regular timer on your phone.

Leave it to the bell to remind you when the time is up. Tell your mind that it can return to thinking as much as it wants as soon as this brief exercise is over.

When you are ready, sit cross-legged on the floor or on a chair. Make sure you're comfortable before you start. You can close your eyes or keep your focus fixed on a point just in front of you. (Placing a candle in your sight line is both helpful and calming.) Try not to let your gaze drift around the room looking for distractions. Remember, this short time is about peace of mind.

Now just breathe in through your nose and out through your mouth, slowly and gently.

Try to let your outbreath take slightly longer than your inbreath. Notice the gap between each inhale and exhale. Relax. Don't worry about any thoughts that come—just try not to engage with them, gently returning your attention to the rise and fall of your breath.

Although two minutes may not seem very long, it is enough to start creating a very important space and a very important habit. Remember that from tiny acorns grow mighty oaks.

If your mind objects to this practice, that's great news. It means it knows it's about to be rumbled. The mind likes to pretend it knows everything, and, sadly, too often we believe it. The truth is that the mind is an excellent servant but a terrible master. It's great at solving crossword puzzles or reading train timetables, but it's not so good at helping us to find fulfillment or love.

So for just two minutes every day, you're going to suspend its operation. You're going to ask your mind to take a short break and then see what happens when you give yourself this brief vacation from your thoughts.

Don't worry if this doesn't make any sense. Don't worry if nothing seems to be happening. This is not about sense or meaning, and there is no right or wrong way of doing this. It is about very gently starting a new and vital habit: training your mind and body to get used to being still.

Each day, when you have finished your two minutes of silence, read the affirmation that corresponds with the chapter you're reading. Allow what's written there to seep in gently as you continue to breathe in and out. Then say the affirmation to yourself softly.

You might like to commit it to memory or jot it down in your journal, so that in moments of doubt and indecision you can return to your affirmation and use it as a way of keeping yourself calm and centered. It will help you to recall your safe place, as well as reinforce the lesson contained in the chapter you've just read.

It's simple. All you have to do is do it!

TIP: *Try to meditate in the same place each day. Create a special place for yourself to sit, whether it's cross-legged on the floor in a corner of your bedroom or on your favorite sofa. Try to make it feel special. Lighting a candle before you start helps to create a ritual around the process. Or, if you like, you can burn incense or place a fresh flower in a vase just in front of you. Assail your senses so that your body and mind learn that when you sit in your special place and the candle is lit, this is their time to switch off and allow something else to take over.*

Before I started meditating, I used to think, "When I'm in the right apartment, I'll create the perfect space, and then I'll do it on a regular basis." Eventually I started anyway, and then it became about the perfect conditions. I had to be facing in the right direction, there could be no distractions, the candle and incense lit, my legs crossed. Then at one point, I was away working and had none of my usual crutches. I remember sitting on a hard floor in a fluorescently lit corner of a kitchen and experiencing one of the most blissful meditations of my life. Now I do it anywhere: in the midst of a crowd, on a bus, at work. My need for meditation to be a part of my life is greater than my need for it to be perfect.

—GA

When I first tried to meditate, I was scared of it. It felt like I was being put in a torture chamber where all the thoughts I'd been trying to suppress would appear and torment me. But knowing that I had to sit for only two minutes made it possible. It might not have sounded like a very long time to anyone else, but to me it was a lifetime. Over time my mind learned to quiet for that period. Just that brief respite gave me a glimpse of what was to come: peace of mind and a way of being in the world without the noise in my head constantly destabilizing me.

—JN

Reflection

It feels good. Kinda like when you have to shut your computer down when it goes crazy, and when you turn it on, it's okay again. That's what meditation is to me.
—ELLEN DEGENERES, comedienne, actress, and talk-show host

Meditation is the way I achieve real, lasting change. I breathe in deeply and I breathe out, and as I do so I return to the present moment and remember the truth: I am a spiritual being on a human journey.

Action. Today I will take time out. No matter how busy things get, I will create a moment to honor myself and the spiritual path I am on.

Affirmation. As I breathe in and out deeply, I feel myself return to who I truly am.

A Note on Addiction

An addiction is any behavior you are unable to stop repeating despite its negative impact on your life. It's a medical illness, like cancer or hepatitis—not something you can heal through will-power alone—and it's impossible to make much real progress if you're actively using.

The good news is that there is great help out there. There are now twelve-step fellowships that can help with any addiction. At the back of this book are links to their websites where you'll find self-diagnosis questionnaires and information about how to access the support that is freely available.

One of the most cunning symptoms of addiction is denial. If you find yourself tempted to minimize your behavior, please don't. Ignoring it will cheat you out of a whole new way of life.

Addiction to substances such as drugs, alcohol, and food are widely known, but you can also be addicted to behaviors: excessive shopping, exercising, gaming, gambling, caretaking, loving, and sex. Basically, you can become addicted to anything that changes how you feel. A temporary period of abstinence from a substance or behavior doesn't mean you no longer have a problem. Addiction is a progressive illness, so, in its early stages, you may be able to kid yourself that you've got it under control. Long term, though, it only gets worse. So if you find you're unable to control yourself around a particular substance or behavior, you should jump straight to the resources section.

Congratulations.

You now have four Essential Practices in place that will hold you steady for the journey ahead and, we hope, for the rest of your life. Often we start this journey feeling alone. But the truth is that there are many of us—across the globe—searching for a happier, more meaningful way of living.

PART 2

The 9 Principles

Look into your own heart, discover what it is that gives you
pain, then refuse, under any circumstances whatsoever, to
inflict that pain on anyone else.

—KAREN ARMSTRONG, British author who often

writes about religion's role in the world

The 9 Principles in this book provide a compass.

Without them, life can feel like a losing battle. We can thrash around trying to satisfy conflicting wants and needs. At times we seem to make headway in the "want" department—we get the job or the partner or the home—and yet our deeper needs get buried. Other times we feel like we're in a rowboat with one oar, paddling as hard as we can but spinning in circles.

The 9 Principles in this book guide us forward. They guide us home. When you've learned to incorporate them into your life, you'll be able to live from a place of authenticity and love wherever you find yourself and whatever has happened in your past.

Only if you are ready to change yourself can you be ready to
change the world.

—EDIT SCHLAFFER, Austrian social scientist

and founder of Women Without Borders

The work of transforming our world begins with healing ourselves. If we don't do the work, we risk allowing our egos to run the show. We can wind up acting out our own unresolved issues on those we seek to help, or taking up a cause from a need to feel important rather than from a place of genuine passion and concern. Our world is full of people who inadvertently cause harm while trying to do good.

You may feel tempted to flip through the book until you find the part that deals with a particular issue that especially relates to you—like relationships, for instance—but don't. The 9 Principles are laid out in an order. Each one builds on the last, and if you skip through the others, you'll shortchange yourself. When you finish the book in its entirety, you may want to keep it close for reference, but until then give yourself the gift of committing to the whole process. You may choose to complete a chapter a week or take it more slowly. You can also work through the chapters with friends or other women who are also interested in taking the journey.

There's no timescale, but the sooner you do the work, the sooner the miracles will manifest.

Doing Versus Thinking

Action is the antidote to despair.

—JOAN BAEZ, folksinger and activist

WE is an experiential rather than an intellectual process. Most of us exert a lot of mental energy trying to understand ourselves, but with little permanent result. We may have plenty of insights, but insights alone rarely lead to change, just as reading a recipe doesn't result in a cooked meal—there's still all the measuring, chopping, and stirring to do.

For change to work, ACTion is necessary.

ACT is one of the acronyms we'll repeat again and again:
Action
Changes
Things

Right action leads to right thinking. Not the other way around. It's not enough merely to know or understand. You don't get to experience swimming by sitting on the edge of the pool. And once you're in the water, if you want to stay afloat, you'll need to move your arms and legs rather than just think about it.

Action is also what will enable you to make the journey from the head to the heart. So throughout this journey, you'll be reminded to ACT.

Each chapter's exercises are actions in their own right. Don't forget them—they are an integrated part of this journey, as they'll help you to integrate what you're learning.

For decades, I tried to work things out in my head. I lived with a mountain of self-help books by my bed. I'd read a chapter or two until I found an insight that made me feel better momentarily. Then I'd recommend it to someone else as a brilliant read. I thought I could get rid of my pain by understanding and knowing. I'd lie awake at night looking at things from every angle, stuck in analysis paralysis. In the end, a combination of whiskey, sleeping pills, and tranquilizers was the only way I could get any peace from the constant noise in my head. It was revolutionary to me when someone suggested I move a muscle to change a thought. I thought I had to wait for my thoughts to change before I could act. Now I know it's the other way around. Right action creates right thinking—and self-esteem to boot.

—JN

I have to say that even though I was introduced to these practices decades ago, I still find it hard to do them. Even though I know what's best for me and have experienced firsthand the difference they make in my entire life, my brain still wants to forget that I feel better when I practice them daily. Maybe it's the fact that they work that makes the challenge greater; my ingrained, stubborn self-sabotage doesn't want me well, or maybe it's my internal rebel that says, "Don't tell me what to do!" or perhaps it's just plain laziness. Whatever my resistance is, the fact is, when I do it, it works.

—GA

Commitment

There's only one thing you need to agree to for the Principles in this book to work: a commitment to be willing. Willing to try. Willing to pick yourself up when you mess up (which we all do) and to try again.

Anyone can make this commitment. It doesn't require education, status, or wealth. And it certainly doesn't require perfection.

Nothing in this book needs to be done "right" or "perfectly." The P-word, perfectionism, should be banned. It causes all of us monumental problems in society's expectations of us and the demands we make on ourselves. We are not cardboard cutouts. We are individuals. That means each one of us is complicated and real, with our own unique and often messy layers of emotional wounding.

Your head will present you with a thousand excuses, but you can and will find the time. You can and will find the space. You can and will find the courage. Those things that are no longer necessary to your well-being will fall away.

The 9 Principles that follow are for you personally and also for the world you inhabit. The Principles are not just for your yoga mat or your place of worship; they are for decisions both big and small. They work just as well in helping you decide how to vote as they do in the grocery store aisle and as they do in your intimate relationships. Nothing is too important or too mundane for them to have an impact. Don't keep them just for crises—they will work in every aspect of your daily life. We promise.

This is a journey toward love.

Prepare to be amazed.

Principle
1

HONESTY:
Getting Real

*My true identity goes beyond the outer roles I play . . . there is an
authentic "I" within . . . a divine spark within the soul.*
—SUE MONK KIDD, author of *The Secret Life of Bees* and other novels

---

Honesty is the guide that leads us home. It returns us
to our true selves and enables us to live authentically,
courageously, and congruently.

Most of us do our best to tell the truth. We might tell the occasional
white lie to avoid hurting someone's feelings or exaggerate a story
for the sake of effect, but otherwise we try to be honest.

And yet there is one person we lie to on a regular basis, perhaps even without realizing it: ourselves.

We all do it. We tell ourselves we're okay when we're not. We tell ourselves we don't mind when we do and that we can't when we can. We say yes when we mean no and no when we want to say yes. We override our instincts in the name of being practical or polite. We bury our dreams and then help others fulfill theirs. We disguise, shave, and shape ourselves to conform to an artificial feminine ideal only to suffer the consequences: depression, relationship problems, anger issues, addiction, and despair.

WE's 1st Principle takes us inward. It involves digging down beneath the surface of who we think we are, in order to reclaim our true selves.

It's a process that involves discovering and discarding the lies and myths we've accumulated over the years, which have left us estranged from ourselves. It requires courage, commitment, and self-care.

Most of us are called to this journey when we hit an obstacle in life: a relationship that's ended badly, a betrayal or disappointment, or when one of the distractions or addictions we use to cope stops working. When our lives are ticking along and appear to be functioning, it's easier to ignore that niggle deep in our soul, pleading for our attention.

But wherever you are in your life, and whatever is happening, *WE*'s 1st Principle will bring an enormous sense of relief and freedom. There is nothing quite like being able to say, "This is who I really am," and to feel truly glad about it.

Losing Ourselves

Severe separations in early life leave emotional scars on the brain because they assault the essential human connection: the [parent-child] bond, which teaches us that we are lovable.

—JUDITH VIORST, author and poet

From early childhood, most of us start to lose touch with our authentic selves.

Our instinctive need to be loved, feel safe, and belong leads us to adapt. Sometimes consciously, sometimes not, we shift in response to our parents', teachers', and peers' perceptions of who we are and what we should be. And in the process, we naturally abandon parts of ourselves.

The extent to which we do this depends largely on how well we are cared for in our early years. We rely on the world we're born into to reflect back to us who we are. If the message we receive as babies and toddlers is that we're loved and "enough" just as we are, we'll have a much greater chance of developing a resilient sense of self. The less secure we are during those early years, the more we will adapt ourselves to try to win that missing approval.

We create false selves to ensure our emotional and sometimes physical survival—*subpersonalities* that are almost us but not *quite* us. They help us get our needs met at a time when we are too young and dependent to have any other choices. The problem comes when we continue to rely on them long after they've fulfilled their use. Often they become so habitual that we no longer realize they're not who we really are.

Exercise 1: Would the Real Me Please Stand Up?

This exercise will help you begin to reconnect with your authentic self.

Pause for a moment and think about which false selves you may have developed over your lifetime. Remember that each one came into existence to keep you safe. They're not bad, they've just outlived their purpose, and they prevent you from living authentically. Take out your journal. Close your eyes and allow yourself to slide backward along the timeline of your life. Be as honest as you're able about the subpersonalities you've developed.

For example, perhaps as a girl, you relieved household tensions by making people laugh, so as an adult you continue to clown your way through life—never showing your tears and keeping everyone else smiling at your own expense. Or maybe you were the "good" girl who was rewarded for working hard, and now you're at the top of a career ladder, and you have no idea why you climbed it.

Perhaps you gained your sense of worth by caretaking an alcoholic or otherwise sick parent, and now you continue to give more than you have and wonder why you are always running on empty. Or maybe you grew up in an environment where there was nobody you could rely on, and so you developed a mask of independence that leaves you seemingly invincible but horribly alone.

It may be difficult to draw sharp distinctions between the characters you've played, whose boundaries may conflict and overlap. Were you Mommy's little helper or Daddy's princess? Were you the intellectual or the dropout? Were you the peacemaker or the truth teller (or both)? Were you a people pleaser, a party girl, a loner, or a saint? Were you Miss Perfect, a rebel, or a critic who sat on the sidelines? Or were you invisible? Write down every subpersonality you find.

Each of us will have developed a number of selves to ensure our survival. Normally, you'll find five or six dominant ones that are still with you in adult life.

Now take every one that you've found and visualize her as a separate person. Greet her and thank her for the protection she has given you. Each of them has helped to keep you safe.

When you've worked through your list, take five deep breaths in and out and congratulate yourself. This is an important step you've taken. Even though these subpersonalities will emerge and sometimes still be useful, from now on, you will see them for what they are—masks that you've needed to wear—and you will not mistake them for yourself. Who you truly are lies beneath and beyond them, and you are now on your journey to meet her.

....

As you go through your day, try to notice when you slip into one of your subpersonalities. Practicing honesty will enable you to identify them and then let them gently drop away, in the same way that a husk drops from a seed.

> When I told the school careers advisor that I wanted to be a secretary at the British Broadcasting Corporation—I didn't dare tell her that I wanted to be a reporter, because I didn't think it would ever be possible—she laughed at me and said, "Don't you think every girl wants to do that? Why don't you be a bit more realistic and work at the insurance company? They're always looking for typists." When, years later, I found myself reporting for the BBC, I always carried a sense that I should be in the typing pool rather than on air. While the men around me had a sense of entitlement and clearly planned their career trajectories, I always felt as if I were begging to be allowed to do what I loved rather than claiming my rightful place at the table.
>
> —JN

Other People's Stuff

When she stopped conforming to the conventional picture of femininity, she finally began to enjoy being a woman.
—*THE FEMININE MYSTIQUE*, by Betty Friedan
(1921–2006), feminist and author

How we are seen by others and society as a whole informs how we see ourselves. The messages we're given as women about what is and what isn't "okay" for us to do, feel, look like, or want, get absorbed.

Whether the message is that we need to be passive and wait to be chosen or that we should try to have it all—children and the seat in the boardroom—the complex truth of who we are gets obscured. Our sense of what is possible is limited, and we bury parts of ourselves, fearing we won't fit into the world as we truly are.

Similarly, our perception of our physical self gets distorted by the constant messages we receive about what we should and shouldn't wear, weigh, and eat, and how we should and shouldn't look. No matter how hard we try, it's difficult not to be affected. They're all around us in what we read and hear and in the images we see on a daily basis. Whether it's scantily clad, airbrushed models staring down at us from billboards or magazine covers, or images on social media, the message is the same: it's not okay to be who we are.

....

THE PRICE OF SOCIAL MEDIA

The stress that social media is causing young women is heavily implicated in a dramatic rise in mental illness. Levels of self-harm, post-traumatic stress disorder, and chronic mental illness are all on the increase.[1] According to UK government-funded research,[2] one in five women ages sixteen to twenty-four have anxiety, depression, panic disorders, phobias, or obsessive-compulsive disorder (OCD). And the proportion of young women self-harming tripled from 2007 to 2014.

....

At this stage of *WE*'s journey, your goal is to discover and know your true self. Becoming conscious of those messages is the first stage to escaping their toxic power.

When I was broadcasting, I felt obliged to don the "uniform" of power suits and heels that my news editors and the industry expected. I was very conscious that I was perpetuating the stereotypes I hoped my work would dispel, but I felt trapped. If I didn't look the part, I wouldn't get to play the part. And I desperately wanted the part. So I dressed up and pretended to be someone I was not in order to get the chance to tell the truth— one of the many acts of hypocrisy that I engaged in to become "successful." I became part of the problem that I was hoping to solve, and each time I put on one of my work suits, I felt myself getting more and more estranged from my real self, and my levels of internal self-hatred grew.

—JN

I agreed to participate in photo shoots when I was younger that I would advise myself against in retrospect, where my desire to be liked or found attractive overrode that small voice that

61

wanted to say, "I'm not okay with this." Whether it was not want-ing to upset the male photographer or letting my ego get caught up in the attention, I hadn't yet found that part of my brain. Not just the part that could stand up for myself and say I will not participate in an act that feels shameful because it is exposing too much of myself for a stranger's gaze, but also the part that might recognize that what I was participating in was a bigger issue, and that by agreeing to do the shoot, I was colluding in a far darker message about women and our objectification.

—GA

It's easy to forget how relatively recently women—even in the developed Western Hemisphere—won basic legal rights. Until 1920 and 1928, respectively, women in the United States and the United Kingdom weren't allowed to vote; until the 1990s, our hus-bands could legally rape us. For the bulk of legal history, we've been treated as inferior, and the legacy of centuries of inequality continues to exact its toll on our sense of who we are.

Leading female scientists, politicians, and commentators still find that if they speak publicly, their looks and clothes are dis-sected in ways that simply don't happen to men, reinforcing the sense that beneath the talk of equality, we remain objects to be lusted over, dominated, and possessed, rather than equals.

To get a snapshot of the extent to which equality is still resisted, take a look at the comments that women who write about equality generate online: threats of sexual assault and even death are com-monplace. As a result, whatever strides the world is making toward equality, the mirror we're reflected back in is distorted and in turn can corrupt and limit how we perceive ourselves.

....

UNDER COVER

Too often we can feel we have to disguise our real physical self to match artificial notions of femininity that have been created largely by men. Whether we're forcing our feet into heels so high they damage our backs or suppressing what we think or feel in order not to upset our other half, we're often left feeling worse about ourselves.

The rise of porn has compounded the problem, giving both genders warped perceptions of what is normal. Young men expect girls to look and behave like porn stars, and girls find themselves under pressure to oblige. Plastic surgeons have seen a surge in the number of women seeking labiaplasty—a painful procedure to alter the appearance of the folds of skin around the vulva, which can permanently damage nerve endings—as women try to conform to damaging cosmetic norms perpetuated by the porn industry to make themselves desirable.

Of course, changing our outside appearance doesn't get us any nearer to being loved and wanted for who we authentically are. Applying *We*'s Principles enables us to know our identity from the inside out rather than the outside in, and realize that who we are lies beyond what we do, how we look, and what we own.

....

When you are clear about who you are and who you are not, it's a lot easier to be clearer with the outside world. If you adopt rigorous self-honesty as a way of life, the false selves and labels that have disguised your true self will gradually start to fall away.

Curiosity is our friend that teaches us how to become ourselves.
—ELIZABETH GILBERT, author of *Eat Pray Love* and other books

As children, we're all emotionally super-porous. In addition to the messages we receive from our families, peers, and society at large, we also absorb our caregivers' fears, frustrations, and beliefs, and mistake them for our own. We start receiving most of them before we're old enough to be able to scrutinize and reject those that don't serve us or belong to us. This will especially be the case if you come from a family in which there are secrets or traumatic events. You may not know the facts, but you'll still absorb the feelings. It's possible to carry emotions such as shame, fear, and sadness for decades, even though they have nothing to do with you.

I've always lived with a fear of catastrophe and could never define what that "terrible" thing I feared might be. As a girl, I'd squirrel away my pocket money so that I'd be ready for whatever it was that was going to happen to us. It was only years later, when I discovered my father's secret past, that my behavior made sense, and my fear started to evaporate.

When my father was a child, he'd fled from the Nazis during the Second World War. Later, wanting to protect his own family from anti-Semitism, he never told us that he was Jewish. But it turned out that he inadvertently left me a different kind of legacy: a sense of impending catastrophe and a fear of saying who I really was.

—JN

....

GENES WITH MEMORIES

The new and fast-evolving field of epigenetics research suggests that trauma can be inherited genetically. In one study, male mice that were taught to fear a smell passed on that fear to their babies—which in turn would bequeath the same sensitivity to their offspring.[3]

Another study found that baby rats who received insufficient nurturing from their mothers matured to become more prone to disease and anxiety than their well-groomed counterparts, and then passed on that predisposition to their descendants.[4]

....

We can live our whole lives with a particular sensitivity, fear, or trait that doesn't belong to us—that's been internalized from the outside world. Now we can start challenging the assumptions we've made about ourselves and ask, "Is this mine? Do I own this? Is it part of me? Is it serving me, or can I let it go?"

Exercise 2: Getting Beneath the Surface

This exercise is to help you discard the ideas about yourself that no longer serve you.

Think about the labels you'd use to describe yourself. They might be about your job, how you look, your race, your background, or your sexual preference.

Now think about the messages about yourself that you were given growing up. It doesn't matter whether they were good or bad—we internalize them when we're young and impressionable, and as we get older, they can be hard to shake.

As a child, were you told you were lazy, smart, or a show-off? Were you criticized or praised for how you looked—told you were too fat, too skinny, too tall, too short? Or maybe you were ignored and grew up with the belief that you were worth nothing at all.

Write a list of the ten most prominent messages about yourself that come to your mind—from your past and your present.

Look at each label on your list. Really ponder it. Is it true? Does it really represent who you are inside?

Now make sure that you are comfortable and have time to sit for a few moments. Close your eyes. Breathe in and out five times, letting your outbreath last for five counts and your inbreath for four. Imagine that you are in a boat floating far out at sea and that you take the labels you have written and scatter them onto the surface of the ocean. Watch the words floating there, bobbing up and down on the waves. Now imagine diving into the water so you're beneath them. As you look back up at them, you see that the paper is wet and the writing is starting to smudge so you can no longer read the words.

Dive deeper and look back up again. The paper is dissolving into the ocean, and now it is gone. As you swim deeper, you find yourself resting on the seabed. It is calm and peaceful and still down there. No turbulence, no waves. Any notion of who you are or are not is just a distant memory left on the surface. Inhale and exhale. You are free. Deep down, beneath the words, beneath the ideas and judgements of yourself and others, you are perfect and whole just as you are. Allow yourself to really embrace what that feels like. To be truly free. To be truly yourself.

When you are ready, slowly float up to the surface and open your eyes.

Take your list and crumple it up. If you'd like, you can throw it in the trash or even burn it and scatter the ashes. You don't need those labels any more. Your true self—the part of you that dived into the water—exists beyond and beneath all words. When you reside in her, you will feel utterly safe and loved.

This is a great exercise for when you're feeling off balance or upset. It's not necessary to repeat all of it; just imagine yourself diving deep down into your own internal ocean and resting there for a while until you feel restored. You can even add this calming imagery to your daily meditation practice.

Finding Ourselves

To be oneself, simply oneself, is so amazing and utterly unique an experience that it's hard to convince oneself so singular a thing happens to everybody.
—SIMONE DE BEAUVOIR (1908–1986), French author

Now that you have started to shed who and what you are *not*, the really exciting work of discovering who you really *are* can begin in earnest.

It's time to get curious—about yourself. Forget all those messages you may have been given as a girl about not being nosy or not asking too many questions. Give yourself permission to question everything and assume nothing. Then be ready to be amazed.

In my working life, I was dedicated to uncovering the truth in the world around me—first as a barrister and then as an investigative journalist—but it was a whole new journey when I was told to start asking myself the questions that I'd normally throw at others. I realized there were all sorts of truths in my own life I didn't want to get too honest about for fear of unravelling. Eventually I did, and that's when I discovered a new level of emotional freedom.

—JN

This is not a straightforward, linear process. You'll find false leads and dead ends. You'll have surprises and tough choices.

Think of yourself as an archaeologist in your own life. Let curiosity be the tool you dig with. Ask yourself questions as you would someone you were studying. When was the last time you were really happy in your life? Why was that? What music did you love in your teens, and do you ever allow yourself to listen to it now? What is your favorite food? What do you hate about your life and what do you love? Write down your answers in your journal.

Sometimes we simply don't know. We've dulled our longings and our wants out of necessity. They've become what often feels like a painful luxury. But the truth is that they are the nerve endings we need to bring back to life. So listen for the stirrings of what you love and what you want, and then expose and explore them.

There are no rules, and there's nothing that says what you discover has to be coherent or logical. Whoever said we had to make sense? We are all complex and multifaceted.

Born in the United States, I lived in London from the age of two. I naturally spoke with a British accent and felt British but was

68

teased in school for being a "Yank." I wanted to fit in but was confused about where my loyalties lay because my parents were American and I loved the States—where the sun always seemed to shine, and I was plied with candy. When I was eleven, we moved to Michigan. I was so excited at the prospect of living in the land of milkshakes and hamburgers. But the reality was, I was still the kid with the "funny" accent. I eventually modulated my speech to fit in, but I still felt like the outsider, and I deeply missed my other home.

Today I still feel torn: the UK has my heart and soul, but the US is in my genes. I've lived in London again now for fifteen years, and it is second nature to go back and forth with the accent depending on where I am and to whom I'm speaking. This has confused people along the way, and the question of falseness has meant that I've had to look at it closely. It would be easy for me to attach a "bad" label to my intentions or to judge myself as being disingenuous, but I've come to accept that adapting to my mixed cultural identity has been vital to my well-being, and despite the fact that it's confusing and awkward sometimes, I have come to own the reality that they are both the authentic me.

—GA

You may discover that you've abandoned your own desires and even your tastes for those of your family, friends, or partner. Maybe it was easier that way, or perhaps you never allowed yourself the space to develop your own likes and dislikes to begin with, and it was a relief to have a ready-made set of preferences handed to you. Or perhaps you never allowed yourself the chance to hope for what you really wanted because it seemed too impossible to achieve.

Ask yourself: "Whose life am I currently living? What

would my life look like if I could have anything, be anything, do anything?"

These can be really scary questions to answer truthfully. Don't censor your answers or limit them with practical considerations. During this early stage, getting to know yourself can feel unsettling, daunting—even frightening. What if you're overwhelmed by longings and hopes that you suppressed in childhood? What if you discover you're married to the wrong person or that you hate what you do for a living? Or maybe you worry that you won't be able to do anything about what you find. Change of this magnitude can feel terrifying, but see if you can start to take small steps to move toward where you want to be. Fears will inevitably surface, and they can at first seem paralyzing or overwhelming. Do your best to move through them at your own pace. Trust, just as you would if you were pregnant, that within you is a living, breathing being whom you are absolutely going to love.

Allowing yourself to discover your true longings will reset your internal GPS system. You can't even begin to get to where you'd love to be if you haven't yet entered the real destination.

Noticing and Naming

Seldom can it happen that something is not a little disguised or a little mistaken.

—*Emma*, by Jane Austen (1775–1817), English novelist

Noticing and *naming* are two of *WE*'s most important tools. You'll be using them for the rest of this journey and, hopefully, the rest of your life. The answers lie within each and every one of us, and noticing and naming provide the mechanics with which we start finding them. Your journal will continue to be a valuable tool throughout this whole process, so keep it close for all these new discoveries.

Noticing

Noticing is like a flashlight in the dark: it leads you to awareness. Allow yourself to notice what's going on inside and around you. Don't judge it or be impatient for answers. Just be curious. You can't be honest about something you don't know exists. Noticing will bring insight. You'll spot contradictions, you'll spot inconsistencies, and then over time you'll start to spot what's congruent with the real you and what isn't.

Perhaps you don't actually want the promotion you've applied for, because it will leave you with even less time with your kids, but you're scared to admit it lest you look like you're giving up on your feminist ideals.

Or maybe deep down you know you don't want children, but you pretend to be broody because you fear the dismay and pain coming clean will evoke in your parents or partner.

Remember ACT. Well, noticing is an action, so notice what you tell yourself, notice what you tell other people, notice how you feel, and allow yourself to become aware of what the reality of your life is.

Naming

Once you've noticed an uncomfortable reality, it can be easy to want to slip back into denial. If you spot buried and painful emotions or truths, it can be tempting to sweep what you've noticed right back under the carpet. Naming is how we stop denial from creeping back in.

Sometimes acknowledging what you've noticed feels like it will be enough, but it isn't. Things become more real when you name them. Write it down in your journal so it's there in black and white. If you have someone safe to talk to—a therapist, a nonjudgemental friend—then say it aloud to him or her too.

Out the truth. *Notice* it and then *name* it—in writing and, if you can, out loud.

Of course, *notice* and *name* what brings you joy and peace too. Take nothing for granted. You are on a mission to chart your own internal territory. It is an eye-opening and profound experience being this honest. Do your best to embrace the process and enjoy the wonder of meeting yourself anew.

....

PEOPLE-PLEASING

It's natural to want to be liked and to want to be kind. But people-pleasing—saying yes when you mean no or pretending you like something when you don't—is a form of dishonesty. We all do it, but if we do it without noticing and naming it, sooner or later we lose sight of what we actually do want and need.

When we deny any aspect of ourselves, we almost always pay a price further down the line. We may think we're being nice, but, as you'll discover when we get to looking at anger in the 3rd Principle, courage, often you're furious, boiling with rage, but simply don't know how to recognize or access it.

....

As you use noticing and naming to become more honest, you'll inevitably discover parts of yourself or your life that you want to change. Try to resist doing anything right now. This early stage isn't the time to make major changes. This is simply the time to get honest with yourself about what areas of your life might need attention.

When you've completed all 9 Principles, you'll be able to make whatever alterations you need. Answers to problems that at the moment seem intractable will come. For now, your job is just to notice and name what's within you.

It's no longer necessary to hide from truths that are inconvenient or difficult, because you are now on a path that will enable you to resolve them.

Exercise 3: Inconvenient Truths

This exercise will help you identify truths you may have had to bury. Take a moment now to write down in your journal anything in your life that you find difficult to be honest about because you wish it wasn't there. Ask yourself what you'd change if you could. Maybe you don't want to stay in your job, but what on earth can you do about it? Maybe you haven't enjoyed sex with your partner for months or even years and don't know how to stop pretending. Or maybe you don't like the way a close friend treats you, but you don't want to have a row.

Maybe it's an aspect of yourself that you would rather avoid facing. Perhaps you keep ignoring the voice inside you that says you're drinking too much, or there's a conflict between how you think of yourself and how you behave.

Whatever it is, write it down. Don't let denial creep in and mask the truths that will lead you to a more fulfilled and meaningful life. The act of noticing and naming is all the action that is required of you right now. As you work through *WE*'s Principles, you'll discover more truths—add them to your list whenever you spot them.

Don't panic about the things that feel wrong or impossible to deal with. The following Principles will guide you to solutions. But all meaningful change begins in the same place: becoming honest with yourself. The truth will set you free, but only if you allow yourself to see it.

Feelings: The Good and the Bad

As you uncover issues and parts of yourself that have lain buried for years, you'll find some challenging feelings come with them. If you notice yourself feeling unusually sad, anxious, irritable, or needy, these are signs that the process is working.

In the next Principle, you'll also be shown how to release difficult emotions, but for now, focus on becoming aware of them by noticing and naming. The more conscious you become of your own internal landscape, the easier it will be to live with integrity.

To nurture yourself during this process, try to be rigorous about your self-care. Make sure you're allowing time for the Essential Practices you learned earlier. Go through your checklist: Have you written your gratitude list? Are you keeping to your two minutes (or longer) of meditation? Have you said your affirmations, and are you getting enough food, rest, and exercise? Now isn't the time to cut corners.

Taking care of yourself is the substructure of this serious work. That includes making sure you have the support around you that you need. That could be a counsellor, a support group, or like-minded friends. Or if you know other women who want to apply these spiritual Principles to their lives, you can explore supporting and encouraging one another. It's common for women in our culture to think it's strong to be self-reliant, but it's a signal of great strength when you are able to truly open yourself to receive. This is a *WE* process, not a *me* process—there are no medals for going it alone.

If you haven't found your sister travelers yet, you will. As you practice the Principles in your life, you'll find that like-minded women are increasingly drawn to you. You don't need to make it happen. Keep walking this walk, stay open, and it just will.

But remember, there's an important person who is already on this journey with you who can nurture you and encourage you through it: you.

Inner Girl

When we're hysterical, it's often historical. It has been estimated that 90 percent of the distress we feel in the present can, in fact, be attributed to our past.[5]

Inside every one of us is a wounded self, carrying hurts and needs. If we're to have any hope of living honestly and happily, we need to learn how to soothe and heal ourselves.

Picture that wounded part of yourself as a small girl. You may think her feelings don't have influence because you've adapted so effectively to the adult world, but they're still there just beneath the surface. Until they're uncovered and taken care of, you're at their mercy.

The time to get childhood needs met from your parents or caregivers has now passed, but you can do the work yourself by showing that wounded inner girl the unconditional love she didn't get the first time around.

Talk to her: the frightened, hurt part of yourself. Encourage her, praise her, and coach her through situations as you would your own child. Tell her she doesn't need to be scared, she's not alone, she's not abandoned—you are there to love, support, and protect her. Talk to her out loud, or if you're in public, have a silent internal dialogue with her. This is your chance to re-parent yourself by replacing any harmful messages you got as a girl.

Take this process gently and at a pace that feels right for you. Powerful emotions can surface as you uncover these past wounds—and that's normal. If you feel at any time that it's becoming too much, it's important to seek support from a friend or a professional.

Just as with a real child who's clamoring for attention, if you take the time to meet her needs, you'll find that she settles down and lets you get on with whatever it is you're doing.

> When I find myself reacting to a situation in a way that is out of proportion to what is actually happening (which is still way too often), I try to have a silent dialogue with myself. I ask myself how old I'm feeling. An answer normally comes back pretty swiftly. Often it's three, sometimes it's six, and sometimes I feel like a newborn baby. I then ask that younger part of myself what she needs, and I try to find ways of soothing and comforting her that are age appropriate. It sounds crazy, but it really does work. Often I want to be held, so I'll either ask a friend for a hug or wrap my arms around myself and give that younger "me" a

loving embrace. I'll chat to her and tell her everything is going to be all right and that I'm here for her and that I love her—just as I would a real child. Once her needs are met, I find that I've miraculously grown myself back up again. The adult part of me can then get on with my day or respond to whatever is happening with the grace of a woman rather than with the tears or rage of a wounded child.

—JN

Picture your inner girl each morning before you meditate and then try to carry a mental image of her held tight and safe in your heart as you go through the day. You could even start carrying a real-life photo of yourself at a young age in your purse.

Take your inner girl out to play whenever you can. The healing benefits are miraculous. Be curious. Find out what she likes and doesn't like, because they will be clues to unlocking your joy. Try to give her a treat at least once a week. Maybe she likes to spend time in parks or listen to live music. Maybe she likes baking cookies or shaping figures out of clay. Have fun with her and allow her to breathe and be happy. Really get to know her as you would if you were fostering a young child. If you have children, let her play with them. The better care you take of your inner girl, the better you'll be able to respond to life's challenges with grace and maturity.

Both the good and the bad news about this journey is that you get to connect to a whole palette of feelings. Some are pleasant, some painful, but all of them are absolutely vital. They are the clues that will lead you back to yourself.

One of the main reasons we abandon parts of ourselves in the first place is to avoid painful feelings—not realizing, of course, that we're paying a far greater price in losing ourselves.

At some point along the way, a therapist referred to my lack of self-care as neglect. When she said it, I was shocked. That's a strong word. But she was right. I am and always have been the last person I take care of, if at all. I push myself so hard and pile so much onto my plate and have for so long that I don't know how to do it differently. I've barely paused to ask my adult self what I need, let alone my inner child. But it is my inner child and her fear from decades of being neglected by her adult self that is the real victim here. It is only when I stop to ask what she needs and how she would like to see things play out that I can see another way that involves space and gentleness and laughter.

—GA

Trust the Process

Some of us live in cultures, countries, and communities where it simply isn't safe to be honest. Some of us grew up in families where we had to hide who we were to survive emotionally, and even decades after we've left home and the danger's long gone, we can still struggle to reveal the truth. Sometimes it takes a lifetime to say, "This is who I am. This is what I think. This is what I feel. This is what my body looks like and—you know what?—I'm happy about that!"

It takes as long as it takes. This journey back to ourselves is not over and done with in a finite period of time. More will be revealed to us about the parts of ourselves we've buried or abandoned, as well as the parts we thought were integral to us, but which, it turns out, were actually just ways of coping with life.

78

Ultimately our intention is to be ourselves wherever we are. We'll still be complex and multifaceted, but each aspect will be a reflection of our true selves rather than characters we pretend to play. We may be less perfect, but we'll be a lot happier and a lot more real.

Honesty in the Wider World

There are no shortcuts. Being true to yourself and what really counts is the only route that leads anywhere.

—DR. SARAH FANE, founder of the charity Afghan Connection

Telling the truth is for many of us a political act as well as a personal act. It says, "I'm real—not a stereotype."

As women, we've been obliged to hide our feelings and our desires for centuries. Although many of us now live in societies that are—on the face of it, at least—a lot more equal, it is still difficult for us to tell it like it is. To really be honest out loud with others.

It's a new muscle. Many of us have been conditioned to seek consensus rather than challenge it. That's one of the things that make women so awesome to be around: we're not constantly picking fights for the sake of it or entering into unnecessary competition. But it means that often we've lost the habit of speaking up.

At this early point in our journey, our primary responsibility is to be truthful with ourselves, not to slip back into denial and lose ourselves again. But when you're ready, you can start practicing honesty out loud.

A good starting place is with the truths that are nearest home.

Imagine what it would be like if we all told the truth about what it is to be female.

If we stopped pretending to be fine when we felt vulnerable.

If we stopped hiding our needs so as to appear "likeable."

If we could say we found being a mother tough or that we hated breastfeeding while everyone around us said they loved it.

If we could speak openly about the menopause and what it involves.

If we could say that we hate the dating app Tinder but are afraid of loneliness.

If we could talk about how it can be difficult or impossible to orgasm.

If we could talk about stress incontinence.

Imagine what would happen if we collectively decided it wasn't okay that we had to make ourselves look sexy in order to feel accepted; that we had to pretend we don't bleed or have body hair or unequal-sized breasts.

If we didn't feel we had to interrupt the aging process to hold our place in the work force or society.

Imagine if each of us—one woman at a time—said, kindly but firmly, "Enough. No more pretending. This is who I really am."

And once we've started to tell the truth about those aspects of ourselves that we've been made to feel aren't acceptable, we can start to tell it like it is in all sorts of other areas.

In the past, many of us tolerated injustice, discrimination, or abuse for fear of rocking the boat. Increasingly, we find we can no longer tolerate the unacceptable—we see it as a distorted form of people-pleasing.

In 2016, I made public that I was initially offered half the amount my male costar was offered for a job that is famously a "duo" and an equal amount of work. I eventually got parity, but I knew that one day I would have to "out" what happened for the sake of, well, women. I can't tell you how nervous it made me. Even though everyone on my team and everyone I had told since was shocked and appalled at the audacity, until the moment when it slipped out in an interview, every time I even thought about saying it publicly, I felt afraid and nauseous. It was, I think, purely the fact that the subject of pay equality had been broached fairly recently and on a very public scale by numerous well-respected women in my industry that gave me the strength to get into it. Even though I'd had the same "fight" for parity with the same network two decades earlier and won. Even though it was insulting and disrespectful and sexist of the company that I'd helped to accumulate billions. Even though it was the truth! I was afraid of angering The Man and embarrassing the *woman* in charge.

—GA

It may not always be necessary to tell our truth out loud. We don't need to grandstand or court attention. Not all of us will be physically or economically safe enough to speak out. But when we are, and truth and honesty are called for, increasingly we'll find ourselves telling it as we see it.

Slowly but surely, we'll find it harder not to speak out, and we'll discover that as we change, the world changes too.

Reflection

Self-respect has nothing to do with the approval of others.
—JOAN DIDION, author

People-pleasing is a dangerous game. When I focus too much on others, I abandon myself. I may start off by trying just to be nice, but before I know it, I'm trying to be whoever I think the other person wants me to be.

Often my need for approval comes from unmet childhood needs. But if I spend my life trying to manipulate others into making up for it, I will lose touch with who I really am.

Action. Today I will have the courage to be me, irrespective of what others think.

Affirmation. I am true to myself.

Principle
2

ACCEPTANCE:
Making Friends with What Is

How wild it was, to let it be.

—CHERYL STRAYED, author of *Wild*, among other books

Acceptance gives us the ability to handle whatever life throws our way. It asks that we sit with what is—even when it's painful. In return, it transforms our relationship with reality and enables us to find peace.

Life hurts. Sometimes it hurts unbearably. Few of us are called to this journey unless we've suffered heartache, and many of us arrive at its start laden down with loss and disappointment.

As adults, we know that painful emotions are an inevitable part of being human. But what many of us don't realize is that much of the suffering we experience isn't inevitable at all. It comes from our not knowing how to use a vital spiritual Principle: acceptance.

Like all of *WE*'s Principles, acceptance works just as well for the small things in life as it does for the big ones. You can use it to deal with minor irritations or howling pain. Whenever you find yourself struggling with difficult emotions or obsessing about how to change something, acceptance is the Principle to reach for.

Surrender to Win

Surrender affirms that we are no longer willing to live in pain.
—DEBBIE FORD (1955–2013), self-help author and coach

Without acceptance, we find ourselves in conflict with reality. We resist what is and then make ourselves the victims of it. We get stuck in the drama, the pain, and the rights and wrongs of what *should* and *could* have happened.

We spend our precious energy begging, pleading, and fighting against our lot rather than working out what we can do about it, and, in the process, we generate a lot of unnecessary pain for ourselves and others.

This is true even when we have the best of motives. "If you loved me, you'd stop drinking," we tell an alcoholic loved one whom we know is powerless over his or her addiction to alcohol. "Please come back," we beg an ex who's clearly moved on. We become attached to outcomes, and when we can't make them happen, we're miserable. Even if it's just the rush-hour gridlock or the rain, our default response is to rail against it and want it to be otherwise.

This approach to life doesn't work. It leaves us emotionally battered and unhappy.

Being in conflict with reality is no different from banging your head against a brick wall and wondering why it hurts. Until you accept that the wall is there, you'll get bruised again and again and again. But once you accept it's there, you begin to have choices. You can work out how to get over it, under it, or around it. Or you might decide to grow roses against it or use it for shade.

....

SERENITY, PLEASE

The Serenity Prayer by Reinhold Niebuhr is used by millions of people all over the world. You don't have to have any sort of faith to benefit from it. At its heart is a simple formula: change what you can and accept what you can't. When you apply it to your life, you can feel at peace no matter what is happening. If you find yourself obsessing about a problem, instead of trying to work it out in your head, repeat this prayer to yourself:

"Grant me the serenity to accept the things I cannot change, the courage to change the things I can, and the wisdom to know the difference."

....

Acceptance is a process that we often have to repeat again and again.

You don't need to believe that acceptance will help for it to work. You just have to be willing to give it a try. When you apply it to your life—no matter how imperfectly—things miraculously get a whole lot easier.

Acceptance takes real courage. It ultimately involves grieving losses you'd rather deny. It involves hitting the pause button, so that you can feel whatever you need to feel and then not only let go of how you wish reality was but ultimately make friends with it, just as it is.

Until you accept things as they are rather than as you'd like them to be, you'll remain stuck in a prolonged emotional tantrum, battling with what's happened. It doesn't mean you like how things are. Acceptance isn't capitulation or resignation. It's a vital step in the process of transformation and finding peace.

It's only once you've accepted reality—shorn of your wishes and wants—that you can start to bring about change.

Whether you're struggling with a breakup, a loved one's harmful habits or behaviors, or just the daily rough-and-tumble of living, acceptance provides a new way of handling life that brings lasting emotional freedom.

Exercise 1: The Acceptance Cup

For this exercise, you'll need your journal and a cup. (An empty pot or jar will do just as well.) Draw a large *A* on the front of your cup—nail polish works well—and, if you have the time and inclination, decorate it.

Take a moment to center yourself and then make a list of anything that is upsetting you right now. It can be large or small. A rejection or a loss. Anything that, when you think of it, makes you feel a live jolt of emotion. You don't need to write explanations—just a word or a name to denote what you've found that hurts.

You don't need to refeel what you're writing down. This isn't about getting stuck in your emotions; think of it more as detective work. What you're jotting down are clues. Keep going until no other charged thoughts come to you.

If you do find yourself becoming upset, pause to do something kind for yourself: perhaps take a short walk or make a cup of tea.

If you're someone who shuts down and finds it hard to know what you feel, then ask yourself, "What would I be feeling sad about if I let myself?" Perhaps a bereavement or loss, or something you wish had turned out differently.

Once you've come to the end of your list, it's time to start the acceptance process. Look over each item and ask yourself this one simple question: "Is there anything I can do about this situation?"

If there is, jot down on a separate to-do list any actions you could take. Try to be brutally honest. Often we're tempted to imagine we can change things we have no control over. You may want to check your to-do list with someone you trust to make sure that you're being really honest.

If there is nothing you can do—or you're not sure—write the letter *A* beside the entry: *A* stands for "accept."

Now look at every item that has an *A* beside it. You'll find they are all linked by a common characteristic: they are all things over which you have no control. Absorb that fact. When we're most in pain, it's often because we're trying to change something over which we are powerless.

One by one, tear off each *A* item and place it in your cup. As you do, take a moment to acknowledge that it is painful to accept this loss or sad feeling, but that there is nothing you can do. Try not to get sucked into the pain. Just nod to it, as you would to a familiar face or acquaintance, and say, "This is as it is."

Accept with your heart as well as your mind that you are powerless. Surrender. Give up the fight and allow yourself to experience the relief of not having to be in control.

You are handing over the person, situation, or event to the flow of life, which is deeper and stronger than you are.

Put your Acceptance Cup somewhere safe and use this process whenever you bump up against a situation you can do nothing about. If you find yourself dwelling upon any of the items in your cup, remind yourself that it is not yours to worry about or to fix now.

When we let go of a problem, it creates the space for solutions to appear.[1]

Accepting "what is" is like letting go of the rope in the middle of a tug of war. You remain standing, and what you've been battling with tumbles to the ground.

Once you agree to stop being in conflict with reality and accept it just as it is, you'll experience a huge shift.

That doesn't mean that you like or condone what is. It isn't about saying that something is okay when it really isn't. But peace of mind will elude you until you let go of bargaining with things that you can't change.

The Things We Can't Change (The Past, People, Places, and Things)

We can't change the past, and yet many of us spend years thinking about how things could have or should have been. When we accept that the past has happened and there's nothing we can do about it, we give ourselves permission to move into the present.

88

Similarly, we can't really change people, places, and things. When we try to control someone or something, even if it's with the best of intentions, we often end up being controlled by that other person, thing, or situation. We abandon ourselves in pursuit of an outcome and rob ourselves of the chance to find peace.

So if you're struggling with one of these, ask yourself whether there's something in the situation that you need to accept. If there is, get out your Acceptance Cup and use the exercise you've just learned to free yourself.

The more we start to accept the things we can't change in our lives, the more effective we become at changing the things we can: namely, our own attitudes and actions.

When we're able to bring back the focus to what we do have power over, we can then connect to our own sense of power and grace.

Exercise 2: Step into Your Light

This exercise will help you stay in your personal power. Find yourself a space where you won't be disturbed. Stand with your feet hip-width apart, so that you feel stable and grounded. Close your eyes and imagine that a spotlight is shining down on you. The light is bright and full of love. You are standing in a shower of affection and warmth. You are standing in the glory of being you, and it feels right, enough, and very, very good.

Now imagine drawing a circle on the ground around the edge of where the light falls. If you were to hold out your arms and turn in a circle, the light would reach about that far from you in all directions and encircle you. Inside your circle is what you can control: yourself.

On the other side of the line is darkness and, within it, all the things that you can't control. Every time you step outside of your light to try to change a person, place, or thing, you abandon yourself and step into darkness. Sometimes you may mistake someone else's light as your own for a time. When you enter the dark, you lose yourself and your power. When you stay in your light, all things are possible.

Imagine for a moment that you are stepping out of your light to try to force someone else to see things your way. Feel how destabilizing it is and how your power fades. Now step back into your light and reexperience the feeling of standing in the warmth of love and wholeness. Feel how empowering it is. Enjoy standing there for as long as you like. Breathe it in. Savor its richness. Try to connect with this feeling during your daily meditations.

As you go through your week, notice when you step out of your power. For instance, when you find yourself experiencing pain or discomfort, look at where your feet are—have you stepped into someone else's circle? If so, step back into your own light. Return home and know that you are loved and that all things are possible.

....

Accepting Responsibility

As women, we often accept responsibility for things that aren't our fault. This can be a convenient but destructive way to avoid reality. If you label something as being your fault, then you don't have to accept that the other person might not be able to give you what you want or need. If you pretend to yourself that you're the cause of another person's dysfunction or cruelty, you may be keeping hope alive, but the waltz of denial will have you avoiding responsibility for yourself and will likely cause you excruciating pain.

Acceptance allows us to stop making excuses and start making tough calls. Do you want peace of mind or just to carry on taking the path of least resistance? Yes, you can go to a party your ex is throwing, if you really *are* okay with the pain that will induce. You can say yes to a promotion you don't want in order to get the pay raise, but you have to be willing to accept the frustration, stress, and lack of spare time that comes with it. You can date someone you're not attracted to in order to avoid feeling lonely, but only if you're willing to deal with the pain that it will generate for both of you further down the line.

Acceptance asks that we get real about what we're up to and accept our truth now, rather than spinning fictions for ourselves or others.

Accepting Reality

The Principles build upon and support one another. For instance, honesty and acceptance walk hand in hand: you can't solve a problem unless you admit it exists. And you can't get over an emotion that you deny you're even feeling, so stay vigilant for any signs of self-deception.

Whenever you feel uncomfortable, notice and name the feeling and then get honest about what you might not want to accept. For example, if you notice you feel really crazy when you spend time with a particular person or in a specific environment, name it to avoid slipping into denial or self-blame, or trying to fix it when it may have nothing to do with you. When you find yourself constantly excusing someone else's bad behavior, notice and name it. Again, you may quietly think "It's me" when someone repeatedly disappoints you or stands you up. Noticing and naming opens you up to accepting the reality that he or she is simply unreliable.

None of this is about blame or judgement. It's just about getting truthful, connected, and real. That's not to say you won't feel furious and rebellious about what you're noticing and naming. It's entirely natural not to want to accept that your partner is an addict, or that someone you love is ill, or that you can't change a decision that an institution or a politician has made.

If you're experiencing a lot of internal resistance, try accepting that you are refusing to accept. Often, *wanting to want to* is enough to begin the process.

Feelings: The Price Tag for Acceptance

No one likes crying, but tears water our souls.

—XUE XINRAN, Chinese-born journalist and advocate for women's issues

Acceptance is the gateway to peace of mind, but there's one very powerful reason we resist it: our feelings.

The majority of us try to avoid or minimize our emotional pain. In fact, for many of us, avoiding our feelings has become a way of life.

But as difficult and as painful as those emotions are, in order to access the miraculous peace that acceptance brings, we need to learn how to negotiate them.

Living on the Run: Avoidance

We bury things so deep we no longer remember there was anything to bury. Our bodies remember. Our neurotic states remember. But we don't.

—JEANETTE WINTERSON, British writer

Many times, instead of feeling our pain, we act as though emotional discomfort is some kind of subterranean monster we can trap beneath our constant activity and motion.

We do it with substances, overeating or undereating, or spending hours online. Perhaps we avoid it by compulsively socializing or overscheduling so that there are no nasty gaps through which the pain can emerge. We might hide in work or parenting. If you're already on a spiritual path, you might use your journey as a form of avoidance—constantly looking for new tools and new teachers to help you avoid pain rather than feel it.

Even self-hatred can be a form of avoidance. The pain hits, and you immediately start trying to work out what you've done wrong. You beat yourself up and imagine that if you were smarter or prettier or luckier, you wouldn't feel what you're feeling. Maybe you try to change your body so you'll be a bit more lovable. Perhaps you buy another self-help book and make a fresh set of resolutions that you fail to keep. Thrashing around, looking for answers to give the illusion of control.

Other times we get drawn into the drama of our story and find ourselves bogged down in blame and self-pity. We feel wronged or rejected. We start to believe that fate has stacked the odds against us. We'll never get what we want and need. "See?" we say. "I'm not worthy of good things," or "Nothing good ever happens to me."

We blame ourselves, and we blame others. We may blame our parents, our friends, politicians, or life events. We try to change things. We try to find satisfaction, and when that doesn't work, if we're not careful, we descend into a negative spiral of despair.

In an attempt to avoid feeling, we obsess about what might have been and torture ourselves with thoughts of "if only." We make deals in our head as if we can control reality with our thoughts alone.

Some of us deny we're hurting at all. "I'm okay," we'll say. "It doesn't bother me really." Then, when the pain breaks through our protective wall of denial, we deny it all the more vociferously.

The problem is that not only does avoidance not work but also it actually makes things worse.

The Two Types of Emotional Pain

When it comes to emotional pain, there are no shortcuts. It has to be felt. If we try to duck out of experiencing our natural feelings, we don't escape them at all; instead, they just mutate into something more damaging.

Also, what many of us don't realize is that there are two kinds of emotional pain. One is the legitimate pain of being alive: *real pain*. The other, *synthetic pain*, is highly toxic, and yet most of us live with it on a daily basis.

Real Pain

Real pain is the price we pay for being members of this extraordinary race. At its most extreme, it is the anguish at the loss of a loved one or the betrayal of a lover. It can sweep over us like a storm. At other times, it's a prick of disappointment that burrows under our skin like a splinter.

The only healthy way out is to move through it. But as difficult as that path can be, when we emerge, we find that not only can we endure and survive, but also that we are infinitely stronger for it.

Synthetic Pain

Synthetic pain is an impostor. It is real emotional pain's toxic clone, and while it feels urgent and necessary, there is nothing noble or inevitable about it. Whereas feeling real emotional pain is ultimately healing and leads to growth, compassion, and wisdom, synthetic pain leaves us stuck and riddled with anxiety, resentment, and regret.

Synthetic pain is what we experience when we try to bargain with or avoid reality by refusing to accept what is. It is to real pain what self-pity is to grief, or resentment is to anger. Think of real pain as being akin to the pain of giving birth: it's agony but productive. Synthetic pain is what you'd feel if you crossed your legs and tried to prevent yourself going into labor.

Telling the Difference Between Real and Synthetic Pain

When we're in real pain we feel it in our body: our guts, our solar plexus, our hearts. But synthetic pain resides in our heads.

Obsessive thinking—replaying an event or situation—is a symptom of synthetic pain. Our minds can resemble a tumble dryer, tossing things around and around and around to try to reach a different outcome. We can think we're trying to solve a problem through the power of our intellect, but usually we're digging ourselves deeper and deeper into a painful mental rut.

Obsessive thinking is an attempt to bridge the gap between how we wish things were and how they actually are. We keep a fantasy alive in our thoughts to avoid the feelings that need to be felt and the actions that need to be taken.

For example, instead of leaving an abusive situation, we may obsess about how we wish it were better. Instead of accepting that something we longed for hasn't happened, we may replay events over and over again, hoping that we can make the outcome different through the sheer power of our thoughts. Bargaining is a natural part of the grieving process, but if we're not careful, we can get stuck there, avoiding legitimate sorrow and replacing it with layers of toxic synthetic pain.

....

THE FIVE STAGES OF GRIEF

While each of us will find her own unique way to face grief and loss, most of us will go through what are now commonly known as the five stages of grief: denial, anger, bargaining, depression, and, lastly, acceptance. Often we find ourselves moving back and forth among the first four stages before we finally get to number five. Acceptance won't reverse our loss, but it does bring us peace.[2]

....

A Toxic Legacy

When we fail to feel our *real pain*, it remains buried alive inside us. Sometimes we suppress our emotions so effectively that we don't know they're there—but our bodies always know. These feelings manifest in our lives as illness, chronic unexplained pains, anxiety, or rage. They lie dormant until they're suddenly ignited, and we find ourselves losing all perspective and self-control.

The good news is that when we step out of avoidance and into acceptance, we can begin to defuse the emotional land mines from our past that can trigger distorted emotional reactions in our present. As we release the bottled-up pain gradually and appropriately, we find we are no longer victims of our histories.

When emotions are functioning healthily, they act as your guide. They'll tell you when to protect yourself and when to let down your guard and become intimate. When to say yes, when to say no, and when to say you're not sure.

NNFR: Notice, Name, Feel, and Release

Hopefully, you're starting to get the hang of noticing and naming as initial steps to identifying your feelings. The next steps are to actually feel and then release them, enabling you to access a whole new level of emotional freedom and making it much easier to practice acceptance.

Notice, Name, Feel, and Release is not an intellectual process, it is physical. To practice it, you need to become present to what is happening in your body so that you can start to expose the truth of who you are. It is a tool we all should have learned at school, but, instead, most of us were encouraged to bury our feelings and pull ourselves together.

In order to feel and release emotions, you have to allow yourself to experience them without a story—with only the physical sensations in your body as your guide.

Initially, you can use the following exercise to feel and release. In no time at all, you'll find yourself incorporating the process into your everyday life. Sometimes you'll do it in the moment, while at other times you may have to pause and wait until you have the space and safety you need. But from now on, you'll have a technique that will enable you to feel your emotions and move through them to a place of acceptance of what is.

Exercise 3: Feeling and Releasing

This is a great exercise for any time you need to free yourself from difficult or painful emotions.

Lie down somewhere quiet and safe. Close your eyes and take five deep breaths in and out. Now imagine that your mind is a laser. Send it down into your body to explore. Allow it to scan, looking for areas of tension. When it finds one, let its light rest there. Try to breathe into it, into the knot of tension that it has found. If that knot were a feeling, what would it be?

Eastern medicine practitioners would say that if it is in your neck or shoulders, it might be anger, as this emotion often gets trapped there just before the point of release—that is, before it roars out of your mouth. If it's in your chest, it may be sorrow— that's how heartbreak got its name. If it's in your stomach, it's likely to be fear—no different from having a knot in your tummy before an exam or presentation.

Breathe into each feeling that you encounter. Let your mind remain silent. If you're stuck as to what you might be feeling, see if your inner child is around. (See Principle 1: Honesty.) She's likely to know the answer. Ask her if she's okay. If not, what is she feeling and why? Trust the first answer you get back; it's often right.

When you've worked out what feelings your tensions are hold- ing, breathe deeply into every one of them until each knot has started to diminish. You might need to release a few tears as well. Let them flow. There's no need for thoughts to get involved. Now isn't the time for words. You're diving down beneath the narratives you tell yourself. Just feel and release. Feel and release.

It's important to take this work at your own pace and pause if you start to feel overwhelmed. There's no need to push yourself—take this journey one step at a time.

Pause for a moment to congratulate yourself each time you allow yourself to Notice, Name, Feel, and Release your emotions. You're doing a beautiful thing, not just for yourself, but also for the people in your life. Imagine how many times you have said or done something hurtful because you haven't taken the time to address what's really going on inside. Imagine what it might be like to make this a regular practice so that you can move into your life from a more grounded, connected, and less agitated or distracted place.

This is an exercise you can come back to whenever you have noticed and named feelings that need to be felt and released. If you have limited time or are worried about being overwhelmed, you can set a timer for five to ten minutes. Or you may choose to take as long as you need to process what surfaces. Either way, release whatever comes up and be gentle with yourself when you've finished the exercise.

This is a journey. Each Principle enables you to take more steps in the direction of wholeness. What you're learning and practicing is vital to a life of integrity and meaning. This is important work. When you take responsibility for your own emotions, you can be a better parent, partner, daughter, sister, or friend. It also becomes easier to forgive others when they are unable to process their emotions because, in this simple exercise, you have come face-to-face with your humanness and your vulnerability, and shown compassion to yourself.

When I'm having really strong feelings, I sometimes remind myself that I've given birth to children and treat the feelings as I did labor pains. I breathe into the heart of whatever is hurting me. Trying to think my way out of the pain of a contraction never would have worked, and it's the same for getting through difficult emotions. Thinking just puts off the feeling and stores up masses of synthetic and toxic pain. Of course, I still try to bargain with reality or enter into judgement about what should or shouldn't be happening, but I increasingly find myself remembering that there's no point. Until I've released whatever feelings need to be felt, I'll be off center, and my perspective will be distorted.

—JN

I'm not sure exactly when low-grade anxiety started in my life. I do recall that waking up with a sense of panic became an everyday occurrence in college, and the full-fledged attacks started when pregnant with my first child. It's safe to say that getting a handle on this is what initially led me to meditation. But despite the fact that I have lived my adult life with some form of it either in periphery or front and center, the only way I have been able to step into my life as a student, a parent, or an actor who does live stage performances is to feel the fear and do it anyway. To say yes to life in all its complexities and terrifying twists and turns, despite potential paralysis behind every corner.

—GA

....

DRAMA QUEEN

In feeling and releasing, your goal is not to prove to yourself, or to anyone else, how upset you are. It is to allow the feelings to pass through you, just as you would a fever or a bout of physical pain. As described earlier, getting too caught up in the drama of a situation is another way of avoiding real pain or its solutions.

When we witness friends doing this, it can sometimes feel disloyal not to join in and agree that, yes, things are really awful. But jumping into the maelstrom can destabilize your newfound process. Next time, take a deep breath and see what happens if you don't participate in feeding the fire of their distress. You can still be there as a calm, loving presence, but you don't need to costar in their production.

....

It may be the case that you can't actually work out what it is you're feeling. You try noticing and naming, but nothing recognizable comes up to feel and release. If you've spent a lot of time trying not to feel, it's completely natural to have difficulty working out what it is you *do* feel—all you know is that you feel bad. And if you're depressed, your feelings may be buried quite deeply.

Don't panic. If you create the space, they will start to surface when they are ready.

Remember that you'll find your feelings in your body, not in your head. Many of us have grown up thinking that thoughts and feelings are one and the same. Part of this process is learning to distinguish between them. Later on, in the 6th Principle, peace, the focus will be on stilling your mind, but for now, your concern is with feeling what needs to be felt so that you can move into acceptance.

In the meantime, if your head starts throwing in unhelpful or negative thoughts—that you'll never feel better, or you'll always be alone—try to ignore them as you would a noisy neighbor or a loud drill. It is, in fact, just noise.

....

SHAKE AND RELEASE

If you've ever seen two ducks fight on a lake, you'll notice that when it's over, the ducks shake their wings and then swim away. The shaking serves a biological need: it releases the stress chemicals that built up during the fight.[3] Similarly, possums play dead when a predator is near, and after the danger passes, they'll shudder to release the stress chemical.

Whenever we've had an argument or received bad news, we too can experience the feeling and then shake our arms and legs to release the stress. We can go for a walk or a run. We can play music and dance. What we don't want is for the trauma to stay trapped in our system, so take your lead from the animal kingdom: shake, release, and move on.

....

Changing What We Can (Accept and Thrive)

If you don't risk anything, you risk even more.

—ERICA JONG, author

When you move through your feelings and into acceptance, you'll discover that you have the space to focus on the things you have the power to change. Or as the Serenity Prayer puts it, you'll start to be able to "change the things you can." (See page 85.)

You can change your outlook, your attitude, your responses to life, and your actions and reactions. You'll discover that when you practice acceptance, answers exist right alongside the problems you've been fixating on; you just haven't known where to look for them. You'll notice many doors are open and available to you that you just didn't see before—often because you were so busy focusing on the one that had closed.

You may, of course, have to wait to see the answer or the open door before you take further action. Waiting is an action in its own right. As you wait, you get ready. You let go of what you can't change to make way for a life full of possibility.

Many of us have spent years wanting our lives to be different. When we release ourselves from that burden and accept ourselves and our lives as they really are, anything becomes possible. Before long, amazing things will come to pass.

....

ENJOY, CHANGE, OR ACCEPT

Life is not an endurance test, although it can often feel like it—especially at the start of this journey. Over time we discover that there are three options in any situation: enjoy, change, or accept. Notice that *endure* isn't one of them! The first choice is always enjoyment, but when that isn't possible, we either change the situation or practice acceptance.

....

Many years ago, I was in so much emotional pain that I sought out a spiritual teacher to help me get to the other side of it. This teacher had written a book that, among other things, was about transmuting emotional pain. I discovered he was holding a retreat and, armed with his book, made my way toward it. It took two planes and a long car ride with many others heading to the same place, but I was so focused on my story of loss that I didn't lift my head out of the book for the entire journey. It was as if somehow the words alone were holding me together and the planes in the air. This "stance" of mine continued for the first couple of days. I absorbed and was moved by the teacher's talks, but was so locked in my head and my pain that I barely managed to engage with anyone, struggled to make eye contact, and definitely didn't acknowledge the beauty of the landscape around me. I was supposedly there to release, but I was completely unable to experience the joy that was manifesting for others before my eyes.

On the third day, I received an invitation to a one-on-one meeting with the teacher. I was very excited, I had so many questions and was sure that he would be able to see the particular "depth" of my story and help me toward understanding why it was so painful. I was led to the teacher's cabin, and there he was: this little man with bright, smiling eyes—the embodiment of pure love, pure joy, and presence. I sat before him looking deeply into his eyes, gathering my questions, and there in the presence of what many agree is an embodiment of higher consciousness, I suddenly had nothing to say. All the questions melted away and meant nothing. They were all based in ego and my inability to let go and just be with what was.

In that moment, there was nothing wrong. Nothing was happening to me. I was not ill or being tortured by anyone—except myself by perpetually hashing over and over the wrongs and the misunderstandings, the self-pity and the pain. I left that cabin with the broadest smile on my face and the deepest sense of joy I have ever experienced. Not a word had been spoken. More miraculously, I was then able to face the "painful" circumstances in my life with nothing but love and acceptance. There was no more story left; it had been transformed.

—GA

We all notch up losses and heartaches as we walk through life, but when we allow ourselves to feel the necessary pain and learn the accompanying lessons, we grow in dignity, grace, and wisdom. They become part of our journey, and in time we discover that what we've suffered can be used to help someone else.

We come to understand that real pain can make us useful as a midwife for another woman's sorrow or fear. When this happens, we start to regret less what we've lived through. Any residual feelings of hopelessness and victimization start to fade as we realize we are taking our place in a chain of women—stretching back through history—who have felt deeply and been there to hold a light for another walking in darkness.

Acceptance in the Wider World

When you invoke the agent of change called acceptance, you must accept all that you are, all that you've been, and all that you will be in the future.

—DEBBIE FORD (1955–2013), self-help author and coach

Politically, the idea of acceptance can bring up strong reactions. Because in many cultures and in many different ways women lack power and freedom, we are often forced to accept the unacceptable.

But this Principle is not about accepting the unacceptable. It is about coming to terms with the problem, however ugly, so that we can begin to change it.

As the old saying goes: when it's raining, let it. Once you've stopped trying to prevent the raindrops from falling, you can put up an umbrella and take shelter while the storm passes. Or, better still, find a way of collecting and reusing the water!

Our goal as activists is simple: to reduce the amount of avoidable suffering that exists in the world. Practicing acceptance in our own lives prepares us for the work ahead.

You can start right now by feeling what needs to be felt, avoiding self-made dramas, and then making yourself available to walk with another as she does the same.

How different and more peaceful would the world be if we all took responsibility for feeling our sorrows? If we sought change from a position of wholeness and spent our energy on the issues where we can really make a difference?

Reflection

*The greatest illusion we have is that denial protects us. It's
actually the biggest distortion and lie. In fact, staying asleep is
what's killing us.*

—EVE ENSLER, playwright and performer,

and author of *The Vagina Monologues*

I used to think that accepting reality was giving up the fight. I
didn't want anything to do with it—I wanted a world where pain
and suffering didn't exist. Now I know that when I accept life on
life's terms I can find peace no matter what.

Action. Today I will embrace life as it is and feel whatever emotions
need to be felt.

Affirmation. My feelings guide me home.

Principle
3

COURAGE:
Ending the Victim Trap

*We don't develop courage by being happy every day. We develop it
by surviving difficult times and challenging adversity.*

—BARBARA DE ANGELIS, bestselling author and
authority on personal growth and relationships

Courage is the Principle that frees us from our past. It
enables us to live fully in the present by shedding the stories
and unresolved anger that can keep us trapped. It puts us
firmly on the path to wholehearted, authentic living.

This is not the courage of stories we heard in our childhoods,
which often focused on public (and almost exclusively male) acts
of heroism—complete with dragons and angry crowds. The courage
that's called for here is no less brave, but it's far more profound. It

involves becoming the heroine of our own lives and rescuing ourselves from the internal mechanisms that have held us captive.

Without courage, we remain trapped by attitudes and habits that reinforce our sense of powerlessness and we risk being the victims rather than the heroines of our lives.

The Story Trap

Life shrinks or expands in proportion to one's courage.
—ANAÏS NIN (1903–1977), French-born author

The word *courage* derives from the French word for "heart": *coeur*. In each of our hearts are stories that we think define and protect us but, in fact, keep us trapped.

As we start to notice and name the emotions, masks, and labels we've accumulated, we become more aware of the stories that lie beneath them.

Our stories are based on our experiences and our attitudes toward them. They're the narratives through which we try to understand and make sense of our lives, and they're part of what makes us human. The problem is that they're rarely accurate. They're almost always distortions of the truth that can leave us feeling as if we're victims of events.

Your story is not who you are, but it is often who you *think* you are. It is one of the tricks the ego plays on us. And the stories each of us have about ourselves separate us from our real self, leaving us struggling to feel at ease in our own skin.

Plus, we don't have just one story. We have entire collections that we layer over one another, fundamentally distorting how we see ourselves.

Of course, not all our stories are bad. But it doesn't actually matter whether it is good or bad; if it's a story, it's not actually the truth. It's a racket: a subterfuge under which our real self hides.

It takes courage to step out from behind these yarns and own your reality. Even when our stories hurt us, we can be reluctant to let go of them because we don't know who we'll be without them—our self-identity has become so entangled with them.

"Who am I," we might wonder, "if I'm not the child who was neglected or the woman whose partner deceived her?" Who are we if we're not the mothers who gave up everything for their children and then were abandoned when they left home without a backward glance?

Who are we if we let go of everything that might have been or we believe should have been? Fundamentally, who are we if we shed our wounds and our defenses? This path is about finding out. But before we can find out who we are, we have to summon the courage to let go of pretending to be who we are not.

Exercise 1: What's Your Story?

This exercise has two parts. The first will help you to identify and shed the stories that keep you trapped. The second gives you a wonderful tool to transform them.

Part 1: Identify Your Story

Have your journal ready. Take five deep breaths to center yourself. What is your dominant story? This isn't the story you'd give at a job interview or if you were speed dating. It's more likely what you'd say if you were having a heart-to-heart with a kindred spirit or a first session with a therapist.

Your story will have an emotional "charge" to it—usually sadness, regret, or anger. It will hurt.

It may center on a childhood event or a loss. It could be that you've been single for a long time, had an abusive marriage, or have never been able to conceive.

Often it feels as if our stories about ourselves are hardwired. They are tattoos or brands burned into our souls—something that we'll never be able to change or erase.

Once you've identified a dominant story, sit down and write it out in your journal. Write it over and over, as if you were a child writing lines: "I was abandoned as a girl." "I'm a single mother." "I'm long-term unemployed." "I was left." "I was betrayed." Keep writing until it becomes as meaningless as any phrase does when it's repeated enough.

You may need to cry while doing this exercise. But write through the tears, write through the pain, and write until you are out the other side. And then *still* keep writing. Write until there is no emotional charge left to what you are writing and then, once it feels as if the pain has gone, write another full page's worth. Write until it is as meaningless as gibberish, because that is what it is.

You might think it's damaging to keep repeating a negative message, but the odds are that you've been reinforcing it all along, countless times a day—to yourself and to everyone you meet— whether you were aware of it or not.

We tell our stories over and over until they are worn out. We repeat them and repeat them, often until we die. Writing it out like this is an intervention. You drain the emotion out of it so that you are left with empty words on the page. But within those empty words, which feel like history, is hidden vital information that you can use to finally set yourself free.

Now it's time to mine the gold that lies at its heart.

Part 2: Rewrite Your Story

Look closely at the sentence you wrote in the last exercise. It contains a message for you. What is the belief about yourself that lies within it? Not the detail, but the essence.

If your story is that you're alone, perhaps your underlying belief is that you are worthless or unlovable. Perhaps it's that you're just plain unlucky in love or doomed in some way. If you recognize the message as one you were given in childhood, that's a clue, because that's when most damaging messages are imprinted.

You'll know when you say it to yourself that it's true in the same way that you know you've got a splinter. The source is a sharp, clear pain.

Now write yourself an affirmation based on that sentence. You may have written one before, but if not, it should be short, simple, positive, and stated in the present tense. It's not a statement of longing; it's a statement of fact. Here are some examples, but it's better to tailor one for yourself:

"I exist."

"I am loved."

"I am resilient and strong."

"I am perfect just the way I am."

"I am enough."

Put it where you can see it—maybe on a Post-it note stuck to the edge of your computer screen, your bathroom mirror, your car dashboard, or inside your journal or iPad cover. Say your affirmation whenever you start to wobble or revert to your story or the emotional reactivity or shutting down that comes with it. Use it as a spiritual shield to protect yourself throughout your day.

Notice how many times a day you're tempted to draw on your story as a resource for defining yourself. Perhaps you're in a line for lunch, and someone pushes in front of you: "I'm invisible" might pop into your head. Or perhaps you hear that you haven't been invited to a party that others you know will attend: you might automatically think, "I'm unlovable" or "I'm alone." Use your affirmation to neutralize and replace your story.

....

For many years, whenever I was doing a mundane task like cleaning or packing, there would be a constant argument in my head. I would be defending myself about something or telling somebody what I really wanted them to know about themselves; whatever it was, it was fraught, and I was in attack mode. Fortunately, that is no longer my experience, but it reveals something about where my head was and what was essentially my default stance in the world.

Today what I notice more is my attachment to a particular story. It's more likely to be something that I want others to feel sorry for me about. Sometimes I hear the refrain of "Poor me" or "You don't understand," which at times heads into "How dare you!" territory. Much of it is an attachment to being right.

When I notice that this type of thinking has taken over, I need to interrupt it. It becomes important to get to the root of why I feel misunderstood. It's really easy to allow something like that to fester and to replay my side of events over and over in my head. Undoubtedly, that type of built-up emotion will affect everything I do and get projected into my conversations with everyone I see. How can it not?

—GA

Our stories keep us captive and mesmerized. We're like hostages who've become bonded to our captors. It takes courage to break the bond.

If you find yourself tempted to tell your story—good or bad— remind yourself, "This is just a story, these are just words. The real truth is that I am [loved/worthy/beautiful/a regular human being]," and then carry on with your day. Your ego may put up a fight and want to revert to its version of you, but firmly and kindly use your affirmation to protect yourself from damaging narratives.

Be vigilant. Like weeds, stories can grow back, but if you're disciplined, you'll start to see results. You'll experience a sense of possibility and expansiveness. You'll start to recognize your true nature: the essential self that doesn't change and isn't shaped by events or challenges. You'll start to see the truth.

Yet no matter how much awareness we practice, sooner or later we're likely to pick up another story, so use the "What's Your Story?" exercise whenever you have a persistent negative thought or tale in your mind. Interrupt it and neutralize it with an affirmation. The only story that ultimately serves you is that you are enough just as you are.

The story I carried with me from growing up in an alcoholic home was that I was invisible. I told myself that nobody saw me and nobody cared, and I discounted any evidence to the contrary. I took the story into adulthood. No matter how many people watched me reporting on TV, no matter how many friends I had, deep down I felt as if I didn't exist. I was a leaky sieve: as soon as I was filled up with attention, it drained out, and I needed more. My childhood story drove me into a life of constant striving for more and more success and love that was doomed to fail.

My most recent Post-it says simply, "I exist." Every time I'm tempted to people-please or do too much, I remind myself, "I exist." I don't need to do, say, or prove anything to justify my space in this life or to be worthy of love. I exist whether I do or do not clear a particular hurdle I've chosen for myself. I exist whether or not I'm told by anyone else that I'm wonderful or that I'm loved. Pure and simple, I exist.

—JN

Having started the practice of freeing ourselves from our stories, we now turn to the courageous work of freeing ourselves from the resentments we've accumulated.

Expect resistance. As with our stories, we often become attached to our resentments, despite the devastating harm they cause.

Releasing Anger Safely

Holding on is believing that there's only a past; letting go is knowing that there's a future.

—DAPHNE ROSE KINGMA, therapist and author

specializing in love and relationships

When we don't process our anger properly at the time it arises, it can fester and has the potential to poison our outlook and our lives.

Anger is a vital and necessary emotion. It drives us to protect ourselves and others, to set boundaries, to say enough is enough. When properly harnessed, it can drive change in our own lives and in the wider world. But for a host of reasons, many of us have problems feeling and expressing anger in a healthy way. There have been social taboos against women expressing anger. We still risk being dismissed as hysterical, shrill, or strident. For example, think of former British prime minister David Cameron's dismissive "Calm down, dear" to a female colleague in the House of Commons, or the highly personalized attacks Hillary Clinton attracted, which never would have been leveled at a male colleague.

Similarly, for many women, it isn't safe to be visibly angry—either culturally or if confronted by an abusive partner.

Even if you're alone, it can be terrifying to experience your own anger—especially if you're not used to it. You can fear it'll overwhelm you or make you go crazy; that once you let the genie out of the bottle, you'll never be able to get it back in again and return to your status quo.

So, for a whole panoply of reasons, many of us bury our anger, shoving it deep down inside, where it becomes trapped as resentment. Before turning to how to release long-held resentments, first it is vital to understand how to process anger safely. It takes courage to release anger, especially when it has been trapped inside you for a time—sometimes from early childhood. Anger, when felt and released in a healthy manner, is the engine that will drive you to sanity. It will give you the power you need to move yourself out of destructive patterns and into emotional freedom.

So call on the tools you learned in Principles 1 and 2. Notice and name anger whenever you feel it. Then, as soon as you can, feel it and release it.

Of all the emotions we experience, anger carries and consumes the most energy. Different techniques to release it will work best at different times, so experiment. You can hit pillows, punch beanbags, go for a fast run, box, dance, or stomp, kick, and smash things that you don't mind breaking. Shout, write, talk—do whatever it takes to release the feeling. But stay in your body; stay in the feeling. It's an emotion, not a thought, so ignore any stories your mind is telling you.

Now is *not* the time to communicate directly with the person you feel caused your anger. If you speak in the heat of the moment, you risk causing harm. Better by far that you wait until you are calm, powerful, and in your center before you engage. Plus, by the end of this work, your perspective will have undergone a radical change. Old certainties will crumble, and new ones will emerge. So for now, keep the focus on yourself.

When your mood is low or you're depressed, you may not even be aware of your anger. Trying to connect with it can be like trying to untangle a ball of knotted wool. But if you find the loose end—the flicker of emotion—no matter how small or hidden it is, and then follow it, you will be able to unravel it.

....

ANGER BUCKET

Imagine that you have a bucket deep inside you for storing anger. Over your lifetime, you accumulate a lot of it! If you empty your bucket regularly—by releasing your anger in healthy ways—it is a lot easier to handle. But if you let it get too full, even the smallest event can cause it to overflow. The result is unpredictable and volatile behavior or depression. You want to be calm and gentle, but, out of nowhere, you find yourself raging.

....

When you don't express your own anger, you may find others doing it for you. You may wonder why you're locked in so many similar situations of conflict—not realizing that you are generating the angry responses you encounter. Or, if you're depressed, you may wonder why others are short-tempered with you when you're clearly suffering.

At the height of my worst depression, my son started getting very angry. We sought professional help. "It's very simple," the therapist said. "He's expressing your anger for you." Once I began to own my anger and find safe ways of releasing it, his behavior returned to normal. Anger works similarly to personal power. If we don't own and harness it ourselves, someone else close by will use it—often against us!

—JN

Connecting with and then releasing your anger can have a dramatic impact on depression, but supplement this process with professional help if you need it. It's extraordinary how reluctant many of us are to allow ourselves to access the support that's available. We'll go to the gym for our bodies, but we resist doing the same for our minds.

··

CLINICAL DEPRESSION

There's a world of difference between the feeling of depression, which is a normal part of most people's emotional range, and *clinical* depression, which is a medical illness.

A prolonged period of stress, a major loss, a repressed childhood trauma, or a genetic predisposition can leave you vulnerable to clinical depression. If you've felt low for an extended period of time and can't seem to shift out of a negative mindset, check it out with a doctor. You wouldn't battle through a serious physical ailment without seeking medical help, so treat your mental health with the same respect.

Seeking help when we need it is an act of courage, not a sign of weakness. There aren't any medals for trying to tough it out. We're lucky to live in an age where there are excellent therapists and medications to treat clinical depression. Our grandmothers and even our mothers were not so fortunate, so make use of the help that is available for your sake and the sake of those around you.

··

After my first marriage ended, I buried my anger and tried to behave as if what had happened hadn't affected me. I was proud, and I told myself I was taking the spiritual high road by not getting angry. To me, feeling angry couldn't change what was happening, so it was pointless. Two years later, when I developed severe clinical depression, I discovered that all the anger I thought I'd avoided lay trapped inside me. My route out of depression involved both medication and a lot of work connecting with and releasing the anger I'd been too "spiritual" to feel at the time.

—JN

Releasing Resentment

You wanna fly, you got to give up the shit that weighs you down.
—TONI MORRISON

If we don't process our anger properly at the time it arises, it churns and becomes the most toxic of all emotions: resentment. The word *resent* comes from the French *ressentir*—meaning literally to *refeel*. When we resent, we refeel events that have hurt and angered us again and again.

We think it's the events themselves that leave us feeling victimized, but, actually, our own *attitude* to events often causes us far more pain and, in particular, the resentments that we hold closely. Resentments leave us trapped in the past, and either depressed or simmering with rage, hurt, and bitterness. They can fuel self-pity and make us act mean as we think about or actively try to even scores. Like boulders obstructing a mountain trail, resentments block acceptance and letting go.

Each person whom we believe has let us down or caused us anger stays with us. That makes the going heavy. When we work through our resentments, we are like weary travellers who stop to unload their baggage to rid themselves of what has been weighing them down.

While real anger is felt in the body, resentment starts in the head. It begins with a "They shouldn't have!" or an "It's not fair!" or an "If only . . ." It justifies itself by listing wrongs and spiraling deeper and deeper into us until we're totally consumed.

Most of us are incredibly sensitive. We often hate admitting how much we're hurt by tiny things. Big things we somehow often know how to handle, but the little hurts can burrow their way into our psyche and skew our whole perspective.

Resentment is the most harmful form of the synthetic pain you read about in the previous chapter. It doesn't matter whether your resentment is big or small, it can steal your peace of mind and leave you obsessing, weaving yet more stories in your head. Before long, those stories, too, can start dictating your reality.

....

HONESTY REQUIRED

Each time you refeel a hurt from your past, you tell yourself the story of what happened to you. Each time you tell it, as with repeating any story, the version is likely to shift, particularly if it involves resentment. Each time you retell it, even if only to yourself, you're likely to make what the other person did to you a little more wrong and how you behaved in response a little more right. So you have to really practice rigorous self-honesty.

....

There'll be signs if you're resentful. You might be passive-aggressive: an angry nice person who smiles and says yes while inside she's screaming "No!" Someone who is nice to everyone else in the hope that they'll be nice to her and carries within her a fury that people aren't treating her as she deserves.

You might be depressed, your life force blocked by layers of hurt and anger that have been compressed within you for so long that you can no longer "feel" beneath their weight.

You might be volatile and emotionally super-reactive, bristling with real and imagined slights to the point where others walk on eggshells around you.

Or you may be a combination—an exploding doormat—who yo-yos between being passive and easygoing one moment and suddenly erupting into rage the next.

If you're dismayed at how angry or hurt you can get over something that seems relatively small, it's likely to be the back catalogue of incidents you've suppressed breaking through the surface of your "niceness." When we're resentful, our past hijacks our present.

Being Right or Being Happy

Hanging on to resentment is letting someone you despise live rent-free in your head.
—ANN LANDERS (1918–2002), advice columnist

The most damaging resentments of all are those that stem from events where your initial anger was justifiable. If you've been betrayed, assaulted, or misjudged, it takes extraordinary courage to let go of that resentment.

Resentment creates the illusion that we can somehow right the wrong that has been done if we just hang onto it for long enough.

But the reality is that it's like drinking poison and then waiting for the other person to get sick. You may get a temporary high from your outrage and a relief from your hurt while you anticipate revenge, but as you wait, the poison starts to take effect and makes you, not the culprit, sicker and sicker.

....

THE MONKEY TRAP

According to an ancient Indian fable, the easiest way to trap a monkey is to put a piece of fruit inside a container with a narrow hole in it. The monkey slides its hand into the container and grabs the fruit. But its fist is now too big to pull back through the hole. The monkey, reluctant to let go of its find, holds on to the fruit and so gets caught by the hunter. To survive, the monkey needed only to let go and move on.

....

You can't change the past, but having courage makes it possible to change your attitude to it.

You can't live a fulfilling and happy life and keep your victim status. The two are incompatible.

It's really a simple choice: Do you want to be right? Or do you want to be happy?

If you want to be happy, then it's time to clear out all the resentments that may be backed up and festering inside you.

Letting Go of Resentment

Spiritual Surgery

Releasing resentments is akin to spiritual surgery. It's the most exacting of all *WE*'s processes. It involves having the courage to step back into your past—not to blame but to go on a fact-finding mission. The process which is outlined follows the exercise that is adapted from a highly effective system used in most 12-step fellowships. It involves listing anyone or anything in your past that causes you pain and releasing yourself from it. This process can be used again and again whenever you realize you've been resentful. It is an intense but very powerful and effective experience.

As with physical surgery, you need to take really good care of yourself before, during, and after this work. So make sure you're using the Essential Practices every day, as well as scheduling in some extra "you" time. (See the exercise "Befriend Yourself," on page 22.)

Exercise 2: Releasing Toxicity

This exercise is set out in three parts and will help you release any toxic resentments you may still be holding. You will need to pace yourself, as you may not be able to deal with all your resentments in one sitting. However, it will be worth the effort. Once you've finished, you'll have turned a huge corner and gained newfound energy and optimism.

You can choose to work on a single, particular resentment to start with or on everything and anyone you have ever had negative feelings about. Just make sure you use a fresh page in your journal or notebook for each resentment. The more thorough and detailed you are in writing out the source of the resentment, the more paper you'll get through, and the better it will work.

Part 1: The Source

Write the name of the person, organization, or event that you have negative feelings about. Beside it, write a few words what he, she, or it has done to hurt you.

It doesn't matter whether what happened is large or small. There doesn't have to be any logic or reasonableness as to why you were hurt. All that matters is that you were. Nobody else will read this, so you are free to be completely honest. It could be someone not picking you to be on her team at school, or it could be a lover who was unfaithful.

Write quickly and don't dwell on or get stuck in the pain. Reliving the drama is a form of avoidance. Your task is not to re-experience the experiences but to list them. So, as the saying goes, glance back but don't stare.

If you find it particularly difficult not to get drawn into the past as you write, invite a friend—perhaps one who is also on the *WE* journey—to sit with you as you do the work. Alternatively, you can write in a café or public place so that you remain anchored in the present while making this excursion into the past.

If you start feeling overwhelmed, treat yourself as you would anyone else you love and pause to do something nurturing for yourself. But don't abandon the process altogether—just as you wouldn't walk away from an operation once an incision has been made.

When you've finished, congratulate yourself and, if you need to, take some time out. You're about to start making the turn-around: to stop being the victim and to start reclaiming your life.

Part 2: Your Role

Now your focus is going to shift away from the other person, organization, or event and onto yourself, leaving behind the (sometimes exhilarating) surges of anger, to turn your focus inward.

This is not about blame. It's about identifying what you can change. If it helps, imagine that each resentment is like a thorn you've trodden on that needs removing. The flesh around it may be tender, but you'll feel so much better once it's out!

So take each resentment and note down what part you may have played in the wrong that was "done" to you. It might be your actions, words, or attitude. Ask yourself: Did I rely on someone I knew to be unreliable and then end up distressed when he or she let me down? Was I expecting someone to give me something he or she was never able to give? Was I looking to hang on to something or someone that wasn't really mine? Have I behaved in a way that might have courted retaliation—for example, by being arrogant or judgemental? Did I do something that might have hurt the person who hurt me? Was I dishonest in any way? Have I distorted the event so that I can look more blameless and someone else more culpable? Have I ever done to someone else what was done to me?"

It may be that you were completely blameless because you were just a child. In this case, look only at your attitude now.

Am I hanging on to this injustice and keeping it alive with my attitude? Have I allowed that event to become my defining story?

What is making it impossible for me to move on? Am I unwilling to relinquish the fact that I've been wronged? Am I choosing to be right over being happy? Am I unwilling to accept that something unfair or unjust has happened to me?

Am I keeping myself a victim in the hope that someone else will make it better or that the person who wronged me will suddenly realize this and make amends? And if so, why?

Am I tormenting myself further by pointing out how much better other people's lives seem to be?

As you do this work, you will identify the ways in which you've stoked and fed your hurt and resentment; how you've compounded it through your thinking. You'll see how when you can let go of having to be right, you can accept and move on.

You didn't choose the hand you were dealt, but thanks to the work you're doing now, you'll have the power to choose how you play it.

When you have worked your way through every aspect of the resentment, you are nearly there. The spiritual surgery is complete, but your wound still needs to be stitched.

Part 3: The Release

The final part of this process provides the gateway to a new relationship with a part of your history and, through that, your life. You'll be identifying what you need to feel and release so that you can move into acceptance.

Ask yourself: "How do I wish it had been?"

In just a few words, write down how you would have preferred things to turn out. Feel the feelings that come up and then release them. This takes courage. But as you allow yourself to release your sorrow, anger, and disappointment, you let go of the past and truly start to move into your present with meaning and purpose.

Acknowledge the loss and say quietly and respectfully to yourself, "This is how it is."

If you want, you can add the page describing your resentment(s) that you wrote in part 2 of this exercise to your Acceptance Cup. (See page 86.) Once it is there, it is over.

Repeat this process with each resentment that you feel is holding you back. It may take awhile or even a few days or weeks. Don't be afraid to pace yourself. Take breaks when you need them. Go for a walk or sit in a park. There is no rush, but the sooner you do the work, the sooner you'll be free

When you have completed part 3, congratulate yourself for having the courage to confront and liberate yourself from an aspect of the past that wasn't serving you. You are now well on the road to freedom.

When we use spiritual surgery, extraordinary shifts occur.

You will cease to see yourself as a victim. You will find that you're able to pick yourself up and get on with your life. You'll no longer carry the burden of others' actions.

Repeat this exercise whenever you feel hurt or angered. It allows you to have a centered emotional response to a situation and then move on. Use it regularly to prevent further pockets of resentment from building up. You can do it at any moment in the day when you notice a resentment starting to niggle away at you: on the bus, when dropping off or picking up your children from school, in a meeting, before bed. Once you've done it, write a mini gratitude list to wash away all traces of it.

Like many of the tools you're learning here, this one has a magic multiplying effect. The more rigorous you are at spotting and then releasing your resentments, the fewer you'll start to have. It will change your outlook and your attitude. You'll start to recognize how you fed your sense of woundedness and outrage and how disempowering that was. You'll see how you took the unfairness that life inevitably entails and made it worse by hanging on to it.

> The longer I walk this path, the more essential it has become to get to the crux of what those building resentments are. The only thing I can control is how I react to situations. If I can look at my own behavior in this scenario, for instance, and see where I have impacted another human being, then I can choose to apologize. I have no control over whether that person accepts my apology, but I do have control over how I choose to let go of any resentments I may harbor.
>
> —GA

EXPECTATIONS

When we expect that someone will behave in a certain way, we set ourselves up to resent the person if he or she doesn't. As the saying goes, expectations are the mother of disappointment and the father of resentment.

They are like contracts that the other party hasn't had a chance to read or sign, and yet we expect people to abide by them. Then when they don't, we're upset. It's a setup. What's more, people often sense the weight of our expectations and experience them as demands or attempts to control, which they naturally bridle against. Once we let go of expectations, we're amazed at how others respond.

While you can't change your history, when you change your attitude toward it, a whole new future opens up.

You'll find that as you let go of the hurts you've been carrying, your journey becomes a lot easier. You'll have new responses to situations and feel hurt less often because what's happening in the present is no longer being inflamed by resentment from your past.

Having the courage to release yourself from the burden of your past frees you up. It creates internal space for your intuition and instinct to find solutions you couldn't have imagined previously.

You will also start feeling less alone. Resentment and false narratives distance us from others. They put a barrier between us and reality, which distorts what we see and blocks real connection.

When new hurts arise, deal with them quickly. Notice, Name, Feel, and Release your anger (see page 97) and use what you've learned to let go of any residual pain. As you do, hope and optimism will become your travelling companions.

Courage in the Wider World

Memories of our lives, of our works, and our deeds will continue in others.

—ROSA PARKS, 1913–2005, civil rights activist

When our lives are dominated by resentment, we find ourselves lurching from one upset to the next.

Open any newspaper, and you can see the consequences of unhealed and unconscious emotional responses playing out in the world at large: brawls, murders, and wars often waged in the name of self-defense but that in reality are the result of emotional wounds accumulating in intolerable feelings of umbrage and impotency.

Hurt people hurt people. When we're not healed, we do to others what has been done to us. We react with rage rather than with compassion and insight.

How much more peaceful would the world be if we each took responsibility for processing our hurt feelings so that we didn't act them out on others?

How many more solutions would be found if we let go of our personal need to be right?

How much more powerful would we be when we engage with others if we harnessed our anger instead of raging about our suffering?

When we have the courage to let go of our rage and resentment, we discover we are powerful beyond measure.

Reflection

Above all, be the heroine of your life, not the victim.
　　　　　　　—NORA EPHRON (1941–2012), author,
　　　　　　　playwright, screenwriter, film director

If I'm upset by someone or something, I have to be diligent and process the anger or hurt it provokes. If I don't, I'll be in danger of acting out my resentment on those I come into contact with. That could be my child, who is nagging me to play while I'm busy, or it could be the shop assistant I snap at because I'm preoccupied.

Action. I will take responsibility for feeling and releasing my anger safely.

Affirmation. Today I let go of being right so that I can be happy.

Principle
4

TRUST:
Living Without Fear

You can never leave footprints that last if you are always walking on tiptoe.

—LEYMAH GBOWEE, Liberian peace activist

Trust is our antidote to fear. It aligns us with the flow of life—a magnificent energy that guides and directs us so that we can live expansive, happy, and fulfilling lives.

With trust, life starts to open up. We're able to embrace opportunities, have fun, and make the most of our time on this earth. Trust fosters cooperation and compassion rather than competition.

Without trust, we live in fear and anxiety. We doubt ourselves, we doubt others, we worry, we compete, and we try to control outcomes. We live small when we could be living big.

A miracle is sometimes defined as a change in perspective—a moment when suddenly everything shifts. That's what trust leads us to: a completely new perspective on our life.

Choosing Trust over Fear

The most difficult thing is the decision to act, the rest is merely tenacity,

     —AMELIA EARHART (1897–1937), barrier-breaking aviator

Trust offers us freedom from fear. But, as with all of *WE*'s Principles, there is just one thing that's required from us if we want to experience its magic: willingness.

To start with, choosing to trust can feel foolish, giddy, and maybe even ridiculous. Trust can seem irrational, illogical, and irresponsible. We want to know what we're trusting and how it's going to work.

But the truth is, you already know how to trust; you've been trusting for many years. It isn't new to you, it's just that you have been trusting the wrong thing—you've been trusting in the negative outcomes that fear tells you are just around the corner.

When we adopt trust as a spiritual Principle, we do the opposite. Instead of assuming negative outcomes, we assume the best. And, crucially, we accept that we don't necessarily know what "the best" looks like.

Often it is only with the value of hindsight that we get to see that what we thought would be disastrous has actually turned out for the best.

Exercise 1: Living Proof

This exercise will strengthen your capacity to trust by showing you that, despite your worst fears, you have been taken care of in the past.

Close your eyes and breathe in and out deeply at least five times. When you are centered, scan back through your life. Look for situations where you were absolutely sure that something terrible was going to happen, but things actually turned out okay. Maybe you were in an accident that could have killed you. Maybe you had a brush with a serious illness that you survived. Maybe you thought you'd be alone forever but met someone and fell in love. Maybe you took risks with alcohol or drugs and lived to tell the tale.

Write down in your journal as many unexpectedly good outcomes as you can remember. It's your proof—when you need it—that things don't always turn out as you feared. And that even events that seemed catastrophic at the time can still lead to positive outcomes.

When I wound up in treatment for clinical depression, I thought it was the worst thing that could ever happen to me. I thought my life was over. Now, more than two decades later, I can see that it was actually the best thing that could have happened to me. It was where I was introduced to a spiritual way of living and began the journey back to my true self. Without it, I'm not sure that I would be alive today. So now when something upsetting happens, I try to replace my instinctive response of "How terrible!" with "How interesting," and then trust that somehow it will all work out.

—JN

I feel like I have so many examples throughout my life where my assumption was that things were undoubtedly going to go wrong. There used to be (and on the rare occasion, still is) a bit of catastrophizing. The relationship was going to fall apart. I was going to be fired. The desired event wasn't going to take place. And yet more often than not, I have looked back and thought, "Actually, thank God that didn't happen! How things have turned out is so much better for everybody." What has gradually changed over time as I've become more trusting is not that more things have gone the way I've wanted them to but that I've come to trust that, no matter what happens—even if the relationship does fall apart or the job goes away—I will be okay. More than okay.

—GA

Unmasking Fear

Fear has always been the driving force behind all dictators' repression.

—MARJANE SATRAPI, Iranian-born graphic
novelist, illustrator, and film director

Fear is an interloper. It pretends to be our friend, but, in fact, it plays a highly destructive role in most of our lives, inhibiting us and preventing us from reaching our full potential.

Of course, fear has a healthy biological function: to keep us safe. It stops us from sticking our hand into a fire, and reminds us not to have unprotected sex or walk in front of fast-moving traffic. The problem is that for many of us, it has ceased to be a tool we use to help us assess real risk and has instead taken control.

Fear often comes disguised as common sense. It focuses on the future: on what could happen or, more specifically, what could go wrong. When we try to make changes or move outside our comfort zones, fear pipes up with advice such as "What if it doesn't work out?" or "What if you never meet anyone better?" or "What if you're not good enough?" It tells us that if we just live a little smaller now, we'll be a little safer down the line.

You might think that worrying keeps you safe, but it's an illusion. It's like sitting in a rocking chair: it provides constant motion that doesn't actually get you anywhere. In reality, fear robs us of our sleep, our perspective, and our self-belief.

None of us can know the future, and yet fear has us in anguish over what it might be like. It can sound convincing, but it peddles lies. Think of it as an acronym for:

*F*alse

*E*vidence

*A*ppearing

*R*eal

When we rely on fear, we undermine ourselves and inflame any underlying self-esteem issues. Fear has us worrying about what other people think. It calls our abilities and decisions into question and makes us doubt ourselves.

It tries to protect us by preparing us to be disappointed, and it keeps us stalled when we could be moving forward. It persuades us to say no when we should say yes and steals our peace of mind.

There are plenty of valid reasons for our levels of fear. Many of us have learned to live fearfully from an early age. Perhaps bad things happened, and we now cling to fear to try to prevent them from happening again.

Or maybe we see the suffering that exists in the world and try vigorously to avoid it for ourselves. Fear can offer the illusion of control, convincing us that if we live small enough, we can prevent bad things from happening.

The problem is that allowing fear to govern our lives doesn't work. We can't control the uncontrollable—no matter how hard we try. Even if we lock ourselves away like modern-day Sleeping Beauties in our apartments instead of towers, there'll always be a metaphorical spinning wheel somewhere that pricks us.

....

THE BODY-MIND CONNECTION

Fear produces a stress reaction in the body: the fight-or-flight response, designed to get us out of immediate physical danger. We can have a similar response when we watch a TV drama or the news or browse the internet; if what we're seeing makes us fearful, our body becomes flooded by the stress hormone cortisol, even though we are not in any danger at all. Unfortunately, chronic or prolonged circulating cortisol can give rise to health problems such as elevated blood pressure and insomnia. The body-mind connection and its implications to our health is now well established,[1] so while it's important to be an informed citizen where current events are concerned, you also have a responsibility to carefully monitor the diet you feed your mind.

....

What we focus on grows. The more we focus on possible negative outcomes, the more fearful we become, and, ironically, the more likely they are to happen. Instead of protecting us, our fear often seems to become self-fulfilling. We stay in relationships we should have left for fear that nothing better would come along—and then the relationship falls apart anyway. We overwork and neglect nourishing our personal life to keep our job—and then get made redundant. We play it safe and turn down opportunities, and wonder why we're lonely, unfulfilled, anxious, and afraid.

As you saw with *WE*'s 2nd Principle, acceptance, we can manufacture unnecessary pain by being attached to how we *think* things ought to be. When we fear, we similarly generate unnecessary suffering. As the expression goes, we "borrow" trouble. We imagine bad outcomes that might never happen. We think we're protecting ourselves, when we are actually trapping ourselves in a place of negativity and fear.

Of course, bad things do happen, but living in constant preparation for them is like always keeping an umbrella above your head to be ready for the day it will rain. All that time we spend sheltering beneath it, we're unable to enjoy the blue skies that exist between the storms.

There is another way to live, and it involves replacing fear with trust.

Exercise 2: An Upgraded Operating System

This exercise will help you reprogram your fear-based response system.

Find a sheet of paper and a pen. You're going to create a new map for your life. Center yourself by taking at least five deep breaths in and out.

On one side of the paper, write the word *fear* in the middle. Scan your mind for situations that stir up a lot of fear for you. It could be that you're scared of public speaking, asking your boss for a raise, being honest with someone you're close to, or being alone. Perhaps you have bigger fears, like dying or getting sick. Jot down each one in a circle around the central word *fear* so that you create a mind map of what your life looks like when it's governed by fear. Add in any feelings that those situations evoke: anxiety, hopelessness, despair, indecisiveness.

How does it look? Not pleasant! Okay, now you're going to upgrade your operating software.

Use colored pens if you have them. Turn over the page and write the word *trust* in the middle.

Ask yourself, "How would my life look if I wasn't afraid? How would I feel? What would I do differently?" Jot down key words about how each situation would be transformed if you weren't afraid.

What would you do if you weren't scared to say how you felt? How would you live if you weren't scared of losing your job? What would you try if you weren't scared of failing? If you didn't tell yourself you were too young or too old, what would you be doing? Be really honest.

Visualize what your life would look like if you weren't afraid.

Make those visions more vivid and real than the lies fear has given you. Enjoy them. Write down words that sum up how your life looks without fear: *free, big, adventurous, bold, safe, courageous, happy.* Enjoy these feelings.

Congratulations! You've just mapped out a new direction for your life. The map marked "trust" is how your life is going to become. Look at it each morning to set your direction for the day and to give your subconscious a goal to aim for.

Notice that when you're looking at the side of the page marked "trust," you can't see the one marked "fear." The choice is as straightforward as that: you can live either by fear or by trust. Flip between the two images and decide which one you prefer!

A New Direction

I am learning to trust the journey even when I don't understand it.

—MILA BRON

When you face a choice, picture yourself standing at a crossroads with two roads pointing in opposite directions. You can either choose the one marked fear, which will lead you straight back to where you've come from, or you can choose to trust and head toward your vision and a courageous, rich, fulfilling life.

Any time during your day when you face a choice, simply ask yourself, "What would I do if I wasn't afraid?" And then do it. Take the leap, and the net will appear.

This new way of life takes practice. The chances are that you've been ruled by fear for most of your life. So don't be surprised when you encounter resistance. Fear won't necessarily go, but your response to it will change dramatically.

....

THE THREE-SECOND RULE

You can't stop fearful thoughts from arising, but you can choose what to do with them. You have roughly three seconds to interrupt a negative thought. Allow it to rest in your mind any longer, and it starts to take hold. The faster you decline its invitation to engage, the less likely it'll be to take up permanent residence. So when you have a fearful thought, don't invite it in and offer it tea and sympathy!

....

Happy Talk

When you're feeling fearful, allow the adult part of yourself to talk to the frightened part of yourself, as you would talk to a scared child. Connect with your inner girl (see page 75). Notice and name what's happening to her. Encourage her, praise her, and coach her through situations. When she doubts she can succeed, remind her of all her successes so far and encourage her to trust her instincts. Tell her when she's doing a good job or when you think she's being brave. Celebrate her achievements and console her with love when she's disappointed. And when you're done, congratulate yourself for trusting enough to try something new even though it makes you uncomfortable.

Growing up, the rule at home was that children should be silent. I wanted to please my father, and so I was virtually mute in the company of adults. In school, I'd freeze with fear whenever the teacher asked me a question. I was so scared of speaking out loud that I'd answer in whispers. Nobody would be able to hear me, and the whole class would erupt in laughter. Now, of course, I'm no longer that terrified, silent child, but occasionally, when I'm in a particularly challenging situation, I can find myself becoming mute again, and I have to work extra hard not to slip back into that early role of being a silent player in my life. The fear can be enormous, and I have to take a real leap of faith, open my mouth, and trust that I won't be humiliated in the way that I was as a girl.

—JN

Trust in What?

Trust in exactly the opposite of what you fear. Trust in the flow of life. Trust that you're glorious, that you're enough, that you're lovable. Trust that life will unfold as it should. Trust that the lessons others need to learn will be taught without your needing to intervene.

Remember fear's acronym: *False Evidence Appearing Real?* Well, trust has a much better one:

To
Rely
Upon
Spiritual
Truth[2]

Trusting is really a commitment to believing that love has more power than fear.

If you're not convinced, experiment. Try trusting for a week and see how it plays out. Each day, choose to do what you would do if you had no fear. Refer to your mind map. Assume the best in every situation, even if you can't fathom how anything good will emerge. Say yes when previously you'd have said no. Take risks. Know that you're capable. Take setbacks as signs that a better opportunity awaits. Be aware of how it makes you feel. Notice how much more resilient and enthusiastic about life you become.

Trust allows you to live in the present. The future will unfold as it needs to. The space you previously spent worrying and strategizing becomes available to enjoy. When you wake up each day, think of your mind as a garden. See how many wonderful, fine-smelling plants you can put in it. If fearful thoughts reappear, uproot them as if they were weeds before they can choke out the blossoms you're nurturing.

If you lapse back into fear, be gentle with yourself. Learning a new behavior is not always smooth. You'd never have learned how to walk if you hadn't fallen down many times.

....

THE SUBSTITUTION RULE

Every thought and behavioral pattern you have creates a neural pathway, or groove, in your brain. That's why breaking a habit can be so hard—you are literally wired to keep repeating your past behavior. With the Substitution Rule, you don't just try to stop doing something negative, you actively substitute a positive behavior or thought to take its place. By doing this you actually create a new neural pathway.

Recent research suggests that it takes on average just over sixty days to create a new behavior,[3] so each time you replace a fearful thought or action with a trusting thought or action, picture the neural pathways in your brain changing.

When you catch yourself saying something fear based, such as "I'll never be fit," substitute it with a positive thought: "I am getting fitter and healthier each day." And remember, what you focus on grows, so focus on what you are choosing, not on what you're giving up!

....

When my long-term relationship broke down, other long-term single friends seemed to pounce on me. "There's nobody out there," they told me. "It's a jungle. All the good ones are taken." Of course, everything they said reinforced my deepest fear: that I'd be alone forever. I became desperate. I was a single mother with two kids and in poor health—who was ever going to want me? I started making some bad choices, which reinforced my fear that I was unlovable.

Then someone told me to start doing the opposite of what fear wanted me to do. So I took a six-month break from dating to give myself time to recover and to prove to myself that I could be happy on my own. Each time someone asked me how I felt about being single, I repeated my new affirmation: "I trust that the right person will come when the time is right." And the more I repeated it, the more I started to believe it. What I discovered during that time was life changing: a source of happiness within me that wasn't dependent on another person. When I stopped trying to run the show, it somehow, magically, makes room for something more powerful to work its magic.

—*JN*

What If?

Once you decide to start practicing trust, be prepared for fear to launch a tirade of what-ifs. What-ifs are the fear-based questions that your mind will pose once you start to even think about making positive changes.[4]

Maybe you ask your boss for a raise, or you ask out the girl or guy in the coffee shop, or you enroll in the dance class full of people who look like they know all the moves perfectly. Well, those are exactly the moments when a what-if might come thundering into your head: "What if she fires me?" "What if he rejects me?" "What if I make a fool of myself in front of the whole class?"

The moment you hear a thought that starts with "What if," interrupt it. Halt it right in its tracks and answer it head-on with this short phrase: "I'll handle it."[5] Whatever the what-if, use "I'll handle it" to neutralize it. Remember, you have only three seconds to stop the what-if from taking hold, so be vigilant.

....

TYING UP YOUR CAMEL

Trusting doesn't mean that we stop taking action. We still have to take responsibility for our own well-being and do the footwork: put the stamp on the envelope, go for the breast examination, check out someone's online profile before agreeing to meet him.

What shifts is that our decisions are made on the basis of a rightsized assessment of risk—not the exaggerated versions we've often lived by. Fear had us trying to control outcomes. Trust asks that we let go of that control and simply do whatever needs doing. Then we let go of the outcome. There's an old saying that goes, "We trust in God, but we still tie up our camel."

Resistance

Some of us experience huge resistance to trust. If that's you, ask yourself whether it benefits you in any way. How does not trusting serve you? What's the hidden payoff?

Many of us discover that we use fear as a form of avoidance. We cling to fear because if we let go, we'll have to feel emotions we're trying to avoid. Maybe we don't want to trust that we'll meet someone more appropriate because we want to avoid the pain of saying good-bye to someone who's not treating us right. Maybe we don't want to trust that we'll get a better job because that will mean admitting we're in a bad situation.

If you find yourself getting stuck, talk to a trusted friend or therapist. Sometimes we can take a perverse comfort in clinging to fear. It might be corrosive, but at least it's familiar. We can trap ourselves in a better-the-devil-you-know mentality. Feeling that you're a victim of life is painful, but fear, with its twisted logic, can convince you it's safer than daring to believe things could be better.

The problem is that refusing to trust puts you in a catch-22 situation: you won't know how much better life will be until you try. The net only appears once we've leaped. So if you need support from others before taking the leap, ask for it.

....

FAKING IT

It takes time and repetition to establish those new neural pathways in the brain, so while they're still under construction, there's nothing wrong with "faking" a new behavior until it becomes authentic. Try acting as if you're not afraid. It sounds improbable, but it works!

....

There was a time when I didn't know how I would pay all my bills and was pretty close to losing everything. The fear was crippling. I couldn't sleep, and the stress was affecting every area of my life. Finally, I called a good friend and asked her for advice. "Your job is not to worry about the bills later this month," she told me. "You have this debt, and it is your responsibility to pay it. If you pay them what you can today, the money will be in your account when you need it for the next payment and for your future bills. Take responsibility now and then let go and trust."

Those words changed everything for me. Each month, for many months, there was the same situation, and, each time, I paid what was in front of me or negotiated to pay in installments, and every month, somehow, there were sufficient funds. The fear wasn't gone entirely, and some days I still found it hard to smile, but taking responsibility and seeing that I was taken care of changed my understanding of letting go and trusting. And I've found since that this works in so many areas of my life. So often I want to hold on tight to an idea or a plan, and every time I fight against the change, it causes pain. And every time I let go and trust that there is a greater plan that is out of my hands, and my only job is to show up and do the footwork. It alleviates the stress and the fight, and my life flows more smoothly.

—GA

Exercise 3: Moving from Fear to Trust

This exercise will give you a taste of the freedom that trust brings. You'll need your journal and to be undisturbed for about twenty minutes for this visualization. Take at least five deep breaths to center yourself, read through the following instructions, and then close your eyes.

Imagine you are walking up a mountain. Try to make the scene as vivid as possible. Breathe into it. Think about what you might be smelling and hearing as well as seeing.

You started your climb in good time. The sky is clear, the air is fresh, and the sun is warm but not too hot. The path curves around, and you discover you are higher than you thought. You sit down for a moment to savor the view and to think about how your life looks now that you're learning to trust.

Take out your journal and write a list of things you trust. They can be things you already trust or things you'd like to trust, if only you could make the leap. (Remember, you're allowed to fake it to make it!) Our subconscious listens to the messages we give it—whether they're true or not. So you can plant trusting thoughts here, even if you don't yet believe them. Make your list as uplifting and beautiful as you can.

As you write your list, remember that you are not alone: there are women everywhere right now making the same journey from fear to trust.

Here are some examples. I trust that . . .

I am in the right place at the right time.
Things happen for a reason.
I will be able to handle whatever life throws at me.
I am lovable just as I am.
I am worthy of respect and dignity.
I can live without active addiction.
I am trusted.
I am honest.
I am safe.
I am powerful.
I can make a difference.
I have a voice.

If you get stuck, look for where you have fear and then choose to substitute its opposite.

Here on the side of the mountain, as you look out across the beautiful view, give yourself permission to really believe each affirmation and to experience the relief that brings.

Your list can also include fears that you might want to dismiss as petty, but they can nevertheless steal your peace of mind. For example, I trust that . . .

If I'm not invited, I'm not meant to be there.
If I'm rejected, I am being protected.
When one door has closed, another will open.
My kids are learning exactly what they need to.
My body is perfect just as it is.
I am glorious and deserve to experience joy.

Make your list really positive. Allow your spirit to soar.

Transfer the statements that give you the most joy onto Post-it notes. Stick them places where you'll see them frequently to remind you that today your beliefs are shifting, thanks to having trust as your guide. .

....

People often tell me how brave I am because I seem to fearlessly jump into challenging and sometimes terrifying situations. But there are certain areas of my life where I am not brave at all: usually in the more personal zones. It has taken a lot of work, concerted effort, trial and error, and awkwardness to actively do things differently and face things head-on despite my deep-rooted reluctance, pessimism, and desire for anything uncomfortable to just go away. And it is still a work in progress. It is hard to say "I'm sorry" or "I was wrong" or "Can we please make time to talk about something difficult?" or "When you say that to me, I feel shamed/uncomfortable, and I don't want you to say it anymore" or "Thank you so much for doing that today; next time it would be really great if you could do it this way" or "I'm sorry, I don't think I was clear in my description. What I meant was . . ." Each requires a deep breath and a degree of humility, which certainly doesn't come easily to me. But it is transformative. Trusting the process and putting aside fear to take responsibility for one's own communication and quality of relationships is truly miraculous in its power and scope. It will change your life.

—GA

It takes time, but slowly, if you use *WE*'s tools, trusting can become your automatic response. When something unexpected happens, you'll be curious rather than frightened. The fear that used to paralyze becomes transmuted into excitement. You'll wonder how situations will turn out, rather than your old habit of presuming a disaster.

The more you leap, the more you'll learn that life really does catch you and takes you to exactly where you need to be.

When we trust, we discover how limited our vision has been and how much more there is to look forward to when we allow life to flow through us, instead of constantly trying to control and contain it.

Trust in the Wider World

Every time you replace a fearful thought with a loving thought,
you make the world a better place.

—DENISE LINN, spiritual teacher

From early on, most of us have been taught to compare and compete with one another, feeding our fear that we're not enough. We've been culturally encouraged to view one another as rivals—to try to work out who is prettier, who is smarter, who is more likely

154

to win love or to succeed. Fear leads to a binary system of winners and losers, of haves and have-nots.

Trust liberates us from that scarcity mentality. It tells us that we're enough and that there *is* enough. We no longer need to fear or be jealous of another's success because we no longer see happiness as a finite resource whose stock is diminished by other peoples' gains.

It gives us permission to substitute cooperation and compassion for competition and to see one another as allies rather than rivals. Before long, the magic multiplying effect that attaches to all spiritual Principles kicks in, and we discover that the more trusting and open we are with others, the more they respond in kind.

What's true for us as individuals is also true for the world. Trusting that there is enough, for us all, is a political as well as spiritual act. It's also factually true.

For example, we could feed every person on the planet if we just chose to. There is more than enough of all that is essential to life to go around. The problem is that when fear governs our decision making, we believe the lie that there isn't enough, and so we hoard and grab and leave those who are less able to fend for themselves to go without.

Trust gives us a new approach to life. Instead of competing, we can now cooperate—it's a much more efficient way to allocate our planet's resources.

It's also a much more peaceful and sustainable way to live. When fear drives our choices, it creates conflict, fuels overconsumption, and generates avoidable pain. So next time you're making a choice—whether it's about how to vote, how to live, or what to do with your evening—ask yourself, "What would I choose if I was able to trust?" And then allow love rather than fear to be your guide.

Reflection

Nothing in life is to be feared, it is only to be understood.
—MARIE CURIE (1867–1934), French chemist

When I'm frightened, I live smaller than I am. I clutch and I cling because I fear that I will get hurt or I will fail, or that there won't be enough to go around. This creates a circle of negativity as others become wary and distance themselves from me. Today I live a different way. I hold my face to the light and trust that my needs will be met, and if they aren't, I will have the courage to ask for them to be met. I no longer need to worry about the future; it is being taken care of, and that leaves me free to enjoy my day.

Action. When I feel fear, I will ask myself what I would do if I weren't afraid and then do it.

Affirmation. Today I am safe, and I am happy.

Principle
5

HUMILITY:
Unmasking Our Ego

Humility is freedom from your own driven ego.
—MARTHA KILPATRICK, Christian author and speaker

Humility allows us to be one of many, to know that we are wondrous and enough just as we are. When we practice humility, we have a strong sense of our own intrinsic worth that isn't dependent on anything we do, have, or own.

With humility, we are able to look for what joins us rather than what sets us apart: our common humanity, our wounds, our longings, our joys, and our frailties. Instead of pursuing bleak self-interest, we foster connection. We work to heal division. And as hard as it is sometimes, we choose to assume that everyone is doing the best he or she can.

Without humility, we are at the mercy of our egos. We compare, control, and compete. We worry about status, success, and what we do or don't have.

WE's Principles lead us down the road less travelled—and humility provides us with a spiritual defense against our egos. Humility rightsizes us: we're not the worst, we're not the best; we're just who we are, and that is wonderful.

The previous Principles will have helped you to start clearing away the emotional scar tissue and fear that may have blocked your path. Now with *WE*'s 5th Principle, our focus begins the shift from our relationship with ourselves to how we relate to the world.

Ego: *Edging Goodness Out*

The human ego's motto is "seek but to not find."
—MIRANDA MACPHERSON

We live in a world dominated by the ego—one that holds material status and accomplishments as paramount. One that loves pecking orders and lists of who's who and judges by external appearance, not decency or depth.

Our ego cares deeply about how we look in relation to others. It wants us to be better than others, but it's actually scared that we don't measure up. One moment it tells us we're fantastic, the next that we're a failure. Like the critical parent we can never please, it makes us feel as though nothing we do or have is ever quite enough.

Our ego's ultimate goal is to keep us safe. But its preoccupation with worldly concerns means that it doesn't take into account our emotional and spiritual needs. It drives us to abandon our values

158

in the pursuit of our goals and straps us in for a roller-coaster ride of "I won" or "I got" highs followed by the inevitable "Now what?" lows.

Most of us are so used to the voice of our ego that we have become oblivious to its impact on our thinking. That thinking then influences how we see ourselves, how we see others, and how we experience the world.

A Mental High

The origin of all demons is in mind itself.
—MACHIG LABDRÖN (1055–1149), Tibetan
Buddhist practitioner and teacher

Like a drug, your thoughts can change how you feel.

Close your eyes and think of something that really upsets you: perhaps a disagreement with a friend or a difficult situation you can't resolve. Observe what happens to your mood and energy. Notice the emotional jolt you experience as you think about it, as if the hurt or offense were happening again.

Now think of something or someone who really makes you excited: someone you're attracted to, a child's embrace, an amazing job opportunity, or a vacation. Feel what happens to your energy levels. This positive thought lifts you up.

Thinking certain thoughts can give you a high—whether it's imagining yourself in the arms of someone you really desire or browsing the internet for things you want to buy. But, like eating sugar, it's a temporary lift, a fantasy, and sooner or later, you will come back down to reality. The scariest thing about the drug of fantasy is that we don't need to go anywhere to buy it: it's just there, available twenty-four hours a day, inside our heads.

....

A NEGATIVE BIAS

We have roughly sixty thousand thoughts a day, and as many as 87 percent of them are estimated to be negative.[1] No wonder we find it so hard to maintain our equilibrium!

....

Thinking in and of itself of course isn't bad—it enables us to navigate our way through life—but only a small portion of our thinking is helpful. The rest is driven by our ego and keeps us locked into patterns of conflict and dissatisfaction.

Attack Thoughts

An attack thought is a kind of egoic thinking. It's quite easy to spot and starts with phrases such as "How dare she . . .?" or "Couldn't he have just . . .?"

It doesn't matter whether your attack thought is aimed outward at someone else or inward at yourself. The outcome is always the same: you are the one who gets hurt. If you consciously take your mind off the negative assault on yourself or someone else, you will feel better. You will be let off the hook of negativity that you placed yourself on.

It's not possible to think an aggressive or violent thought and maintain your peace of mind. So the moment you notice yourself mentally criticizing someone—stop! Use the Three-Second Rule you learned in the previous chapter. (See page 135.) Interrupt the thought by telling yourself very simply, "I could have peace of mind instead of this."

Of course, you might not *want* peace of mind. You might want to keep thinking about how wrong someone else is. But you now know that you can't be both right *and* happy. So the choice is yours: righteous indignation or peace?

Self-Blame

> *It's time we start writing a new narrative that doesn't focus on the struggle but on progression.*
>
> —NANCY KACUNGIRA, Kenyan TV news anchor

When our attack thoughts are pointed inward, we tell ourselves we're the worst parent/friend/worker/boss/daughter/person. We get stuck in the awfulness of distorted thoughts about who we are.

Beating ourselves up is subtly addictive. Some of us started doing it in childhood as a defense against situations we couldn't control. It gave us an explanation for the bad things that happened. It was less scary to blame ourselves than our parents or caregivers because if our caregivers weren't to be trusted, then surely we couldn't survive.

Thinking we're bad protects us from disappointment: if we're not good, we don't deserve anything good to happen, so we won't mind when it doesn't. (Except that we still do!)

We're never as bad as we think we are. It's another one of those lies our ego tells us. Pretending to be worse than we really are is just an inverted form of boasting; it's pride in reverse. Sorry to break the news, but you're not actually the worst anything—you're just you!

Compare and Despair

We may believe that everyone is born equal, but how often do we actually act on that belief? Most of us spend a lot of our lives thinking we are superior or inferior to others. We're constantly reading situations and trying to work out how we fit in. Who has the power? Who's the smartest? The most attractive? Who's the loser, or the one who'll make us look like one?

Society, of course, actively encourages us to compare and compete with others. We are conditioned to see ourselves as objects that have to be made worthy of selection: educated, groomed, and honed to the max. We're trained to rake over one another's appearances and told how to copy someone else's look, wardrobe, or lifestyle, feeding the lie that who we are isn't enough. The woman on the magazine cover has always got the body or the job or the relationship that would complete our lives.

It's all too easy to end up feeling as if other women are our rivals and that we're all in competition with one another. That's the work of our ego.

When we compare ourselves with others, sooner or later we end up in despair. Our ego loves to make comparisons, but most of the time it doesn't even compare like with like. It usually contrasts how we *feel on the inside* with how other people *look on the outside*, and it makes no allowance for the fact that most people put up a façade.

Thanks to social media, the opportunity to compare and despair is only ever a click away. We can instantly see what we haven't got and the places we haven't been invited to. We live with our faces pressed up against the windows of the virtual lives of friends and colleagues who seem to have exciting careers, luxurious holidays, immaculate children, and so on, and wonder why our lives don't match up. We forget that most people post only good news: the successes and sunrises, not their daily struggles or the hard slog to pay the bills.

> When I was offered my first pupillage at the English bar by a chambers of more than twenty barristers, I was told, "We're happy to have you as a trainee, but we won't have a permanent place for you because we already have a woman." It wasn't said with malice, more as a statement of fact—they had their token female. It affirmed what many women know already: that our sex is the first thing many employers see when interviewing us. That can make it hard not to feel as if our only real competitors for any job are the other women. Now if I'm in that situation, I make a special effort to connect with the other female candidates and build a bond of solidarity to replace the competition and the comparisons that my ego (and often society) wants me to make.
>
> —JN

The Toxic Cs

There's a handy technique for spotting when you're in egoic thinking. Generally, our ego has five really bad habits—all of which are culturally encouraged and all of which handily begin with the letter C:
- Comparing
- Criticizing
- Complaining
- Controlling
- Competing

These attack thoughts are defense mechanisms, only they don't work. They rob us of our peace of mind and set us apart from others. Each time we pick up one of the Toxic Cs, we cloud our minds and our outlooks.

Humility provides us with a spiritual alternative.

Humility: The Path Less Travelled

The thing that is really hard, and really amazing, is giving up on being perfect and beginning the work of becoming yourself.
—ANNA QUINDLEN, journalist and author

WE's Principles provide us with an alternative way of living and relating to one another. It's a path less travelled but much gentler. In exchange for the 5 Toxic Cs, humility gives us three more power-ful ones:

· Compassion
· Cooperation
· Connection

These three Constructive Cs are important not just for your own well-being but also for the planet as a whole. They give us a new template of how to be in the world, and they help us to stop replicating a system that has caused so many of us to suffer for so long. The fact is, if we gain power and influence and then use the old system we've inherited from men, nothing will change.

Instead of seeing one another as rivals competing for scarce resources, humility asks that we treat each woman we encounter as a potential ally and friend. Where once we might have compared and criticized, humility enables us to practice compassion, cooperation, and connection.

Many of us have suffered discrimination, directly or indirectly. We can be hungry for our chance of success. Humility doesn't mean we can't still pursue our goals, but it does ask that we do so in a way that doesn't cause others (or ourselves) harm. When we find ourselves drawn into any of the Toxic *C*s, we reach for our spiritual antidotes: the Constructive *C*s.

Remember *WE*'s acronym for trust: *To Rely Upon Spiritual Truth*. The "spiritual truth" that humility gives us is that our worth doesn't depend upon externals. When we truly comprehend this fact, we free ourselves to focus on the journey and our experience of it rather than the ultimate outcome. Our sense of identity is no longer wrapped up in obtaining goals. Instead, we judge ourselves by our values.

One of my biggest lessons in humility wasn't voluntary. I loved my working life as a television correspondent. I loved being able to call politicians to account, to be part of the events as they unfolded, to have a voice and a platform. I always had an interesting story to tell over dinner or a cause to galvanize support for. Then overnight I burned out and lost the ability to work. That was it, gone.

For the next decade, I was too ill to work or do much else. I no longer had stories to wow people with. I no longer had the inside track on what was happening in Westminster, the hub of British government. I was chronically sick—that wasn't quite so glamorous! But that period gave me freedom from my egoic self. There was nothing I could do to feed my ego; many days, I couldn't even get dressed. To start with, when people asked me what I did, I'd tell them about what I used to do, but it made me feel ill again. I'd become allergic to my egoic self.

Then I discovered the freedom of telling them the truth: "I don't do anything." I'd watch the look of panic spread across strangers' faces—perhaps they worried we'd have nothing to talk about—but I was no longer scared of not having an external identity, because I'd found who I really was inside.

—*JN*

The rewards of the spiritual journey you're now on are enormous, but the work isn't always easy. It requires honesty, willingness, and commitment. But remember that nothing has to be done perfectly. Perfectionism is banned, but there are other Ps you can use, such as persistence and practice. The more you practice, the more spiritually fit you will become, and the easier it will get.

Exercise 1: Spiritual Gym

This exercise is in two parts. In its entirety, it will help you build your spiritual muscles to tackle some of the ego's worst habits. You'll start to recognize when your ego is in charge and doing the talking.

In the warm-up, you'll need your journal and a dictionary. Using a dictionary, even an online version, may make you feel like you're back in school, but the beauty of working this way is that it harnesses your intellect for spiritual purposes.

Part 1: The Warm-up
Look up the definition of the following words and write them down

in your journal: *arrogance, dishonesty, envy, greed, impatience, intolerance, jealousy, lust, pride, self-centeredness, selfishness, self-pity.*[2]

Some of the definitions may appear to be contradictory. For example, *pride* can refer both to satisfaction in a job well done and an inflated sense of one's own importance. For this exercise, concentrate on the aspects that the ego likes to harness: the negative ones.

Each characteristic has the power to distort your thinking and your response to life events. It can make you feel deeply uncomfortable.

Have a look at this list and see how many of these responses are familiar:

Arrogance—"Why can't they just do things my way?"

Dishonesty—"I'd never behave like that."

Envy—"I want what they've got. It's not fair."

Greed—"I want more [than my fair share]."

Impatience—"It needs to happen now."

Intolerance—"I can't stand x, y, or z."

Jealousy—"I'm going to be replaced by this person or left out."

Lust—"I don't care, I really want him/her."

Pride—"How dare they!" or "Don't they know who I am?"

Self-centeredness—"How can they do this to me?"

Selfishness—"What about me?"

Self-pity—"Poor me; doesn't anyone understand how difficult this is for me?"

These often habitual responses to what life throws at us cause discomfort and pain. They lead us straight into a destructive cycle of attack thoughts and one or more of the Toxic *C*s.

Note down which ones you resort to most often. We all have some that are our go-to responses. "Poor me" (self-pity) or "How could they?" (pride) are usually favorites.

Notice and name them as you go through your day. There is a spiritual cure for them, which we'll look at in part 2 of this exercise.

Our ego focuses on externals. It complains that life isn't fair and looks for someone to blame. But as we do this work, we discover that whether we're happy or miserable is more likely to depend on our *responses* to the hand that life deals us, rather than the actual hand. With humility, we learn to replace our habitual ego-driven responses with spiritual ones.

Part 2: The Workout

Each of the negative characteristics we just examined has a spiritual opposite. When you notice yourself struggling with one, you can defuse it by focusing on its mirror image. It's like a gym, only spiritual. Just as when you have a bad back you're told to strengthen your stomach muscles to reduce the stress on your spine, you want to work with the spiritual opposite of a problem.

Take up your journal and dictionary again. Write down in color the definitions of the following words: *humility, gratitude, acceptance, courage, compassion, generosity, honesty, kindness, tolerance, patience, love*. These are your defenses against the ego's attacks.

As you write them out, focus on where they reside in your body. Ego-centered feelings are experienced as thoughts in the mind, but their spiritual opposites exist in your heart and in your core. As you develop these new muscle groups, the ego will begin to relinquish its hold.

Below is a rough guide to which spiritual Principle to exercise to counterbalance each egoic trait. Adjust it according to your needs. The moment you spot a negative characteristic, replace it with its spiritual opposite.

Arrogance—Humility, Acceptance
Dishonesty—Honesty
Envy or Jealousy—Gratitude, Acceptance, Generosity
Greed—Gratitude, Humility
Impatience or Intolerance—Humility, Kindness, Peace
Lust—Gratitude
Pride—Humility, Acceptance
Self-centeredness—Humility, Kindness
Selfishness—Generosity, Joy, Kindness
Self-pity—Generosity, Gratitude, Courage, Joy

You might notice that we left one Principle off this list: love. That's because you can use love in every single instance. So if you're struggling to remember which Principle to use to diffuse a particular ego attack, choose love, and you'll always have a healthy defense.

Try practicing a different spiritual Principle every day, or every few days. Developing these new muscles and behaviors will take time and patience. This is not a race. We're in it for the long haul.

Increasingly, you will find that the gap between your values and your actions starts to close. Your life becomes more congruent. And this in turn creates another of WE's magic-multiplying effects: the better you feel about yourself, the better you're able to act on your beliefs. As you do, so you become.

....

IDLE MINDS

A healthy habit that will distract your ego from its destructive tendencies is to give yourself intellectual stimulation each day. Read something uplifting or informative, do a puzzle, learn a new skill. Otherwise, sooner or later, your ego will start roaming around looking for something inappropriate to gnaw on.

....

Forgiveness

Forgiveness is the key to action and freedom.
—HANNAH ARENDT (1906–1975), German-born writer and philosopher

Humility frees us from the need to pretend we're better or more perfect than we are. That means we can apologize more easily when we've acted in ways that have hurt others or failed to reflect our values. Humility also provides us with a spiritual skeleton key: forgiveness. Of course, our ego doesn't want us to forgive—ever. It feeds on having enemies and on being right. From its Neanderthal perspective, forgiving is letting the other person win. It stokes both our longing for vengeance and our need for other people to realize just how much they hurt us and that they must make it better. Our ego—if we don't neutralize it with humility—can lead us to rekindle the resentments and stories we processed in Principle 3, courage.

....

A WISH THAT WORKS

If you find yourself craving vengeance, here's a remedy that really can help.

Every time the person who wronged you comes into your head, wish or pray for him or her to have every good thing you want for yourself: happiness, fulfillment, love, peace of mind. Wish for the other person to have it all.

Your ego will naturally try hard to resist it. You may be happier praying for the other person to suffer, but that will just keep you trapped. Your desire for vengeance makes you a prisoner.

If you can manage to do this every time you think of that person for as long as two weeks, amazing shifts will take place. After three weeks, you'll feel free.

....

All too often, we sanitize and simplify forgiveness, when in fact it's an arduous, exhausting task—messy, risky, and unpredictable.

—MARINA CANTACUZINO, British journalist and founder
of the nonprofit organization the Forgiveness Project

Forgiving doesn't mean forgetting, and it doesn't mean that what happened was acceptable. It just means you want freedom. Without forgiveness, you remain bonded to those who've hurt you.

It isn't enough that others want to be forgiven, although that can sometimes help. Forgiveness isn't something you can force or deliver on demand. Be kind to yourself if you are struggling with it.

171

At its core, forgiveness involves experiencing loss: you're letting go of the hope that things can be otherwise or the belief that the other person deserves your anger. Anger can feel like the only way you have to show that you're not totally powerless. But so often we cling to anger in order to avoid the grief or disappointment that comes with loss. Only in forgiving can you give it up.

Ask yourself, "How is this anger continuing to serve me?"

Listen carefully to the answer, and if you're still struggling to forgive, use the following exercise to help you let go of the hurt.

Exercise 2: Emotional Archaeology

This exercise is to help you release your attachment to past hurts. You will need two pieces of paper, a pen, a candle, and a pair of scissors.

In one sentence, summarize what wrong was done to you. Not the details (hopefully, you will have attended to that as you worked through your resentments on page 125), but what lies at the heart of your anger and resentment. Were you betrayed, left out, or maybe you were abandoned? Abused or exploited? What is the nature of your hurt, shorn of all detail and story?

Now ask yourself when else in your life you've experienced a similar feeling. List all the times you can remember. Trace the moments backward and forward until you have a timeline of similar experiences.

It's unlikely that the wrong you're unable to forgive has happened only once at the hands of one person. It's likely to be part of a pattern: the details and magnitude may not be the same, but that core wound is likely to have been activated more than this one time. Some of the instances you find may be more extreme than others, but there will almost always be a connection through time that is keeping you tied to it.

Realizing that you've experienced this wound before releases some of its power instantly. No wonder you've struggled so much. The pain has been repeated and compacted over time.

On another piece of paper, draw a large figure eight. Put the name of the person you're struggling to forgive in the top half of the loop, along with the nature of the core wound. Write your name in the bottom loop. See how you're separate but also tied together.

Now light your candle. Take the scissors and cut the figure eight right down the middle. Burn the half that has the name of the core wound on it. It's over, consigned to your past. You can now start to live fully in your present. If it floats back into your mind, remember that you have cut the cord.

....

....

AN EYE FOR AN EYE

Our jails are overflowing, but many of the people within them don't need to be there. In the United States, 50 percent of prisoners are serving time for nonviolent crimes,[3] while two-thirds of prisoners held in custody awaiting trial in the United Kingdom are likely never to receive a custodial sentence.[4] It's been proven time and again that for the majority of offenses, prison neither deters nor reduces the likelihood of future offenses. Yet instead

of finding more effective ways of rehabilitation and crime pre-
vention, we waste billions and contribute to future offenses[5] in
order to meet our cultures' hunger for vengeance.

Imagine all the good that could be done with that money
if we found more effective options, such as tackling poverty or
providing training in conflict resolution in schools.

....

Living in the Day

Surely the world we live in is but the world that lives in us.
—DAISY BATES (1914–1999), civil rights activist and journalist

The thoughts that cause us the most pain, courtesy of our ego, generally concern events that have already happened or ones that we
fear might occur. As we're thinking about yesterday's slights or
how we'll get ahead tomorrow, we rob ourselves of the chance to
experience the day we're actually living through. Crazy, isn't it?

Humility brings you into the present. When we're genuinely in
the present, the chatter in our head subsides. We feel at peace—for
that moment, we're a *human being* rather than a *human thinking*.

In the next chapter, you'll learn some powerful meditation techniques to help you connect more deeply with the present, but for
now, start with an incredibly effective tool—one that's used to help
beat heroin addiction and alcoholism. Try to live just one day at a
time. In other words, let yourself think only about the twenty-four
hours ahead.

The minute I engage in worry about one thing or another outside of this moment, I become paralyzed. Seriously start spinning in circles in my head. Out of necessity, over time, I've learned to adapt to thinking only of the day that I'm presently in and sometimes, literally, just this minute. That isn't to say I don't plan and think ahead—I can tell you what I'm doing on any given day for the next seven months—but I've trained myself not to worry. The future event exists in time, but I won't think about it until it's upon me. In any day, when I get an uneasy feeling in my stomach, which signals that I am afraid or nervous about something, after naming it it's important to determine if there is anything I can actually do about it in this moment. If there is, I do my best to address it now, even if it's just scheduling a time in the future to deal with it—that in itself is action. Taking care of myself in this way takes commitment and discipline because it's also about showing that I'm trustworthy and that when I say—even if just to myself—I will deal with something at a certain time, I actually do.

—GA

··

TODAY OR TOMORROW?

To help you stay focused on the present, imagine your mind is your desktop, and it has two folders on it. One is marked "Today," and one is marked "Tomorrow." Each time a thought intrudes, glance at it and see whether it's about today or tomorrow. If it's about today, you can think it. Otherwise just pop the thought into the folder marked "Tomorrow." If they continue to intrude, use the Three-Second Rule, so that you don't let unnecessary thoughts about the future distract you from the business of living in the now.

....

Living in the day sets a no-excuses perimeter. If things are tough, tell yourself you only have to get through this one day. If things are good, remind yourself that it may last only for this day, so make the most of it instead of worrying about when it'll end. Nothing—neither good nor bad—lasts. Attend to what has to be done and then set yourself the goal of making the most of the day you have, not the future that hasn't arrived yet.

When you give yourself permission to reduce the time you spend thinking about the past and the future, you create the space for joy, grace, and wonder to emerge.

Rightsizing

I love who I am, and I encourage other people to love and embrace who they are. But it definitely wasn't easy, it took me awhile.
—SERENA WILLIAMS, professional tennis champion

With humility, we become rightsized—in other words, the same size as everyone else. You don't need to be intimidated by someone who has more success or power, and you don't need to be deferred to by those who have less. There is no pecking order in the spiritual world. We are all exactly the same.

176

Often it's those with the biggest egos who have the lowest self-esteem. They overcompensate with material accomplishments and possessions to make up for their lack of internal worth. Like the Wizard of Oz, their ego hides behind levers and screens, hoping to intimidate us.

Observe your own ego rise and reach for the Toxic Cs. Then remember the magical Constructive Cs: compassion, cooperation, and connection. By replacing the one with the other, you prove to yourself and others that you can actively become an equal part of a whole.

My experience of success is that it's like cotton candy. It makes me feel good for a moment, and then I have a postsugar crash and crave more. I remember how great I felt when I had my first book published. Becoming a published author was something I'd dreamed of since I was a child. But then I went to the bookshop and saw how many other books there were—thousands of titles sat like tombstones on the shelves—and I suddenly "got" it. There was nothing I could do that would satisfy the calling of my ego and make me feel special enough. There was no material achievement that would fill the God-shaped hole inside of me. Now I'm grateful for the satisfaction I get from doing a piece of work well, but I no longer take it as any kind of measure of my real worth.

—JN

If you find yourself hungering for more "ego food"—more success, more recognition, more things to make you feel better about yourself—make sure you're still using the Essential Practices, or Four Essentials, from the beginning of the book: food, exercise, rest, and appreciation. When we take care of what our real self needs, the needs of our ego will diminish and ultimately fade into the background.

There's no taking our trophies with us at the end of this life. Everything we hunger for now will turn to dust. So keep your focus on the good you can do and the lives you can touch today and then enjoy the freedom and love that practicing humility brings.

Humility in the Wider World

It is a most certain truth that the richer we see ourselves to be, confessing at the same time our poverty, the greater will be our progress, and the more real our humility.
—SAINT TERESA OF ÁVILA (1515–1582), Spanish
Carmelite nun and Roman Catholic saint

Humility allows us to take our rightful place on this wonderful and extraordinary planet. It frees our thoughts and vision from the ego's petty concerns. To the ego, enough is never enough, and it demands that we possess and accumulate more and more. It always chooses short-term gain, no matter the long-term pain it causes the world around it.

A prime example is how we humans treat our precious planet. Overconsumption drives climate change and harmful emissions. The poorest half of the world is already paying the price in droughts and rising sea levels. At least ten thousand species become extinct each year,[6] and we are ploughing through the earth's resources as if it were a planet three times its size.

Humility enables us to challenge that head-on. If we can see ourselves as one of many rather than as an individual who has to make her mark at any cost, we will change how we consume and how we live.

Imagine what would happen if we each said, "This is enough. I don't need more"?

What would happen if we said, "They don't have enough, and so they can have some of ours"?

What would happen if we all asked, "How can I help?" rather than "How can I win?"

Together we can demonstrate that there is a different way of being in the world that puts compassion and cooperation ahead of competition and status. We can acknowledge that we're here as custodians of our exquisite world and need to preserve it for those who come after.

Your ego may not like it, but your soul will start to soar.

Reflection

It's never about how little we have. It is about what our little has the potential to become.

—CHRISTINE CAINE, Australian evangelist and cofounder of the A21 Campaign, a nonprofit organization that works to stop human trafficking

Today I know that when I feed my jealousy and envy by competing or comparing, they grow. So instead, today I will turn my gaze inward and work on their spiritual opposite—generosity, gratitude, and love. Before long, I will be back in balance and glad to be myself.

Action. I treat every woman I meet as a friend.

Affirmation. My worth comes from within.

Principle
6

PEACE:
Ending the Conflict Within

There is no need to go to India or anywhere else to find peace. You will find that deep place of silence right in your room, your garden, or even your bathtub.

—ELISABETH KÜBLER-ROSS (1926–2004), Swiss-born
psychiatrist and pioneer researcher on death and dying

Peace resides in the stillness beneath the chatter of our thinking minds. In that state of serenity, we experience freedom from inner conflict and a sense of wholeness. We feel connected to the world in which we live, and loneliness begins to evaporate.

Peace leads us to a safe space within ourselves that we can return to whenever we are feeling distressed or unsettled. Over time we discover that when we rest in peace our levels of emotional reactivity are reduced and our capacity to experience joy increases.

Without peace, we are restless, searching, and stuck in a state of almost constant *dis*-ease and dissatisfaction.

And yet, being still in the moment has become so foreign to many of us that it can feel uncomfortable. With our hectic schedules and the demands of modern 24/7 living, many of us have lost the habit. We spend our time *doing* rather than *being*.

In the last chapter, we saw the damage our ego-driven thinking can cause. *WE*'s 6th Principle takes us a step further: to a place that lies beyond our thoughts. It is there that we get to soak up the healing energy that peace brings.

Beyond our Thinking Minds

We've known about the transcendent power of solitude for centuries; it's only recently that we've forgotten it.
—SUSAN CAIN, author of *Quiet: The Power of Introverts in a World That Can't Stop Talking*

Most of us have spent so long listening to our thoughts that we have become completely identified with them. We have become like computer operators who think they are the computer.

We also believe that thinking can bring us peace, but actually the opposite is true. It's by detaching from our thoughts that we find peace. Meditation is our gateway to the extraordinary realm that exists beyond our thinking selves—the part of us that *knows* we're thinking.

Exercise 1: Our Internal Landscape

This exercise will give you a glimpse of the peace that exists within us all.

Set a timer for five minutes. Take a few deep breaths. Imagine your mind is a clear blue sky. Now watch and wait to see how soon thoughts start swarming in. Observe them. How many of them make sense? How many of them really need to be thought? How many of them instigate pain, anger, or fear? How many of them repeat themselves? We live amid that swarm day in and day out.

Now close your eyes again and imagine your mind is a clear blue sky. This time, when the thoughts appear, try not to focus on them. Try to let them fly by as you would a wasp. Gently say to yourself, "Thinking," every time you find yourself trying to grab on to one and instead return to the gentle rise and fall of your breath. Keep your focus on the blue sky rather than the wasps, and soon they'll find it harder to get your attention.

You are the sky. Everything else—it's just the weather.

—PEMA CHÖDRÖN, Buddhist teacher and author

PROOF POSITIVE

Scientific studies show that meditation creates a whole raft of physical and mental benefits: increased energy, reduced blood pressure and depression, better sleep, improved immune system, decreased inflammation and pain, increased attention and memory, enhanced self-control and emotional regulation, and higher emotional intelligence.[1] In addition, a University of California study found that daily meditation for just two weeks helped improve focus and memory: overall, the students who meditated had a 16 percent higher score than those who did not.[2]

....

Meditations

Breathe. Let go. And remind yourself that this very moment is the only one you know you have for sure.

—OPRAH WINFREY, talk-show host and media mogul

The West is finally waking up to the wonders of meditation. Doctors now recommend it. A growing number of businesses provide training for employees to reduce stress levels and increase efficiency. But its benefits go way beyond the physical and mental.

When we meditate on a daily basis, we reconnect with our core: the authentic part of ourselves that lies beneath the defenses and scar tissue we accumulate through life. And with that comes a sense of belonging. We start to feel connected at a deep level to the world of which we are a part.

When we meditate, we reach a higher state of understanding and perception. As a result, what we have in common with others becomes more important than what separates us. Our intuition strengthens and leads us to a sense of purpose and fulfillment.

If you've been using the meditation technique you learned in the start of this journey in Essential Practice 4 and sitting for a couple of minutes each morning, you'll have already started something wonderful for yourself. You'll have established a meditation routine.

The length of time you've been sitting is less important than the habit. But now that your habit is in place, you can start to lengthen the time you sit. Notice your resistance to this idea. You may already be listing in your head how little time you have. So take a moment here to analyze how you spend the time you do have.

....

TIME AUDIT

For one day, make a record of how you spend your time. Note down the times you spend working and doing necessary tasks, but also pay particular attention to the time you waste. Maybe you check your phone repeatedly, or lose hours on Facebook checking out people you barely know, or daydreaming about the distant future. Maybe you fritter away time talking to people you have no desire to speak to, or doing chores that don't matter at all, or watching TV shows you don't really enjoy. Whatever you notice, write it down.

Identify what you could do differently to free up twenty minutes each day to devote to your meditation practice. Your peace of mind will be well worth the adjustment.

....

Many of us are addicted to our gadgets. The average smartphone user checks his or her phone 150 times a day—that's every six and a half minutes.[3]

Our ego likes to pretend that we're so important that we have to keep this connected, but for many of us, there are other factors at play. We use gadgets to stave off an inner emptiness or to fill an awkward pause, or perhaps as an emotional buffer to avoid difficult feelings such as sadness, grief, loneliness, guilt, and fear. And who wouldn't rather be watching the world's funniest cat videos on YouTube than feeling those emotions?

But when we turn to our gadgets to change how we feel, we feed rather than soothe our inner restlessness.

Pathways to Peace

Inside myself is a place where I live all alone, and that's where you renew your springs that never dry up.
—PEARL S. BUCK (1892–1973), author and novelist

There are many ways to meditate. None of them is right or wrong. They are merely different routes to the same place. There aren't any rules other than to find a practice that works for you.

Experiment to see which method you find most effective. Maybe you're a member of a church, have a yoga practice, or attend a synagogue or mosque where meditation is taught. Perhaps you love movement or chanting, or would prefer a technique with strict guidelines. You may want a religious component or something entirely secular. Keep seeking until you find a method that resonates with you.

Be open. Be curious. But don't let seeking become a form of

avoidance. This is not about perfection. It's about action. Whichever path you choose will work if you commit to it.

Exercise 2: Mantra Meditation

This exercise introduces you to a simple and very powerful technique that is used by millions of people around the world. It uses a mantra which is a word or a sound that gives the mind a focus during meditation, and will make it easier to switch off your usual merry-go-round of thoughts.

You may already have a mantra you like. If not, try using the Sanskrit word *om*. Alternatively, a word such as *love* or *peace*—that has a positive meaning—will do. Or you can find mantras online.

Settle yourself, set your timer for five minutes, close your eyes, and take five deep breaths. Allow the mantra or word to appear in your mind. Repeat it to yourself silently.

Imagine that the sound is a magic carpet and watch it rise and fall on your breath. Now climb onto it.

Feel the magic carpet beneath you as you breathe and allow yourself to rest on it. You don't have to concentrate on it. You are safe and supported. This is not about focus but about softness and ease. So just let yourself rest on the carpet as you repeat the mantra silently. It doesn't matter whether you repeat it several times a breath or once per exhalation. Just do it with ease. Let it establish its own rhythm. You'll find that the pace at which it comes to you tends to quicken and slow naturally. As you repeat your mantra, you may also notice that at some point it ceases to be a word that you are repeating and becomes something you are experiencing.

If you find yourself drifting into thought (and you will), gently shift your focus back to the mantra. You may have to do this many times. Thoughts are persistent. Don't strain, stress, or judge what's happening.

Be loving with your mind's antics. Think of your mind as a puppy you are training to "stay." You may have to put it back on its mat numerous times before it learns, and even then it will sometimes stray.[4]

There is no rush, and there is no destination. When your timer goes off, don't open your eyes right away. Respect your practice. Allow yourself to slowly and gently come back to your physical surroundings. Then say thank you to yourself and to your mantra for the experience.

....

When I started meditating, I was in so much emotional pain I couldn't sit for longer than a couple of minutes. So I used a walking meditation. I'd walk for twenty minutes, and the movement soothed me. After that, I used to meditate during morning prayers in a nearby chapel. I couldn't sit by myself, but I could sit when others were around. Then I went through a period of "spiritual tourism": trying every technique that was popular until someone suggested it was time to stop searching and start doing. I decided to commit to a mantra-based technique, and it works. I now sit for twenty minutes on my own each morning. In fact, it's the part of the day I look forward to most. I make my coffee, read a portion of a spiritual text, and then set my timer.

Some days, it's easier than others to find peace, but I try not to judge myself—what matters is that I've shown up and made myself available to the process. Often my six-year-old will come sit with me. He rarely lasts the full twenty minutes, but he finds the stillness comforting and is drawn to it instinctively.

—*JN*

Deepening Your Practice

Surrender to what is, let go of what was, have faith in what will be.
—SONIA RICOTTI, author of *The Law of Attraction Plain and Simple: Create the Extraordinary Life That You Deserve* and other books

To start with, developing your meditation practice takes discipline. As with any form of training, you have to show up if you want to see results. But while it may feel like a chore at the beginning, it will soon become a source of joy, and you'll wonder how you ever lived without it.

If you liked using the mantra meditation, then try it again tomorrow in the regular time you've set aside. If not, use whatever technique works for you.

Each day, set your timer for three minutes longer until you get up to twenty minutes. Then allow an extra minute at the start of the session to settle into your breathing and an extra two at the end to come back into the world. Using your timer frees your mind from needing to monitor time, making it easier to let go.

If you can, try to meditate before your day gets under way. Set your alarm to go off early to enable you to get up before your other commitments start.

Some people add an additional meditation time at the end of their day, but, for now, see if you can commit to the morning.

All you need to bring about extraordinary changes in your life is twenty minutes a day. You'll find yourself becoming calmer, less reactive, less easily hurt. Meditation creates the emotional equivalent of a moat. It's harder for life's arrows to penetrate when you have a spiritual buffer protecting you.

As your practice becomes more ingrained in your daily life, you'll find that activities and people that alienate you from your inner equilibrium become less attractive. Why would we want to do things that make us feel worse rather than better?

Once you've started to taste that sense of peace, you're likely to want more. You'll start to prioritize it. And that will mean making different choices about how you spend your time.

Exercise 3: Your Inner Circle

This is an exercise to help you make choices that will prioritize your inner peace.

Draw three large circles, one inside the other, on a piece of paper.

In the outer circle, write down all the activities that almost always make you feel bad. Perhaps it's looking at photos of an ex's new partner on Facebook. Maybe it's checking out a gossip column, going on a crash diet, or binge drinking. These activities manufacture pain.

In the middle circle, write down behaviors that sometimes make you feel good and sometimes bad. For example, speaking to a close friend who is also close to your ex, surfing shopping sites, being in touch with a member of your family who causes you concern.

In the inner circle, jot down behaviors that make you feel great. For example, spending time with a good friend, meditating, exercising, laughing, playing with a child, walking in nature, playing a sport, painting, writing, dancing, creating, sculpting, or singing. Write down as many as you can.

Take a look at your map. That inner circle is where you're happiest, safest, and most fulfilled. It's firm ground. Your aim is to spend as much time there as possible.

Now look at the middle circle. You can do these activities when you're feeling emotionally robust, but they carry risks and could lead you to lose your center. When you feel emotionally vulnerable, try to avoid them as much as possible and return to the inner circle as soon as you can.

Your goal is to stay out of the outer circle altogether.

Your peace of mind is precious, so use this tool to foster it and keep it safe.

MENTAL DETOX

Most religious traditions insist on a day of rest from worldly engagement for good reason. The idea is that it enables us to return to center and remember what really matters in our lives. You don't have to have a faith to benefit from the practice. Try

giving yourself a day of rest each week when you decline to shop
or actively consume, where you prioritize being in the life you
have rather than getting or having more.

If you enjoy it, how about taking a complete mental detox
by not reading or listening to the news? Think of your mind as a
glass of clear water. Every time you listen to or read a fear-driven
or shocking report, it's like injecting ink straight into it. So why
not make disengagement from it a regular part of your week?

....

Letting Go of Knowing

As you learn to detach from your thoughts, you'll begin to notice
how your mind likes to categorize your experiences as either good
or bad. Whether it's the fact that it's raining again or that a friend
failed to show up, you'll probably discover you have a running
commentary assigning value to it.

You'll almost certainly do the same with people: sorting them
into goodies and baddies, and making all sorts of assumptions
about their motives and intentions.

The problem is that we think we know what's going on, but
actually we have no idea. We don't have a crystal ball, nor can we
read minds. Instead, our assessments are based largely on our past
experiences and fear. We project what has already happened onto
our present and then wonder why the same experiences keep happening to us again and again.

....

NEITHER GOOD NOR BAD

Once upon a time, the fable goes, there was a farmer who had no ox with which to plough his field. One day he woke up and saw a horse grazing in his pasture. He was ecstatic and rushed to the wise man in the village. "Wise man, wise man, I thought we were all going to starve, as we had no ox to plough our field. But now we have a horse. This is the best thing that's ever happened to me."

The wise man replied, "It is neither good nor bad, it just is."

The farmer left, shaking his head. "What an idiot that wise man is," he thought. "He understands nothing of value." Then he and his only son set about ploughing the field.

Suddenly the horse reared up, injuring the son, who broke his leg.

The farmer rushed back to the wise man. "Wise man, wise man," he said. "You are so wise. You were totally right. The horse was not a good thing. It has broken the leg of my only son, and now I have nobody to help me bring in the harvest."

The wise man shook his head and repeated, "It is neither good nor bad."

Exasperated, the farmer returned to care for his son and do what he could with his crop before the rain came.

The next day, an army marched into the village and rounded up every able-bodied young man to help fight in the war. They were taken off to the front, and before long, word came back that they had all died.[5] When the horse broke the son's leg, it inadvertently saved the farmer's life.

How often do we, like the old farmer, think we know what is good and bad in our lives? And how much time do we waste trying to puzzle it out? While we're busy trying to get more of what we think is good and avoid what we think of as bad, we miss out on what happens in between—which is actually the vast majority of our lives.

Living Consciously, Mindfully

What would happen if instead of waiting for the "good" moments to arrive, we remained present for all of life—including the parts we often dismiss as boring and unimportant?

The peace we can find when we meditate at the start of each morning is actually available throughout our day if we open ourselves to it.

Exercise 4: The Miraculous Mundane

This exercise will help you transform your present—no matter what is going on.

Pick one of the activities listed below that you find really boring; perhaps something you barely notice yourself doing:

· Brushing your teeth
· Putting on your clothes
· Getting to or from work/school
· Eating lunch

- Making your bed
- Washing your face
- Doing the dishes

Now, for the next week, do that activity mindfully—in other words, be really conscious of every aspect of it.

Be aware how extraordinary the mundane action you've chosen really is, and how amazing it is that you, with the unique emotional and psychological makeup and genes that you have, came into existence, and are using the instruments that you're using. How many hands have been involved in gathering the raw materials, manufacturing, selling, and delivering them? How many different sensations can you feel in your body as you use them?

Imagine how you'd feel and how your life would change if you lost the physical ability to do these things again. If you are eating, take time to be aware of every single taste and sensation. Chew your food properly. Marvel at the miracle of how the body digests sustenance and converts it into energy.

Say a silent thank-you for the experience, for the growers and the harvesters and the distributors and the makers: "Thank you for nourishing my body so that I may be alive today." Try to imagine that you're from another land or universe and see everything anew, as if for the first time. Connect with the awe and wonder how you'd feel if you'd never tasted food or drunk a glass of water before.

These "normal" tasks can be stress busters. They can be like a church bell or a call to prayer that reminds us to return to the present so that we can encounter the sacred.

When you bring attention to the wonder of the small things in your life, the details of the bigger issues start to assume less importance. And miraculously, when you loosen your focus on them, they often somehow start to slip into place.

I don't know how many times a week I arrive at my destination on autopilot with little or no memory of my journey. The days of my life that I remember the most, even though side by side they appear the same—same bus, train, route to work and home—are the days I was present in my life. When I chose not to multitask—not to be on my phone, listen to music, read a book, think about the weekend—but instead was there on that train and looked around and noticed the woman next to me, who was heavily pregnant; and the man with the handlebar moustache; and the saxophonist busking in front of the coffee shop. When I stopped and was grateful for the moment: for the gift of his music, her smile, my life. That, I've learned, is peace.

—GA

The more practiced you become at switching your focus from your thoughts to where you actually are, the greater the sense of freedom and joy you experience. You no longer rush to get things done. Instead, you get lost in the detail and the glory of them and wonder how you could have missed out for so long.

Consciousness transforms life. Whatever you're doing—making a cup of tea, waiting for a bus, or getting dressed—use it as an opportunity to connect with what is. Decline your mind's invitation to worry and instead focus on the task at hand.

Presence of mind is peace of mind.

The Power of Pausing

Give your morning to God, and he will give you your day.

—CARMEL MURPHY

Life will present countless challenges to your practice of peace. They'll come in the form of relationships, traffic, grocery store checkout lines, and so on. You'll be triggered because you're human. Any strong emotion, such as jealousy, anger, or fear, can catapult you back into anxiety and negative projection.

When this happens, see it as an opportunity to practice. Hit the pause button, fast. Focus on your breath. You have one goal: to preserve your peace of mind while not robbing other people of theirs.

Your mind may tell you you've been offended. It will almost certainly want you to dive into the future or rake through the past. Refuse its pull to rope you into a story and instead stay present.

Notice what you're experiencing and then name, feel, and release it. If you're struggling to stay in the moment, excuse yourself from the room or go to the nearest ladies' room to realign yourself and calm down.

Pausing buys you vital time. It enables you to respond with kindness and curiosity rather than fear. As you do so, how others respond to you will in turn shift miraculously.

If you feel your mind flooding with attack thoughts, wait until you're centered and then wait some more.

Have some useful phrases ready, such as, "I'll need to get back to you about that," or "I'm sorry you feel that way." Stay soft and stay open and remind yourself that whatever the problem is, love, in one form or another, is the answer.

One hasty word or reaction can alter a friendship for a lifetime. I often struggle with inserting a pause. I'm too worried that I won't get my way unless I respond straight away. But over time I've come to see that my way doesn't necessarily help me or anyone else. I think I know what's best, but often I'm just trying to control outcomes to avoid my own anxiety. On a daily basis, I try to observe before I respond—and things always turn out better when I manage to insert a pause.

—JN

....

MOVE A MUSCLE TO SHIFT A THOUGHT

If your thoughts are particularly persistent, try using movement to dislodge them. Remember, *Action Changes Things.*

Shrug your shoulders, wiggle your toes, or even try balancing on one leg. Singing and dancing are great too—anything that allows you to get out of your head and focus on the moment.

Again, watch out for your mind. It is going to use every opportunity to try to persuade you to return to living in your head. It may even tell you this new way of life is lazy and irresponsible. But just remember how many moments you lost as the result of being caught up in loops of obsessive thoughts.

....

Indecision

Pausing is also great for indecision. When you're not sure about something, instead of forcing a resolution, try to put the dilemma in the back of your mind. If necessary, write it on a piece of paper and put it in your Acceptance Cup. (See page 86.)

Accepting that you "don't know" is one of the fastest routes to allowing an answer to emerge. And be careful not to short-circuit the process. It's like baking bread: each time you open the oven door prematurely, you jeopardize the outcome.

Using the pause button for decision making gives you space to hear your inner voice, your intuition, your inner knowing. It usually has answers that the conscious mind can't deliver. Sometimes it will take the form of a hunch; at other times, a coincidence. The more regularly you meditate, the easier it becomes to hear. Learn to trust it when it comes.

When I'm suffering from indecision—which has happened a lot in my life—it's generally because there's a conflict between my overly educated brain and my inner knowing. My father was an academic, so I came from a home where the intellect was prized above all else and talk of intuition was dismissed as airy-fairy. Meditation has proven to me beyond all doubt that there's another form of knowing that has nothing to do with education. It comes in the form of an inner nudge. To start with, it was so gentle that I often overrode it. It would say turn left rather than right, or call this person or wait awhile. Now, whenever I can discern it, I listen—it always leads to something more wonderful than my limited mind could have predicted. It's as if through meditation I've

199

tapped into a collective pool of wisdom that makes itself known through my heart rather than my head. Just as in the Bible it was eating from the tree of knowledge that led to Eve and Adam being cast out of paradise, I can see how I exile myself from a state of peace when I give my thoughts too great a priority.

—JN

Uncertainty

Living with uncertainty—a pause that's inflicted on us rather than one we've chosen—can be incredibly uncomfortable. It can send us into a tornado of antics trying to force a resolution. Be it a job loss, a medical diagnosis, or just a phone call not coming as expected, sitting with uncertainty takes courage.

When one door closes, it can be tough to trust that another really will open. Notice when your ego tries to persuade you to close the gap between what was and what will be by obsessing about possible outcomes. Watch it generate fearful attack thoughts. Do your very best to not engage with any of it. When you allow yourself to rest in the uncertainty of what is, space opens up for answers to emerge.

There is a great deal of uncertainty in the line of work I am in. There have been times when I have scheduled months of child care and schooling and travel only for the job to fall through, or other times when there are three jobs that might go around the same time, but none can be counted on or let go of—yet all will impact the other aspects of my life and my relationships. I have by necessity come to a place of acceptance that uncertainty is just part and parcel of what I do. I try to make sure that no matter what, my time with my children is protected, but beyond that, I have no control and simply have to let go and trust that whichever job is right for me will stick. When I hold on too tight to the end result, I only get disappointed and resentful. As provocative as it can be to not know what the next six months will look like workwise, it's so much better for my peace of mind if I let go into the unknown and let the cards fall as they may.

—*GA*

COINCIDENCES

Some people call them coincidences; others, synchronicity. Start looking out for them in your day-to-day life. The time you spend meditating brings you into alignment with whatever it is that orders our universe, so you're likely to notice them occurring with increasing frequency.

You may think of someone you haven't seen for ages, and suddenly they'll call. You'll finally pluck up the courage to leave the job that was making you miserable, and a fantastic opportunity that you'd never imagined presents itself. Or you'll trust your instinct to take time off work to care for a loved one, and you're offered extra pay for work you can do at home.

Make sure to add these moments to the list you started in the Living Proof exercise in the 4th Principle, trust. They're further proof that this new way of life yields tangible results.

If you take care of your mind, you take care of the world.
—ARIANNA HUFFINGTON, Greek-born author,
columnist, and founder of *The Huffington Post*

Transforming Difficulty

As you get used to pausing when you're disturbed or upset, you'll find that it gets easier and easier to contain your responses and not react inappropriately.

If you find yourself struggling, take the more difficult feelings into your formal meditation practice.

As you sit down to meditate, hold a gentle awareness of what's upsetting you. Don't seek to repress it or puzzle it out; just offer it up to your practice and see what happens.

The secret is not to struggle. It's like learning to float: we think we'll sink unless we do something. In fact, the opposite is true: when you allow yourself to rest in your own consciousness, you discover you can float, and the weight of your worries is taken away.

When you are present to your difficulties and pain in this way, meditation becomes like a magical composter. You actively nourish the parts of your life and yourself that you find difficult and, over time, miraculously transform them.

Being Human

Ultimately, we have just one moral duty: to reclaim large areas of peace in ourselves, more and more peace, and to reflect it toward others. And the more peace there is in us, the more peace there will also be in our troubled world.

—ETTY HILLESUM (1914–1943), Dutch
diarist and victim of the Nazi Holocaust

As your meditation practice develops, when you lose your balance, you'll find that you have a place to call home. A place that doesn't depend on your accomplishments or possessions. A place where you can feel safe and be at peace.

You'll still lose your emotional footing from time to time. When it happens, it doesn't mean you're failing. It's a sign that you're not shut down or anesthetized but open and sensitive and truly alive to life.

When we shift from a state of internal war to one of peace, the change is reflected externally. It's as if meditation helps us chart a course that keeps the wind in our sails.

Life will begin to feel less complicated and problematic. You will start to feel lighter, and you'll laugh more. You'll be less confused by situations and notice a new ease in your relationships with others. The stronger the connection you'll feel with your inner self, the more connected you feel to all humans. Prejudices and judgements will start to fall away as you sense the interconnectedness that lies beneath what divides us.

I used to be addicted to the drama of life. To the rights and wrongs, the "he said/she said." I'd want to get straight into the middle of whatever was happening and try to sort it out. But often, when I do that, I'm really just pouring kerosene onto someone else's emotional bonfire. Now, when I remember, I try not to stoke the embers of any conflict. Instead of fanning outrage, I try to just listen and be a peaceful presence. A port in the storm is more useful than someone fanning the flames.

—JN

Peace in the Wider World

One of the advantages of being born in an affluent society is that if one has any intelligence at all, one will realize that having more and more won't solve the problem.

—JETSUNMA TENZIN PALMO, British-born Buddhist teacher and author

Peace is contagious, and now that you have it, you can help to spread it.

As you take your thinking mind less seriously, you'll find you have the capacity to be present for others in a new way. You might not be able to salve another's pain, but you can sit with the person while he or she processes it.

When you allow your inner peace to light someone else's way, you'll find that his or her pain starts to dissipate and solutions start to emerge.

When we make peace our priority, we can be of real service in the world. If all we do to help change the world is meditate, we will still make a difference. We'll be less likely to react with anger and rob others of their peace of mind.

We all know the power of an unkind or harsh word. Remember: hurt people hurt other people. So if we reduce the harm we do, we will instantly create a ripple effect.

Try—one day at a time—not to cause harm to yourself or others. When you're uncertain, hit pause. Remember that you don't have a crystal ball and don't know what will ultimately be for the best, but if you do the right thing, the right consequences will follow.

If everyone in the world took responsibility for his or her mental well-being, think how much more peaceful the world would be instantaneously!

Reflection

No matter who causes you grief, take your complaints to the
meditation room, where your real friend is.

—MATA AMRITANANDAMAYI (AMMA), Indian spiritual leader

When I find myself getting too caught up with or too hurt by the drama of my life, I can take a moment to pause. I can remember that while the surface of my life may be like a choppy sea on which I get tossed and turned, deep below the surface there is a part of me that remains constant and unaffected by what is happening above. I picture myself as a stone dropping down beneath the surface of the waves, falling deeper and deeper into my own internal ocean until I find a place of peace to rest. When I reside there, I know that everything is actually all right.

Action. Today, if I feel overwhelmed, I will pause and remind myself that underneath the surface, my true self resides.

Affirmation. Whatever else is happening, deep down I know I am absolutely okay.

Principle
7

LOVE:
Transforming Relationships

The cure for all the ills and wrongs, the cares, the sorrows, and the crimes of humanity, all lie in the one word love. It is the divine vitality that everywhere produces and restores life.
—LYDIA M. CHILD (1802–1880), abolitionist

Love knows no bounds. It wants the best for everyone
and doesn't discriminate or judge. Love is our authentic
nature and is always present, but, like the sun,
it can be obscured temporarily.

Love transforms us. It dissolves our prejudices and opens our hearts. It connects us to ourselves, to one another, and to all humanity.

Without love, we feel alone, we erect barriers and divisions—

often without realizing it. We long for connection, but we cut ourselves off from it.

This is a path of love and love is woven through every step of the journey. The essentials and principles you've learned so far have been preparing you to be able to experience true love in its most powerful, spiritual sense.

The Key to Love

I am happier when I love than when I am loved. I adore my husband, my son, and my grandchildren, my mother, my dog, and, frankly, I don't know if they even like me. But who cares? Loving them is my joy.

—ISABEL ALLENDE, Peruvian-born journalist and bestselling author

Many of us come to this journey looking for love. In Western cultures, romantic love has become almost a religion—something we're encouraged to devote ourselves to seeking in the belief that it will bring a perfect union and meaning to our lives. We're raised on fairy tales of girls transformed by the kiss of their handsome prince and bombarded by images of happy couples. Movie after movie ends with a happy couple who, after overcoming the requisite obstacles, look certain to live happily ever after.

It's not surprising that many of us see love as a Holy Grail, something to be sought, found, and won. Something we have looked for in the arms of others or in our worldly endeavors. Often our hearts have taken a battering. Some of us may shut down and turn our back on the very idea of love, while others just try harder.

But no matter how deeply we bury our desire, all of us ache for it to transform and make good our lives.

The good news is that we don't need to search for it any longer. It is available right here, right now, in every one of our lives. If you use the Principles in this book to clear the fear and emotional scars that can block love's flow, you will experience an extraordinary truth: love isn't something you have to seek or win. There is an infinite supply of it—enough for each and every one of us. All we need to know is how to gain access to it.

Love isn't something that we either do or don't do according to how we feel. It's something we can experience at any time. That's because the key to unlocking love's flow is very simple. It comes from realizing that love isn't a *feeling* but an *action*.

It is loving action that connects us to the constant supply of love that exists within us. Every time we act with love, we generate more. It's like a muscle: love may be hidden behind years of righteous anger, fear, or hurt, but we all have it and can choose to exercise it.

Like gratitude, it has a magic multiplying effect: the more loving you are, the more loved and loving you feel.

What's more, it doesn't matter whether you're giving or getting it; you'll experience love either way. It's the flow that counts.

But be prepared for your ego to object. To the ego, love is a two-way street, something to be traded, a transactional relationship. "What about me?" it'll want to know. Your ego will tell you to ration love, to save it up for the special or deserving people in your life. But, of course, when you withhold love, you deprive yourself.

Love, in the inspirational sense, has no limits—it's unconditional. It has nothing to do with how anyone else behaves. Giving in order to get back isn't love—it's a form of manipulation. And giving love only to those you judge to be worthy is a subtle form of discrimination.

With practice, it becomes possible to choose to respond with love no matter how somebody else behaves.

Love Begins with You

The preceding Principles have been getting you ready to love. You can't love if you're a bouncing ball of emotional reactivity or a jumble of unmet needs. Nor can you experience love if you're walled into a fortress of self-protection or wearing boxing gloves.

You can't give away something you haven't got. If you fail to meet your own needs, you risk slipping into codependency and hoping that others will make good your own internal sense of lack. Your home can't be made in anyone else's arms or company. Your true home is right where you are, within you.

Every relationship—whether with a friend or a partner—is like an arch: if each of you stands tall and strong in your own space, love can be the keystone. But if one of you leans, it can topple.

....

LOVING VERSUS CODEPENDENCY

Compulsive helping, or codependency, is now recognized as a serious and sometimes life-threatening addiction. People who are codependent attempt to get their self-esteem from taking care of others; often they think they are just being kind or helpful. They obsess about others and try to control, help, or guilt them into doing what they think is best. Other symptoms include saying yes when they mean no, accepting unacceptable behavior, staying in a harmful relationship to please another, giving unsolicited advice, and trying to save someone who doesn't want to be saved.

It can be hard to say no when we can see that someone needs help, but saying yes when we want to say no or giving what we haven't got is a form of dishonesty, not love. It sets us up as victims and martyrs who then resent the people we've helped or become angry when our "love" isn't reciprocated. It also puts us at risk of depression, anxiety, and chemical addiction.

Encouraging others to rely on us to meet *their* needs can make us feel needed and less immediately vulnerable, but it's the flip side of the same coin. Dependency in either direction doesn't work long term.

....

Hopefully, the work you've been doing since you opened this book has given you a sense of self-connection. Love will never ask you to abandon yourself. As women, we're encouraged to be selfless, but the meaning has become misunderstood. It does not mean to override our needs but rather to love without ego. The very same obstacles that block us from connecting with our authentic selves can block us from experiencing love. Our ego-based thinking, emotional wounds, and fear can all get in the way.

This is a path of love and love is woven through every step of the journey. The Essentials and Principles you've learned so far have been preparing you for love. The very same obstacles that blocked you from connecting with your authentic self can block you from experiencing love. Ego-based thinking, emotional wounds, and fear can all get in the way. As can preconceptions as to where, how, and with whom we will experience it. But with the power contained in the principles we can all clear away what blocks us from love and become a channel through which love can flow.

Loving Others

Love asks that we don't discriminate. That we love those we know and those we don't, those we like and those we'd rather avoid. Our neighbor is absolutely anyone: friend, stranger, or foe.

As women, we're all familiar with what it feels like to be on the receiving end of discriminatory or abusive behavior. But without realizing it, most of us also discriminate against and judge others.

Think about it. In your friendships, do you always go for the cool, popular people? Do you want to be only with the people you judge as being like you? Do you justify avoiding those who come from different backgrounds or socioeconomic strata by saying you're not likely to have as much in common?

Do you let your own agenda and needs influence your engagement? Do you automatically critique the people you encounter—their dress, their class, their race, their appearance? Are you one-upping and one-downing without even being aware? Are you impatient or intolerant with those who aren't as smart as you? How do you treat those you have power over—i.e., dependent family members, newcomers to any social group, or anyone you employ? How do you treat the strangers you pass in the street, the newspaper vendor, the shop assistant, the waitress?

Every one of your encounters gives you the choice to either set yourself apart or to practice love.

The further down this path you travel, the less you will find yourself able to engage in behaviors that were once second nature. How often have you bonded with others by gossiping? Or pretended (even to yourself) that you weren't gossiping at all but assessing a situation to work things out for everyone's benefit? Perhaps you use it as a way of making yourself look insightful. All gossip is a form of attack—no matter how good it might make you feel.

In each encounter, ask yourself, "What would love do?" Apply the Golden Rule (see page 225) and treat others as you'd like to be treated yourself.

....

THE SHAME GAME

When examining our own actions, it can be easy to slip into shame, guilt, or self-blame. Resist the temptation. Beating yourself up is just another racket. This is fact finding. It's about becoming aware, because without awareness, we can't change. The behaviors you're noticing and naming were developed to protect you and get your needs met. They may not be desirable, but they're understandable. Now that you're aware of them, you've got a choice. So use your energy to change rather than blame or shame. Remember, love isn't just for others—it's for you as well.

....

213

Our Template

All of us are in relationships all the time. And whether they're romantic or not, we can find ourselves slipping into old, harmful patterns. With frightening speed, we can re-create our childhood patterns of relating: in the workplace, dropping off or picking up your children from school, or in the bedroom.

The template for how you love others lies in your family and upbringing. What you grow up with, you learn. If you lived with abuse, you'll carry within you the knowledge and capacity to abuse.

If you grew up with compassion, you'll find it easier to have compassion for others. But no matter how wonderful our parents and other early caregivers, most of us carry wounds that interfere with our ability to love.

....

ABANDONED OR ENGULFED BY LOVE

Two of the most frequent ways we can be wounded in childhood is by receiving too little love or too much. Both significantly affect how we conduct ourselves in adult relationships.

Emotional or physical neglect can reveal itself in adulthood as excessive neediness. Whereas being smothered by love, due to our primary caregiver's own neediness or anxiety, can lead to a paradoxical fear of intimacy and a pattern of avoiding the connection that's craved.

Most of us can swing between feeling needy or feeling smothered, depending upon whom we are with and their pattern of relating. Extreme states of neediness and avoidance can be signs of an underlying addiction. The medical profession now accepts that love can be an addiction in its own right, and there are specific twelve-step fellowships one can go to for help.[1]

....

If we don't take responsibility for those early childhood wounds, we can stay stuck in a lifelong standoff. We can find ourselves repeatedly re-creating the same dynamics that we experienced as a child in the hope that the ending will be different.

But when we try to make someone else—a parent, friend, partner, or even boss—heal our early wounds by giving us what we lacked in childhood, we end up getting what we got the first time around: a mountain of pain.

Others can't change our template, but we can. So when you find yourself struggling, look back to see if a childhood wound is being reopened and then use the spiritual tools you've learned to bring about change.

Keep your focus on what you can change: yourself. *Not* your past or your family.

It was many years into my working life before I realized that I was carrying my childhood template for relating into my adult workplace. It was not a good look! My boss (who, this being a newsroom, was typically male) always became my father. I'd seek his attention at every opportunity. Those I worked with became my siblings, and I'd feel rivalry whenever they, too, sought his praise. I'd regress to being the jealous but good girl who overperformed to win her emotionally distant father's attention. I often did win my boss's approval (and became a workaholic in the process), but it didn't do anything to heal my inner girl's broken heart. No matter how much acclaim she got, she wanted more. Because, of course, what she really longed for was to be loved for who she was, not for what she did. Thanks to these Principles, I learned to give her the love she needed, but if I skimp on my self-care, I can easily slip into that pattern of relating when I'm in the presence of a powerful, competent male.

—JN

The stronger the connection we feel with someone, the greater the triggers into our past will be. You may be amazed at how quickly you can regress into childlike feelings. So take time out to connect with the wounded part, your inner girl. (See page 75.) Ask her what she wants and needs. Usually it will be to feel seen and heard and safe. You can provide that for her.

....

INSTANT RELIEF

If you're overwhelmed in the moment by an emotion, try this simple but effective tool. Make a fist and then place it over your heart. Press it gently into your chest as you breathe in and out deeply, telling yourself (silently if you're in public), "Although I'm sad/angry/upset about _____, I am safe, and I'm okay."

It's a great way to self-soothe when you're feeling triggered.

And don't forget the tools you've learned so far: Notice, Name, Feel, and Release your emotions; use affirmations and meditation to help you return to center; look for your part in your resentments; and then bring yourself into the present and ask what love would do.

....

I owe a large chunk of my spiritual growth to my first husband. We had an incredibly messy and painful divorce with lots of horrible conflict, from which it took many years to recover. But if it hadn't been for all that pain, I wouldn't be on the path that I am on now. Looking back, I can see how it led to transformation. I had to learn to love in the face of anger and what felt like hatred—otherwise I wouldn't have survived. I am no longer the wounded child who entered that marriage demanding to be loved. I am an adult woman who is happy in her own skin—with or without a partner. I now refer to my first husband as my greatest teacher and, extraordinarily, I feel genuine gratitude and love, despite the pain we put each other through.

—JN

Understanding

And the day came when the risk to remain tight in a bud was more painful than the risk it took to blossom.

—ELIZABETH APPELL

While much of your life may have been spent wanting to be understood, love turns the tables and asks that you make trying to understand others your priority. With understanding comes compassion and the realization that deep down we are all the same, and have the same needs, wants, and fears.

When we truly understand others and our awareness of differences evaporates, love becomes easy. We see beyond our personal story, prejudices and preferences, and can become truly present and available. We realize that our similarities matter most, and we can start to be able to practice love in every situation.

Exercise 1: Our Enemy's Shoes

This exercise can help you gain more insight, and therefore more compassion, for those who have hurt you.

Pick someone you feel animosity toward. It can be someone from your own life or even a public figure.

Imagine you're an actor, and you are to play the other person's part. To do that effectively, you need to understand his or her motivation. You're a professional, so take the time you need to find out as much as possible about the person's early life and influences. What was their childhood like? Why do they think and act as they do? What has hurt them? What has nurtured them? How have they become who they are today? If you want, you can write it out or, if they are someone in the public eye, use the library or internet to do your research.

If the person is a political figure, try to understand their cause and why they fight for it. What does it mean to them? You are not seeking to excuse or condone anything they've done but to understand, so that you can play your part as effectively as possible.

When you've gathered as much information as you can, center yourself and close your eyes.

Imagine sitting opposite the person. If they are truly someone who makes you feel unsafe, you might prefer to imagine that you are visiting them in prison or perhaps under the protection of a bodyguard or guardian angel.

Hold this person in your mind's eye. Notice and name the strength of your feeling. Is it hate? Is it hurt? Is it a combination of both? Whatever it is, try to allow yourself to connect with the feeling and then release it. Remember, you are not here to judge but to understand. Your antagonist is sitting in front of you, just a few feet away. If you both reached out your arms, your hands would touch. Look straight into his or her eyes. Hold their gaze and then hold it some more. Keep staring straight ahead and hold this imaginary focus for the rest of the exercise.

Now, as you look into their eyes, ask yourself why they've done what they've done. Start your questioning in the present and then move back in time. Keep asking why. Was it because they were abused themselves? Because they were abandoned or their father died when they were young or they grew up in poverty? Let the question lead you further and further back in time. Keep looking into their eyes. What do you notice about their eyes? How different are they from your eyes? How different are they from the eyes of someone you are close to? Now cross the divide between you and imagine you are that person. See and feel what it's like to be in their skin.

This may make you very uncomfortable. It may bring up all kinds of difficult emotions. But it may also bring you one step closer to feeling compassion for this other human being. When you feel you have learned all you can, take your time returning to center. Breathe in and out as many times as you need to. Say your name out loud and maybe shake your arms and legs to return to being you.

Think of your "character" and their motivation. Now try to reconnect with the animosity you felt for them. Notice how much it has diminished. The more we educate ourselves about another, the harder it is to judge. Next time you feel the desire to condemn, try to defuse that natural impulse through understanding.

Those who hurt us can become our greatest teachers. Love—in the form of compassion—shows us that they're usually caught up in their own woundedness, grievances, or fear. We've said it before: hurt people hurt people. So set the boundaries you need to set (see page 252) and instead of retaliating, try to trust that they're doing their best—no matter how it might appear.

Looking for Romantic Love

The crucible of romantic love will stress test your spiritual growth more than any other challenge. If you don't feel happy and complete on your own, you're not ready yet for someone else. So, ironically, we know we're ready for romantic love when we no longer feel a desperate *need* for it.

There is no rush; practicing the Principles in this book will bring you the sense of comfort you ordinarily long for in someone else's arms.

....

SINGLE BY CHOICE

If you find yourself obsessing about when you're going to meet the perfect person, try doing the opposite of what you feel. Step back, take time out, and see what's behind all the urgency.

It can also be liberating to set ourselves a specific time period during which we're not going to look for a partner. Try committing to three to six months. During that period, put down the habits that feed your neediness. Stop scanning and stop flirting. No more placing yourself in locations that might possibly bear results. Give up trying to make yourself lovable, and you'll discover that you already are.

Use this opportunity to seek out friendships with women who are comfortable with themselves and their singledom. But also use this time to really enjoy your relationship with yourself. Take yourself on dates, buy yourself treats, and truly take delight in the only person whom you can guarantee will be with you until death do you part. You'll then be in much better shape when you start dating again.

After your self-designated sabbatical is up, test your readiness by seeing how reactive you are around your family. This may feel like it's beside the point, but if you're still red-hot with hurt and resentment, there's more work to be done. You want your adult woman, not your wounded inner girl, to be in charge of whom you eventually choose to be with.

....

Dating

We are not what other people say we are. We are who we know ourselves to be, and we are what we love. That's okay.

—LAVERNE COX, transgender actress and activist

Dating is the process of looking for someone who is worthy and able to fill an incredibly important and intimate role. It's an information-gathering process that takes time. Do first interviews and then second, third, fourth, and fifth—as many as you think you need. Use it to find out who the person is and whether he might be able to meet your requirements. Treat dates as opportunities to research whether you want what's on offer. Don't try to close that anxious gap between liking someone and not knowing whether it's going to work by pushing things along too fast.

From now on, you're the chooser, not the chosen.

If you find yourself focusing on what your date is thinking about you and whether or not he likes you, hit the pause button, because you're abandoning yourself. What others think of you is their business. What matters is what *you* think of you—and in this instance, of them.

....

HISTORICAL BAGGAGE

It's not surprising that dating can be fraught with anxiety. Historically, as women, how our lives unfolded depended upon whether or not we were taken on by a man through marriage or as a dependent. When women finally won the right to vote in the United

Kingdom in 1918—two years before their American sisters—only married women qualified! Even today, the tax system rewards marriage for both heterosexual and same-sex couples. Add to that the economic and social benefits of sharing a home, the ticking of our biological clocks (if we want children), and the societal stigma that can accompany being single, and it's easy to see how a natural longing for a mate can morph into something less healthy.

....

In the past, you may have worried about whether the person you just met liked or fancied you more than whether you actually liked and wanted them.

But now you have a different attitude. You are a precious and unique being. Instead of worrying about *being* chosen, actively work out what you do and don't want.

....

Exercise 2: Drawing Up a Partner Spec
....

This exercise will help you get clear on who exactly is the right person for you. It is a great exercise whether or not you're actively seeking love. If you're in a relationship, it can remind you to stay honest. If you're looking for a relationship, it gives you a job spec. And if you're taking time out, you can shelve this exercise for when you are ready to start looking.

Take a blank piece of paper and draw a line down the middle from top to bottom. Head the left-hand side "Needs" and the right-hand side "Wants." In your Needs column, write down the qualities of a relationship and attributes of a partner that are nonnegotiable for you. So you might put "mutual attraction" in Needs but "good looks" in the Wants column. "Solvent" may go in the Needs column, but "wealthy" should go in the Wants. The reason to be rigorous about this is that it's likely you have adopted attitudes that reflect your conditioning, rather than your authentic values, without even realizing it.

Fill out both columns with as much detail as you like. Then look at what you've written. Is there anything that you really long for that isn't on your list? Add it to the Wants column.

If you wish, share what you've written with someone you trust to make sure you haven't confused your wants with your needs.

All lists will differ, but there are two qualities that should be in everyone's Needs column: "available" and "kind." If you didn't include these, please add them now. "Available," means that the person is not with someone else and is also emotionally open. That, of course, rules out anyone who is in active addiction. Using addicts, of whatever kind, are not emotionally available. Their primary relationship will always be with their drug of choice.

Everything that is in your Needs column is nonnegotiable. You must get your legitimate needs met 100 percent. Your Wants are less important. They are the icing on the cake—but without the cake, they're meaningless.

Keep a copy of your "Needs" column in your journal or phone. Remind yourself that you're not settling for anything less. Then fold up the original list and place it in your Acceptance Cup. (See page 86.)

You've charted your course, and sooner or later the universe will respond. How will you know when that time has come? You'll meet someone who meets your needs. Your side of the bargain is that you must decline to settle for anything less.

....

THE GOLDEN RULE FOR DATING

The Golden Rule gives us a simple code of conduct. We treat others as we'd want to be treated ourselves. That means not flirting with anyone else's partner. If he's (or she's) with someone else, he's out of bounds, period. If that person is flirting with you, check in with yourself to see if you're reciprocating. Ask yourself how that person's partner would feel if she saw you, and you'll know instantly. Simple, perhaps, but easy to forget.

For years, society has pitted women against one another. The time for this to stop is now! We need to start treating one another as if we are important, precious, and worthy of respect if we want society to do the same.

....

Staying Honest

It's not your job to like me—it's mine.

—BYRON KATIE, founder of The Work

No matter how powerful we may feel in other aspects of our lives, many of us adapt ourselves to fit into relationships that can never meet our needs. We do it out of fear that nothing better will come along. We hide the parts of ourselves we are afraid aren't lovable and alter ourselves to fit into the space we think a current or future partner might want.

Of course, we want to be liked. We want to be chosen. We want to fit in. But if we allow parts of our real selves to be invisible, we eventually erase ourselves, and before long, we're back at the start of this journey—lost and in pain.

Remember your commitment from the 1st Principle to being honest about who you really are? If you catch yourself pretending to be something you're not to please a partner, or saying you like something that you don't, or professing that something is okay when it isn't, immediately notice and name it. Then check in with yourself to see if you're fearful or need to feel and release emotions. (See page 97.) If you are fearful, take time out to reassure the scared part of yourself. Remind yourself that you're loved and loveable as you are. Nobody else matters enough for you to abandon yourself again.

So many of my relationships during my high school and college years went the same route: I met someone, instantly fell in love, and spent every possible waking hour with him, but stopped doing the things I enjoyed doing and stopped taking care of myself. I adopted my partner's interests, friends, music, and tastes, and ended up immersing myself so much that the old me was no longer recognizable. Before long, I'd start to resent him, even though it was me who actively let myself go. I've learned since that one of the biggest gifts we can give ourselves and the person we love—and the relationship on the whole—is our commitment to remain who we really are and to purposefully carve time and space for ourselves to be able to do so.

—GA

When I've met someone I like, I do three things. I make sure he sees me without my makeup on; I make sure I sing out loud (I love to sing but am virtually tone deaf, so he needs to be able to handle that); and I disclose my vulnerability. I don't do this to push someone away but to make sure that he wants me for who I really am, with all my so-called imperfections. Like everyone else, I long to be loved, and I try to keep myself honest by being real.

—JN

....

BEING PERFECTLY IMPERFECT

If we don't embrace our so-called imperfections, then how can we expect anyone else to? If you feel yourself starting to fear that you're not measuring up to contemporary notions of what women are expected to be, remind yourself that they are unrealistic, and instead of trying harder, do the opposite.

If you're ashamed of your singing voice, sing out loud. If you worry about your weight, wear something tight. If you wear foundation because you believe that your skin tone is too uneven, try not wearing it at all.

Do whatever it takes to remind you and those around you that you are real and three-dimensional. You're not a cutout from a magazine, so don't erase those parts of yourself that don't fit the image. Show the world that you are perfect just the way you are.

....

Sexual Love

Sexual attraction is all too easily confused with love. It's often tempting to mistake being wanted sexually for being loved or liked for who we are. And if we're feeling insecure, it can be tempting to use sex to foster a feeling of closeness and bridge the gap.

But sex—and the feelings it releases—can mask underlying issues and blind us to the reality of a situation. By the time we realize our needs aren't going to be met, we can find it hard to leave because we've become invested and/or attached.

So really get to know them first and try waiting for a period of time before having sex. Set yourself a time frame. A month? Two? A particular number of dates? It may seem impossible, but anyone really interested in you will be happy to wait.

....

THE NO-HARM RULE

Once you're sure you want to be sexually involved with someone, use the No-Harm Rule to protect your emotional, psychological, and spiritual well-being. Whatever you want goes, as long as you don't harm yourself or someone else. That means taking responsibility for your sexual and reproductive health. It also means not saying yes when you want to say no and not pretending to like something you don't in order to please another. Lying to someone else to make him or her happy does both parties a big disservice.

The No-Harm Rule means you don't objectify yourself, either. Society encourages us to mistake self-objectification for freedom. But if you're contorting yourself into a sexual paradigm that is designed to please the male gaze, then however powerful it might make you feel, at some level you're still abandoning yourself and therefore harming yourself.

....

Sexting or having anonymous sex with someone you've just met online can similarly feel like an act of freedom, but if you're risking your sexual and emotional health, it's really a form of self-harm. So roll the tape forward. Ask yourself how you'll feel the day after. Treat yourself as you'd treat anyone else you love: gently, kindly, and with respect.

Healthy sex is fun and can be a fantastic release, but it shouldn't be the emotional glue to fix a faltering relationship. And, of course, you don't need a partner to have a healthy sex life. You can learn to self-pleasure so that your unmet sexual longings don't drive you into the arms of someone you wouldn't want to be with otherwise.

....

OMG YES!

Our need for sexual release is no different from any of our other physical needs. It's healthy and natural, but, as women, we've often been taught to fear and conceal it.

Whereas for men masturbation is taken as a given, for women there is still a stigma. Getting to know your own sexual needs and how to meet them will make you feel more of an agent and less of an object. Plus, you'll know what brings you pleasure. It's hard to have an equal and reciprocal sexual relationship if you're not aware of how your own body works.

You can find techniques online at websites such as OMGYes (www.omgyes.com). Your clitoris has eight thousand nerve endings—double the nerve endings in the glans of a penis—and exists solely to give you pleasure.

There are also health benefits. Masturbation is associated with improved cervical and cardiovascular health, increased pelvic floor strength, and better sleep.[2] Remarkably, it can also lower the risk of type 2 diabetes.

So shed any lingering shame and acknowledge and meet your natural needs.

....

Love or Infatuation?

Infatuation and falling in love can both feel like a kind of glorious madness. At first, it can be hard to distinguish between the two. But if it's the real thing, it'll be congruent with who you are. You won't be ashamed to introduce your partner to your friends, and you won't make excuses for him or her. You'll genuinely like the person for who he or she is. And you'll find that sexual chemistry will be less important than soul connection. You may discover that attraction comes *after* rather than before you get close.

Infatuation, on the other hand, relies on fantasy. Its bubble will burst if it comes into contact with reality. Sometimes intense sexual chemistry is an indicator of infatuation—you need the sexual high to feel okay about yourself or who you're with. There's a fantastic saying in twelve-step meetings: if your eyes meet across a crowded room, run like hell. That instant chemistry can be a sign that you've met someone who fits your childhood template rather than someone who feels "right" for healthy reasons. If you find yourself having to stay "high" to keep the fantasy alive, you're probably denying aspects of your partner or yourself. Sooner or later, the giddy phase will wear off, and you'll find out whether it's real or not.

If it is real, you'll like the person you're dating. You'll have a real friendship and want the best for him or her. It's at that point the journey really begins.

The Three Stages of Romantic Love

All relationships go through phases—especially those that last long term. First comes the honeymoon, which usually lasts between six and eighteen months. For that period, we're on a natural high, and our partner can do little wrong.

Next comes the power struggle, where most relationships get stuck. The qualities we fell in love with are now often the ones we find most intolerable. We once loved them for being so outgoing; now we resent them for not being around enough. We loved them for being sensitive; now they appear weak or needy. We can feel shocked at how our loved ones have morphed before our very eyes. Of course, they haven't: reality has just punctured the projections we thrust onto them.

True love is not a strong, fiery, impetuous passion. It is, on the contrary, an element calm and deep.

—ELLEN G. WHITE (1827–1915), author and
cofounder of the Seventh-day Adventist Church

Many couples remain in this power struggle for the rest of their lives or for as long as the relationship lasts. Each tries to get his or her needs met, often dancing to the same emotional tune learned in childhood. Even if one partner gives in, the tension bubbles beneath the surface.

....

THE INTIMACY DANCE

Most of us will have relationship issues with intimacy and will dance the intimacy tango: one partner stepping back as the other steps forward. If you find yourself caught in this dance, notice and name what you're frightened of—it'll likely be fear of abandonment or engulfment. Use the Essentials to self-care (food, exercise, rest, and appreciation) to anchor yourself so that you needn't retreat or encroach.

....

If you're lucky and do the work, you can reach the third stage: where the power struggle is over, a sacred space is created, and the issues that emerge within the relationship are seen as opportunities for the two partners to support each other in healing and spiritual growth.

The Magic of Listening

Listening is love in action.

—KATHERINE WOODWARD THOMAS, marriage and
family therapist, and author of the bestselling *Conscious
Uncoupling: 5 Steps to Living Happily Even After.*

Listening is an act of love that we can practice in all our relationships. But, ironically, the closer the relationship, the harder it can be to really hear what the other person is saying.

A lot of the time, what we call listening is actually just waiting for our turn to speak. And while we wait, we're working out what we're going to say rather than really hearing what is being said to us.

It is only through listening that we get to the truth. Otherwise we just react to what we *think* the other person is asking or doing. And that's how conflict starts.

Exercise 3: Magic Listening

This exercise will teach you a style of listening that will transform your interactions, not just with partners but with children, friends, and work colleagues as well.

Sit opposite your listening partner, near enough to hold hands but not so close that you're invading each other's personal space—ideally a few inches apart, knee-to-knee. Both of you take five deep breaths in and out. Then set a timer for an agreed length of time so that you can each have the same amount of uninterrupted Magic Listening.

You will each have an opportunity to say whatever is on your mind. There's just one rule: keep everything you say to "I" statements. Start each statement with "I feel . . ." or "I understood . . ." Don't accuse the other person. This isn't an argument; it's an opportunity to talk about your thoughts and feelings without blame.

At intervals, the listener repeats back to the person what he or she has said, using that person's own words. It's important that you use the other person's words. If you substitute your own, you're likely to give them your own spin, and the other person won't feel heard. You might start by saying, "What I heard you say was . . ." and when the other person confirms that you heard correctly, say, "I hear you."

When we don't like what the other person is saying or feel hurt, it can be especially hard to listen. You may need to "park" your feelings—that means not allowing them to overtake you, for this isn't the time. When the other person has had his or her say, you'll get your chance to have yours and express your feelings. Remember to stick with "I" statements and stay out of blame.

Be bold. Take the risk. Give up the desire to control through silence, bully through ranting, or wound by sniping, and give yourself and your relationships the gift of open, loving communication.

Empathy

Hearing another person's truth helps us to understand and to feel empathy. You might not agree with what you're hearing—in your mind, the other person is completely wrong—but understanding their reality will help you both.

Set aside your idea of what he or she should be thinking or feeling and imagine how you would feel if you were in their shoes and had that particular interpretation of events.

Allow yourself to truly see things from the other's point of view. You'll see the other person visibly relax when you show that you've not just heard but understood.

> I know I've said hurtful things in past relationships. I know I've reacted instead of paused. And I feel huge shame. In some cases, I've apologized. In others, I am not ready yet, but I feel confident in the knowledge that I'm working my way toward it.
>
> —GA

Appreciation

Often we take people for granted once we've known them for a while. It's easy to spend more time focused on what's wrong with them rather than celebrating what's right.

Try telling someone you love—this can be a partner, a sibling, a child, or a friend—something you appreciate about him or her every day for a week. Make it specific, just as you would a criticism, and include how the quality or action you appreciate makes you feel.

The harder we find it to think of an appreciation, the more we need to do it. If you're finding it particularly tough, write a gratitude list specifically about that person every evening. What you focus on grows, so the more you look for someone's good qualities, the more you'll find.

A spiritual advisor encouraged me to start thinking of an ex-partner as my "beloved." That regardless of our separateness, we will for the rest of our lives be raising two children together, and that makes him one of the most important people in my life, whether I like it or not. As you can imagine, this is not easy, but the times I am able to do it genuinely and instigate my relations with him from a place of love and appreciation rather than resentment, hardness, or, as he says, "againstness," the more my actual perception shifts. When I practice this actively, my casual thoughts about him have a tendency toward, at the least, neutrality, which is something in and of itself, but sometimes even fondness and (miraculously) deep appreciation and gratitude.

—GA

A Nonverbal Solution

When words fail, try hugging. When we squabble, most of us end up regressing—and toddlers are never good at resolving their disputes. So set aside words if they're not working and hold each other until the emotional storm passes. Hugging may be the last thing you feel like doing, but just as an angry toddler can be soothed through holding, so can most adults.

You can even agree in advance that if you can't resolve things within thirty minutes of starting to talk, you'll stop talking and hug. Hold each other until you both feel completely relaxed and then resist the temptation to start talking again. Soothe each other and yourselves by acting kindly. You can also agree in advance that you won't bring up the subject again for twenty-four hours—and by that time, you might not even remember what you were fighting about.

Abuse

Research shows that once someone has crossed the line into behaving abusively he is likely to continue, and the longer women tolerate abuse, the harder they find it to leave.

Research also shows that although most women think they'd never stand for abuse, it takes an average of thirty-five incidents of violence before a woman reports a partner to the police.[3]

If you experience abuse, tell someone immediately. The action of saying it out loud places you one step further away from slipping into denial. If you're unsure whether or not what has transpired constitutes abuse, check it out with someone else or call a specialist help line for advice. (See the resources section.) You are responsible for your own self-care and that includes, as a priority, not allowing someone else to hurt you.

If you were abused as a child, then this may be especially hard. If the relationship you're in now fits the template of "love" you experienced back then, that wounded part of you may convince you that the relationship is "right" even if the behavior is "wrong." Now that you are an adult, you can tell yourself that it doesn't matter what you feel; the facts speak for themselves. Nobody is allowed to abuse you. *Nobody*. There may have been no one around when you were young to protect you, but now there is someone who's got your back 24/7. That someone is *you*.

When I found myself in an abusive relationship, I blamed myself. It catapulted me straight back into being a terrified little girl who wasn't good enough. I needed to try harder, to jump higher, to please. Despite having qualified as a lawyer and written a book on domestic violence, I was so blindsided that I didn't even recognize it when it happened. It took a therapist to point out that the situation was abusive. I wanted to understand my partner, but she was firm: abuse is unacceptable. Full stop. She told me to tell the younger, traumatized part of myself very clearly, "This isn't okay. Nobody is allowed to treat you like this." And it was only then that I found the ability to leave.

—*JN*

....

PROTECTED BY LAW?

Until ridiculously recently, the right of men to abuse women was preserved in culture and in law. Marital rape became a crime in the United Kingdom only in 1991, and in all fifty US states in 1993, so legal protection is only a recent reality in the West and is still absent in a staggering 127 other countries across the globe.[4]

....

Stay or Go?

The key to happiness is freedom. The key to freedom is courage. The key to courage is love.

—KATE TRAFFORD

Pride masquerading as self-esteem can tell us to quit when the going gets tough. The thing is—and this is a big one—what you don't heal in this relationship, you are likely to repeat in the next. So that provided you're not in an emotionally or physically abusive relationship, you can use every relationship as an opportunity to learn.

If your relationship is going through a difficult phase, it can feel like a relief to move on and start afresh with someone new. But if you haven't done the work, you'll be like a guest at the Mad Hatter's tea party in *Alice in Wonderland*: you'll move to a nice, clean place setting, but before long, it'll look as messy as the last.

As the saying goes, you can either have the same relationship with lots of different people or lots of different relationships with the same person. If you keep the focus on your part, you'll grow and heal whether or not your partner changes. When you get to a place where you're no longer triggered by your partner's behavior, you'll know what is right for you in the long term.

As you engage more in your life, with clarity and integrity, the right solutions follow.

Love Goes On

With every good-bye, you learn.

—JOY WHITMAN

When a relationship or close friendship ends, we're often so heartbroken that we feel as if love itself has disappeared. But as hard as it is to remember during those painful times, there is, in fact, an infinite supply of love all around us.

Every encounter we have—romantic or not—has the potential for true love and connection. Be open to experiencing it in all its many and often unexpected guises. It doesn't reside in any one person. While we're yearning for the "special" relationship or wondering how it could have gone wrong, we're missing out on the love that is readily available.

Love is always there—just like the sun hiding behind the clouds on an overcast day—waiting for you. It's an action. It's a choice. And when you allow love to flow through you by taking loving action, not only will you connect to the never-ending source of love that resides within us all, but also you won't ever need to feel its absence again.

Practicing Love in the Wider World

Give light, and people will find the way.
—ELLA BAKER (1903–1986), civil rights and human rights activist

The lessons we learn in our close relationships are easily carried into the world. When we listen, empathize, and appreciate other people, we become peacemakers in our daily interactions.

From early on in our lives, we learn to divide ourselves into groups: genders, families, classes, teams, towns, countries, nationalities, and ethnicities. We work out who is on our side and who is not. But we can't foster a sense of solidarity with one group without fostering a sense of "other" toward another. When we focus on our differences, judgement and intolerance follow not too far behind. Then comes hate. That is how feuds, fights, wars, and genocides begin, by focusing on how we differ. Intolerance breeds intolerance. Violence breeds violence—and ultimately entrenchment and terror.

Love asks that we realize it is our similarities, not our differences, that matter most. Through each of us is sewn a thread of humanity that connects us, one to the other. As human beings, aren't we, in fact, all on the same side?

Love does not discriminate—whatever our color, sex, sexual preference, gender identification, religion, class, disability, cultural background. Love is love is love.

We don't have to know or even like someone to show love. We can act with love even when we don't feel it—the bigger the stretch, the greater the gain. The more you give love, the more love you'll receive.

Think what would happen if we all started to allow ourselves to feel love for everyone—not just for those in our own special tribe of family and friends but also for everyone we encounter.

Try starting with strangers. Look for the common humanity that connects you and do your very best to act with love. Then think of those you actively dislike, park your judgement, and look for the tender, wounded part that is present, often hidden, inside every human—the part that is crying out for love. Ignore the outer casing and seek to connect to their hearts.

Each of us needs and deserves love. You have tools that enable you to process your hurts rather than act them out.

Refuse to hurt yourself or anybody else. In every situation—small or large—ask yourself, "What would love do?" And do your best to follow the answer.

Reflection

Keep your face to the sunshine, and you cannot see a shadow.
—HELEN KELLER (1880–1968), blind and deaf writer and humanitarian

It's often much easier to feel anger, fear, and hate as I focus on the pain and struggles around me. But when I allow myself to settle, I discover that deep beneath my negative emotions, love exists. It's like the sun behind the clouds on a rainy day. I don't have to see it to know that it's still there. If I allow the clouds of judgement and fear to part, and I turn my face up toward it, I will feel love's warmth.

Action. Today I will meet the gaze of all those I encounter with love.

Affirmation. I am love.

Principle
8

JOY:
Living Fully

Let us dance in the sun, wearing wild flowers in our hair.
—SUSAN POLIS SCHUTZ, poet

Joy feels like happiness, only better. It's generated from
within and doesn't depend on what we have or haven't got.
It's vital for our well-being and arises in the moment.
Joy connects us with a sense of the divine.

With so much suffering in the world around us, joy can seem like a luxury, an indulgence, but, in fact, it's the opposite: it is a necessity. When we cut ourselves off from joy we jeopardize our emotional health by leaving ourselves vulnerable to depression and burnout, as well as our ability to connect, which can be of use in the wider world.

So far on this journey, *WE*'s Principles have given us tools to heal our emotional wounds, care for our bodies, and calm our chattering minds. *WE*'s 8th Principle teaches us how to tend to the needs of our souls.

Joy replenishes our spiritual reserves. When we are joyful, we are resilient and able to relish our lives.

The Necessity of Joy

The majority of patients I see admitted for inpatient psychiatric care are there in part because they've cared too much. They've given more than they've got to give.

—HELEN BACKHOUSE

Inside each of us is a pilot light—a life force. It's our job to tend that flame.

When we're depressed, our internal light diminishes. If we allow ourselves to become too fearful, it will flicker precariously. Resentment, jealousy, and ambition can smother it, as can over-work or compulsive caretaking.

But when we feed that flame with joy, it burns gloriously and brightly. Joy is the oxygen we need to keep our inner light aglow. When we find ourselves fatigued, flat, or flagging, turning to joy boosts our energy and our spirit.

Most of us struggle to live in balance. Often we end up living in a boom-or-bust cycle where we're either overfunctioning or over-whelmed. We may be fantastic at dealing with crises, but afterward, we're on the floor because we've given all we've got and more.

There's no virtue in running on empty, no matter how worthy it can make us feel—it risks our emotional, spiritual, and physical health. Life is to be enjoyed, not endured.

Joy nourishes us. It gives us reserves of spiritual strength to meet life's challenges by connecting us to a source that is stronger than any of the battles we face.

Joy Is Always with Us on the Path

I'm singing, oh, I'm singing in my soul, when the troubles roll, I sing from morn' till night, it makes my burdens light.
—SISTER ROSETTA THARPE (1915–1973),
gospel singer-songwriter-guitarist

No matter how difficult life is, joy is always available.

Our job is to be open, to be curious, and to commit to noticing the extraordinary nature of the ordinary. To make sure we're not too busy to hear joy's call.

Perhaps the roses in the garden you walk past on your way home from work invite you to enjoy their fragrance, or the girl singing by the bus stop makes you stop and listen, or the old set of paints on the shelf above the pile of laundry beckons, or a song thrush calls when you wake in the middle of the night.

Take care to respond to joy's call. Each moment will never come again, and every ounce you allow yourself to experience will give you resilience for the road ahead.

It is those who have a deep and real inner life who are best able to deal with the irritating details of outer life.
— EVELYN UNDERHILL (1875–1941), British writer and pacifist

One of the main things that brings me joy in my life aside from my children—who also bring other stuff with them—is meditation. I often access a state of joy when I am meditating, and the chances are that some of that leaks into the rest of my day and therefore my interactions with the world. There is also a good chance that if I have meditated, my experience of my children will feel more joyful, and I will take that away from the interaction rather than the other stuff.

—GA

Creativity

When we open ourselves to our creativity, we open ourselves to the creator's creativity within us and our lives.
— JULIA CAMERON, author of *The Artist's Way* and other books

Creativity fosters joy.

All of us need to create to feel fully alive. We don't have to do it formally or be "good" at it, whatever that means. Creativity isn't about being good or bad or skilled or amateur. It's *not* about what you produce—it's about the process of creating. It's about connecting to the creative flow that pulses through us all.

Every activity contains within it the opportunity to create. It doesn't have to fall into the categories that are traditionally thought of as "artistic" to count. Whether you're tidying a drawer, cooking a meal, or chairing a board meeting, if you tap into your creative flow, you'll find that it restores, nourishes, and rejuvenates you.

Creating—in whatever form—brings us into the present moment. It gives us a single point of concentration, which, like meditation, takes us out of the normal passage of time. And in that creative zone, our concerns about past and future slip away.

....

FLOW

Psychologists researching happiness discovered that when we are completely absorbed in an activity, we enter a state of flow in which we feel joyful, positive, aligned, and full of energy.[1]

For artists and writers, flow is the place where inspiration comes from and ideas arise effortlessly; for athletes, it's the zone where peak performance is achieved. Flow feels like the "state of being at one with things" described by Eastern religions. All of us can access it if we allow ourselves to use our hands, eyes, ears, voices, and bodies to play and create. Regularly entering into a state of flow is a key component to happiness.

....

All of us are artists, but many of us have forgotten how to be. Think of those early drawings you did as a girl, before you learned to label them as "good" or "bad." We often have to strip away layers of conditioning to allow ourselves to create. We have to learn to override the criticisms we received from the art teachers who told us we couldn't paint and the singing teachers who told us we were off-key. We have to rediscover what we once knew and loved as children and then allow ourselves to do it.

Your voice is simply your voice, like your nose is your nose. It's nothing to worry over.

—SHIVON ROBINSON

At one time, creativity was simply part of daily life—whether it was painting, letter writing, or sewing. Before television and radio, families and communities used to sing together, irrespective of whether individual voices fitted into formal musical categories.

The voice that may now be dismissed as off-key would once have had a place and a use. But now we're so used to hearing commercially recorded voices that we can be dismayed at and judgemental of our own and others. The ubiquitous recording processor Auto-Tune, which "fixes" a singer's less than perfect pitch, provides the audio equivalent of airbrushing. It gives us a distorted idea of what's normal.

So reclaiming your voice through singing is a political act as well as a joy-filled activity. It says that we can be active participants in art rather than just passive consumers.

When I was seven, my music teacher announced to the class that I was tone deaf. From then on, she'd leave me out when she went around the room getting the other pupils to sing. I didn't sing out loud from that day onward. In church or at school concerts, I'd lip-sync—I knew all the words and could feel the music flowing through me, but I didn't dare utter a sound. But when I had my first child, I discovered that the only way to soothe him was to sing to him. I was flabbergasted that my tone-deaf, tuneless renditions of the songs I'd mimed to as a child could stop him from crying. To begin with, I was too self-conscious to let anyone else hear me sing to him, but eventually I realized that if my voice could comfort my son, it couldn't be all that bad. Now I sing at every opportunity. I sometimes see my friends who have "perfect" voices wince when I fail to hit the correct notes, but I don't let that stop me. Now that I've found my voice, I'm never going to let anyone else ever shame me out of using it.

—JN

Nature and Beauty

People from a planet without flowers would think we must be mad with joy the whole time to have such things about us.
—IRIS MURDOCH (1919–1991), Irish author

Awe and wonder generate joy.

Connecting with nature and allowing yourself to be uplifted by beauty can give you the same experience that the process of creating provides: a moment out of time. There is joy in finding wonder in the delicacy of each leaf, the trillions of atoms joined to make each one of us, the infinite lapping of waves against the shore.

Every second spent in nature is an opportunity to encounter joy. It is never a waste of time to take the slightly longer route home through the park and allow the leaves dancing in the wind to distract you from your worries.

Next time you are tangled up in a problem, look at the sky and see what the clouds are doing. Or check out the sunset and take in how extraordinary it is that no two are ever the same. Wherever you are and whatever you are doing, find a moment to connect with nature each day. Let the life force in each growing thing inspire and nourish you.

What a wonderful life I've had! I only wish I'd realized it sooner.
—COLETTE (SIDONIE-GABRIELLE COLETTE, 1873–1954), French writer

Think of each day as a blank canvas and try to fill it with things that uplift you. Look for beauty, because joy is never far behind it; whether it's in a spider's web, an art gallery, or the rhythm of falling rain, it is always there, waiting to be noticed.

Be curious about yourself. Notice and name the things that lift your spirits and make you laugh. Give yourself permission to have more of what enthuses and impassions you in your life.

Commit to joy and then open all your senses to the unusual or unexpected. The daisy that insists on growing where it shouldn't, the tattoo on a stranger's arm, the lyric of a song you've listened to a thousand times but never really heard before. These are simple moments we don't notice in our rush, or we notice them but don't appreciate what gifts they are. Committing to joy means that you make a commitment to yourself that you will start to pay attention to those gifts.

Exercise 1: The Artist's Life

This exercise will help you connect with the opportunities of joy that are all around you. Find or make yourself a notebook—one that you can easily carry with you. Use it to record what you find beautiful or uplifting each day. This can be anything you see, hear, or experience—or even something you taste or smell. Describe it in as much detail as you can: sketch or doodle it, take a photo, jot down the name of the piece of music or quotation that made you laugh or weep, paste in tickets to events that you attend.

There's no right or wrong way of doing this.

Artists and writers rely on their sketchbooks and notepads to store inspiration, observations, and ideas. If you already practice this habit, use this as an opportunity to collect examples from beyond your regular areas of interest.

Just as your regular gratitude lists leave you feeling more grateful, so connecting with what inspires and enthuses you makes you feel more inspired and enthusiastic.

When your notebook is full, review it. See whether it reveals any areas of interest you didn't know you had. Ceramics? Music? Architecture? Drawing? If you can, take a class, go to a free concert, find a way of developing that interest further.

How extraordinary is the world we live in. We are all creative, and the more we allow ourselves to connect with our creativity, the more joy we'll feel.

....

My mother tells me that as a child I was happiest when I was painting—apparently I whistled, which, if you knew my usual adolescent demeanor, might startle you. But something in me knows that if I were willing to give up what I think I "should" be doing with my life and do what I know would make me the happiest, I would be . . . happy. But there are so many "buts" in the way! So now I carry a simple sketchpad and a fine-tipped pen, and once in a while I endeavor to sketch something: a corner of a room, a table, a face. Not only does this feel like I'm honoring a long-standing desire within me, but it's also honoring my creative self, honoring moments in my life that so often whizz by, and honoring that part of me that has always wanted to be—were I not so attached to my phone and its camera—one of those people who did things like write letters and drew things in notebooks.

—GA

Creating Space for Joy

It's a helluva start, being able to recognize what makes you happy.

—LUCILLE BALL (1911–1989), comedienne, TV star

Joy requires space, which in our 24/7 lives can be hard to make. When our days are full of the noise of the world—be it radio, TV work, or online chat—we can starve joy of the space it needs to grow.

Children generate joy effortlessly through play, and so can we. Use your Mental Detox day (see page 191) to open up the space to play, create, explore, and tap into joy.

Exercise 2: Joy in Practice

This exercise is to help you brainstorm activities that bring you joy. Think of things that you enjoy doing—that aren't about consumption or end results but about the process of doing them. Ice skating, rollerblading, dancing, making pottery, or collaging? Maybe you like gardening, listening to music, sharing a meal with friends, painting, reading, or going to the movies. Or is it travel, table tennis, or rock climbing?

Think of as many as you can—at least ten. Now, beside each item on your list, write the date when you last did it. How many of your passions are in your life right now?

If it's been awhile, you may feel a pang of sadness at the time you've lost. Often there are good reasons why we've had to stop doing something; perhaps children, work, or financial constraints have gotten in the way. But living in deficit doesn't work. It fosters envy, resentment, and sadness. It makes us cling to others to fill the void in the center of our own lives.

Without thinking about any practical limitations, ask yourself which joyful activity you long to do most. Try picking something you haven't done for a while and that you especially used to enjoy. Put a star next to it. Now find a way of doing it, and do it on your own. Having a companion will distract you and dilute your experience.

If there are practical problems in doing the activity you've selected, brainstorm a way of getting around them. You just need to honor the spirit of what you've chosen. Perhaps you long to walk on a beach but live miles from the coast. Instead, find a lake or even a pond, and take yourself there.

Perhaps you've selected dancing but don't have child care or the money to go out. Instead, you could set aside a half hour, put on some of your favorite music, close your eyes, and dance around your room. Try your best to really let yourself go. Leave your mind and all your worldly concerns aside and let your body be absorbed in rhythm and movement.

It doesn't have to cost anything to have a good time or to awaken the joy inside you.

....

The word "enthusiasm" has its roots in Greek and means "possessed by God's essence." If you feel enthusiastic, go with it. Similarly, the word "inspire" derives from the Latin *inspirare:* "to breathe in." So seek out inspiration and breathe it in!

Once you've created space for joy, protect it.

Seek out the company of people who radiate love and warmth. It's infectious, and increasingly you'll find that you want and need to be around it.

Misery loves company, but you don't have to provide it. You don't need to abandon old friends, but you can choose not to collude with their negative thinking. Set boundaries and protect yourself from situations that rob you of your love for life. Negativity, like positivity, is contagious.

Now that the Principles are generating huge shifts in your life, you'll find it harder to be around friends who are resistant to or cynical about the possibility of change.

> I used to think that anyone who wasn't a pessimist was fooling themselves. I prided myself on my ability to see the possible negative outcome of any course of action. But my experiences on this path have transformed me. I'm now an evangelical optimist, because I know that wonderful things can and regularly do happen.
>
> —JN

....

SETTING BOUNDARIES: LEARNING TO SAY NO AND YES

The word "no" is an essential part of our vocabulary. Setting boundaries is one of the ways we define ourselves. It lets others know where we begin and end and is particularly important to use if we're given to people-pleasing. (See page 72.)

Saying no when someone wants you to say yes can feel brutal—particularly if you're not used to saying it. So apply the Golden Rule: speak to others in the same way that you'd like them to speak to you: kindly. Let people know what is and isn't okay for you. We can't expect others to read our mind. There's always a way to say what you mean without being mean and without levelling accusations.

Of course, others won't necessarily want to hear your "no." People want you to do what they want you to do. But capitulating won't serve anyone, and it will leave you feeling angry, resentful, and overwhelmed.

Saying no to what isn't good for you frees up the space to say yes to activities and opportunities that bring you joy.

....

When you aren't meeting your innate need for joy, you leave yourself spiritually hungry. No matter how good your life is, you end up feeling restless and discontented, and before long start looking for answers in the wrong places.

Just as when you're physically hungry you might pick up junk food to replace the meal you've missed, if you're spiritually hungry, you may end up grazing on unhealthy relationships or point-less activities that leave you feeling empty and more restless still. As you do this, your chances for internal freedom and peace diminish.

Watch out for feelings of restlessness and dissatisfaction. They are signs that your soul is hungry and needs to be fed with joy.

I have to really work hard to create space for joy in my life. Self-imposed misery and sadness and irritability come much more naturally to me. I find it so hard to do something that I know from experience will bring me greater happiness and a sense of contentment. When I know that there is a solution, why do I choose to stay in the struggle? I've learned over the years that being in synthetic pain is so familiar to me that I have become comfortable in the discomfort. That often I don't feel like "me" without it. That part of me feels alive when I have something to complain about or fight against. And that there is a small part of me that enjoys the rebellion of not doing something that I know is good for me. The longer I push against that rebellious self and allow myself the gift of happiness without judging it or feeling like I don't deserve it or that it's sappy somehow, the more space I naturally make for joy to be a part of my life.

—GA

Soul Food

Happiness is not a station you arrive at, but a manner of travelling.

—MARGARET LEE RUNBECK (1905–1956), author

Joy feeds our souls and connects us with a sense of the divine. Everyone has an inner sense of the divine, and when we use the Principles to bring us into alignment, we become increasingly aware of it.

Many of us equate the divine with religion. That can cause problems for those who don't have a formal faith, as it is all too easy to point to the harm that's been done in religion's name: wars, persecution, abuse of power—sexual and material. Not to mention the legacies of guilt and shame that it has burdened so many of us with.

WE's path is spiritual rather than religious. It connects us to a source of power that is stronger than any of the difficulties we face and helps us to weather life's storms.

Your sense of that source of power will grow as you walk this path. Your knowing will develop experientially rather than intellectually, and it will resonate with the same part of you that recognizes love, authenticity, and truth.

You can think of that power as God, but if you don't feel comfortable with that term, try thinking of the power as simply "Love." Or add an extra "o" to God and think of it as the "Good" that exists in all of us. Reclaim that power for yourself and think of it as you choose.

....

THE G-WORD

If you're someone who has a strong reaction against the G-word—
God—you may find it helpful to make a list of why you object to it
so much. See how many of those objections still apply if you substitute the word *Love* instead. Or how about *Goddess*? Religion is
man-made, but God is divine, so don't let your experience of it be
limited by those who've historically laid claim to it.

....

Many atheists experience the divine but call it awe and wonder. Recovering addicts may find the divine in the power of a
group, others in beauty or nature. Still others may return to the
God of their childhood but update it as a loving God rather than
one to be feared.

Keep an open mind. Instead of reasoning about God and love,
experience it in your soul.

Wisdom can be found in traditional faiths and in the many
spiritual teachers who are alive today. (See the resources section.) We're lucky to live at a time when there are so many different routes to developing our faith. They all lead to the same
place, so it is simply a matter of finding a path that speaks to
you and then following it. Almost all faiths and teachers share
common truths—and the Principles in this book are distilled
from them.

PRINCIPLE 8: JOY

....

MORE UNITY THAN DIVIDE

While the world's great religions make war against one another in the name of dogma, cultural differences, morals, and ethics, enter any mosque, synagogue, church, temple, or other place of religious worship, and you might be surprised by the similarities you find.

The same guiding Principles lie at the heart of most religious teaching: kindness, humility, peace. The names and language may be different, the doctrine and ritual unique to each, but wherever we choose to worship, we are reminded to turn toward joy and seek out transcendence and love.

....

It's easy to get caught up in definitions, but they're fodder for our intellects and egos. Spiritual truth is beyond the comprehension of the human mind but not the experience of the soul. It doesn't matter what we do or don't call the source of power, how we do or fail to define it; what matters is our experience of it.

I had faith as a child, but when my father became ill with Parkinson's disease, it evaporated. As far as I was concerned, God either didn't exist or was so cruelly indifferent to suffering that I wanted nothing to do with Him. I became an evangelical atheist and dismissed anyone who had faith as either deluded or intellectually dishonest. And then one day—twenty years later—I found myself in treatment, and we were taken on an outing to a small country church. I was in my usual cynical mode, ready to lampoon the worshippers who'd fallen for a made-up story. But halfway through the service, I was suddenly transfused with the most powerful feeling of love I'd ever experienced. I knew in that moment that God did exist and that s/he was love. It was a knowing that had nothing to do with my intellect—it came from deep within me and has never left. Instead of blaming God for the suffering that exists in the world, I now turn to God for help in negotiating my way through it. I've discovered that I can access that feeling of love any time I pray or am of service to someone who is struggling.

—JN

Asking for Help

Why must people kneel down to pray? If I really wanted to pray . . . I'd go out into a great big field all alone or in the deep, deep woods and I'd look up into the sky—up—up—up—into that lovely blue sky that looks as if there was no end to its blueness. And then I'd just feel a prayer.
—ANNE OF GREEN GABLES by L. M. Montgomery (1884–1942)

Wherever you are and whatever is happening, asking for help is a necessary part of being human. You can't, and don't have to, go it alone.

There are so many paradoxes on this journey. One of them is that the stronger we become, the more vulnerable we can find ourselves. As we come to know ourselves and connect with our true center, we find that we can no longer bury feelings or slip into denial. We need to reach out and connect. Isolating yourself from others does not work, nor does pretending to be okay when you're not.

When we're operating from a place of authenticity, there's a shift in the way we relate to others. We discover that we need people, but we need them in a healthy way. We can ask for help from a whole range of people: friends, other women who are on a spiritual path, professionals.

But there's also another way we can ask for help, which is available any time we need it.

We can ask for help by praying. Prayer is a tool that works for all of us—atheists as well as the devout.

If we're blown off course by disappointment and we pray, it can help to bring us back to center.

We can pray if we're furious. Things haven't gone our way. What we wanted hasn't happened. We can rant and rage at the universe or our God. We can tell it why things aren't fair or how we've been let down.

At other times, we can just confide gently—we can chat to the power that's always there and tell it how we're feeling: good, bad, or middling. As we talk, we start to feel a connection. We come back to center as we disclose our truth—even when we're doing it to a God we don't believe in. It's amazing.

A Word of Warning: Prayer Works

Some prayers are answered after a humble request in the midst of our busy lives. Others are dramatically answered after messy, miserable pleadings shouted with snot and tears running down our faces.

We don't always know what answers prayer will bring. Sometimes it's "Yes," other times it's "No," and often it's "Wait." Whatever the answer, when we look back, we find we've been guided in ways that have led to outcomes that surpass our limited vision.

Each morning when you meditate, add a prayer to your ritual. Rather than asking for things or specific outcomes—as you may have been taught to do as a child—try simply asking to be aligned with what is good and right. If you are able to do the next right thing in any situation, then the right things will unfold.

One straightforward prayer, which can bring us into alignment at any moment, is simply to say, "Thy will, not mine, be done."

Gratitude—saying thank you—can also be a prayer. Try saying it at night before you go to sleep. Try saying it when you're struggling with your reality. When we connect with gratitude, we free ourselves from the burden of unhappiness. Prepare to be amazed. Prayer works. It's an action, and *Action Changes Things*. So try it.

If you hold your head up to the sky, sooner or later you will start to feel the warmth of the sun. And so it is with the light of the spirit.

Keeping an Open Mind

And then in a nanosecond, joy swoops in and in a humungous way clears it all away, just like that.

—MONI VANGOLEN, spiritual teacher

Some of us come to the spiritual path with an active faith, others with a faith that has been broken, and yet others with no faith at all or with an active antagonism against faith.

It doesn't matter what you think you know. If you keep an open mind and seek out joy, you will start to have a spiritual experience.

Spiritual experiences take many different forms. They might be a dramatic, life-changing moment of spiritual awakening in which your whole attitude and view of life change forever. But for most people, the process is gradual. It starts as a result of using the Principles to heal the wounds and attitudes that have blocked you from seeing your own true nature and that of the world.

As you nourish yourself with joy, you will notice that you are lighter in spirit. You will begin to feel a sense of ease and confidence where before you felt awkward and insecure. You will find it easier to enjoy time alone and will start to seek it out.

Increasingly you'll find yourself grateful but not surprised when life meets your yearnings and needs in return for you nourishing your soul with joy and stepping forward into your own spiritual truth.

You'll become aware of coincidences and opportunities that are increasingly difficult to dismiss as happenstance.

You'll notice that the trust you once found hard to practice has crystallized into a faith that you are being taken care of.

You'll notice that others who are walking a spiritual path will be drawn to you, and you will find companions to aid and accompany you on your way.

Then you'll realize that you are experiencing joy and an internal sense of freedom and happiness.

The process may sound magical, but it comes about as a direct result of you applying the Principles to your life. And the more joy you allow into your life, the brighter the spark of the divine burning within you will shine.

Joy in the Wider World

When you shine your unique light, bit by bit, you light up the
world of those around you. And, one by one, you inspire them to
light up too.

           —REBECCA CAMPBELL, British spiritual teacher and author

When we attend to the needs of our soul, we prepare ourselves to be of real use in the wider world. The brighter we shine, the greater the light we'll cast for others.

Joy prepares us for the work to come. *WE*'s final Principle—kindness—leads us out into the world of activism, where we will be called to have emotional resilience, and it's joy that will sustain us.

The more urgent and necessary the work we undertake in this life, the more important it is that we make space for joy. It will prevent us from slipping into adrenaline-driven or ego-based ways of working. It doesn't matter if we're engaged on a micro or macro level, joy makes our work sustainable.

Whether we're battling climate change, volunteering in a hospital, or trying to help a friend deal with her divorce, we have to connect to something stronger and bigger than the challenge we're facing if we are to be effective. That means taking time to connect with the energy that pulses through life and allowing it to nourish and nurture us.

But joy does more than just sustain, it also informs how we work as activists. It allows us to play and laugh along the way. We don't need to be serious all the time. We can scatter joy as we go.

We're told that angels fly because they take themselves lightly. But it is joy that puts the wind beneath their wings. So create, pray, and look for moments to enjoy beauty, and you will not only find yourself soaring high, you'll also beam light into the darkness for others.

Reflection

Lighthouses don't go running all over an island looking for boats to save; they just stand there shining.

—ANNE LAMOTT, writer

When others are suffering and I'm trying to help, I can get so caught up in the urgency of the situation that I can forget to make space for joy. When that happens, I take a moment to connect with nature, beauty, or the wonder of a beating human heart, and that reminds me that there is a much bigger picture. And that joy can shine a light to brighten any darkness I let in.

Action. Today I will seek out joy and let it fill my heart.

Affirmation. I am resilient and filled with joy.

Principle
9

KINDNESS:
Love in Action

Even the briefest touch of kindness can lighten a heavy heart.
Kindness can change the lives of people.

—AUNG SAN SUU KYI, Burmese politician
and winner of the Nobel Peace Prize

Kindness is what love looks like when we take it out into the world. It pierces our hearts as keenly as any arrow, and in doing so, it allows love to flow in and out. Through gentle, loving actions, kindness transforms us into spiritual activists.

Kindness brings a sense of meaning and purpose. As we apply this principle to our lives we discover that love starts to flow through us with increasing velocity and that we now feel truly part of the extraordinary world in which we all live.

Without kindness, no matter how much we do, have, or achieve, there's a hollowness at our core. A yearning that persists.

Most of us have spent our days pursuing goals that don't ultimately bring meaning. What we're conditioned to think matters most often ends up mattering least. As we shift from a state of self-concern to one of inner freedom, we acquire a new perspective.

We see that our ego's quest for "more" will ultimately always make us unhappy. There is no "enough." We have been suffering—individually and culturally—from the disease of more. And each time we've scratched the itch, it has only gotten worse.

The journey has shown us that no amount of material achievements or possessions can assuage our spiritual longing. But the good news is that where self-seeking has failed, kindness steps in to bring meaning and happiness. It is the final step on our journey from me to *WE*.

What Really Matters?

Happiness is not a goal, it's a by-product.
—ELEANOR ROOSEVELT, First Lady of the United
States, 1933–1945, diplomat, and humanitarian

At the center of all our lives is a quest for meaning. When times are tough, all our energy may be absorbed in trying to get by. But when the pressure eases, we find the question there, lurking beneath our daily struggles, calling for our attention. Is this it?

How should we spend the time we've been given, the uncertain number of days between birth and death? What will bring fulfillment and a sense that there is a point to our existence?

Exercise 1: Gaining Perspective

This exercise will connect you to what really gives your life meaning.

Have your journal ready and then center yourself by taking five deep breaths in and five slightly longer breaths out. Close your eyes and imagine you are a much older version of yourself, coming to the end of your life. Look back at your time on Earth and ask this older you what has really mattered. What are you glad to have experienced, and what do you care about most?

Open your eyes and write down what the older you has to say. Stay in this future state with your wiser self until you feel she has given you all you need to know.

Now close your eyes again and allow yourself to time travel back to today. Center yourself in the present. Take a look at what you wrote down and think about how you spend your time now.

How much of your energy is focused on the things on your list? How many of the items on your list have to do with looks, achievements, and material possessions? How many are about relationships and love?

If you keep this list in mind as you go about your days, you'll find that the awareness it gives you will gently result in your priorities starting to shift.

How wonderful it is that nobody need wait a single moment before starting to improve the world.

—ANNE FRANK (1929–1945), German-born

diarist and victim of the Nazi Holocaust

Like love, kindness is an action. It allows love to flow through us so that we become channels for a greater purpose than our own limited wants and needs.

It's the neighbor that keeps an eye on the elderly lady next door. It's the woman who passes a homeless person sitting on the sidewalk and stops to offer him help. It's the mother who offers a home to a stranger's child. It's the student who sets up a stall to collect food for a local soup kitchen. It's the friend who noticed you were looking sad and calls to make sure you're okay.

Before we started this journey, kindness was easy to overlook. It felt limp, small, not quite up to the job, but increasingly we come to understand that if it were to govern our interactions, the world would be a very different place, and our own quota of happiness would increase as a natural result.

Kindness carries within it the potential to overthrow orthodoxies, hierarchies, and regimes. What if we care for those whom we are told are our enemies? What if we give to those we are told are not deserving? It busts the myth that there is nothing we can do to change things.

The previous Principles have prepared you. Now kindness plants you firmly on a path of spiritual activism. Through four simple practices—Choosing, Acting, Giving, and Joining—we discover how to unlock kindness's transformative power.

Choosing

If not me, who? If not now, when?

—EMMA WATSON, British actress

Everyday life involves making choices. Often we feel small and powerless, as if there's nothing we can do to change our world. But there is.

With every choice you make, you have power.

All decisions have some impact. When you use kindness to guide your decisions, you will begin choosing the options that represent your values and beliefs. Your goal is congruence and the inner freedom and outer influence it brings.

Start small. Start where you are. Remember that mustard seeds can shift paving stones. You choose how you spend your time and your money—no matter how much or how little you have of each—so start using those choices.

Our actions, and inaction, touch people we may never know and never meet across the globe.

—JACQUELINE NOVOGRATZ, founder of the global nonprofit venture-capital firm Acumen, which seeks to improve the lives of the poor

Women in the United States control 80 percent of all consumer purchases.[1] Imagine if we used that power to demand ethically and sustainably produced goods, at affordable prices.

....

AN UNTAPPED POWER

In the United States alone about 50 million plastic water bottles are used every year.[2] The plastics used can take over 500 years to decompose.[3] Scientists predict that by 2050 there'll be more plastic than fish in the sea. Plus, it takes 17 million barrels of oil each year just to produce them—enough oil to fuel a million cars for a whole year.[4] Some American cities like Concord and San Francisco have banned the sale of small plastic water bottles, as have a number of university campuses like Leeds in the UK. How great would it be if we got their use banned altogether, first nationally and then globally?

....

Kindness can guide all sorts of choices: who you bank with, who you shop with, who you do business with, who you invite into your home. But don't beat yourself up with it. Change comes incrementally—your job is not to force it but to allow it.

Notice and name when you discover a gap between your beliefs and your actions. Over time, if you create the space and awareness through using *WE*'s Principles, you'll find you're making new choices across the board.

Exercise 2: One Choice a Day

This exercise helps identify the choices you make on a daily basis that you could make differently. How often do you notice something that upsets you, but you do nothing about it? We can get so used to living with situations or avoiding things that are unpleasant or unacceptable that we stop noticing.

For the next week, notice the small, everyday decisions that you make from habit, necessity, or haste that don't reflect your true values, and jot them down in your journal.

Perhaps you are passionate about the environment, and yet you buy bottled water at lunchtime rather than refill a reusable one with tap water before going to work in the morning. Maybe you feel sad every time you rush past the old woman who sits alone in the park feeding the birds. Maybe you never open the emails you get from the human rights organization you signed up to with such enthusiasm. Or you bitch about a colleague rather than stand up for her.

Notice the moments and name them to yourself. Write them down so that you remember them.

This isn't about making you feel bad. It's about becoming aware of the opportunities that exist every day that can help you to feel more powerful.

Think how great you'd feel if you decided—every day—to exercise one small choice that would increase the positive impact you have on the world around you. It doesn't even necessarily mean doing anything "extra"; it can just involve doing something that you already do but in a new way.

Acting

Practice random kindness and senseless acts of beauty.
—ANNE HERBERT, writer

Once we start becoming aware of the power we can exercise through our choices, a space opens up to begin making changes.

*A*ction

*C*hanges

*T*hings

So commit to carrying out one deliberate act of kindness every day and see how differently you start to feel about your life.

It can be as simple as picking up a bit of litter or giving a compliment to a stranger on the bus. Perhaps it is making someone an unexpected cup of tea or paying for the unknown woman behind you in the line for coffee. Small is beautiful. Often we feel that, unless we can do something big, there's no point in doing anything at all. This is not true. The more of us who hold up candles, the brighter our combined light will be.

Pick little things that fit into your life as it is now. If you're stuck for ideas, you can look through the list you made in the previous exercise and choose just one of them. Or you might like to check out the website recommended in the resources section, which is devoted to ideas for random acts of kindness.

Starting small is important. If you give yourself lofty or ambitious goals at this stage, you can set yourself up to fail or be burdened by yet another thing to add to your to-do list, in the process creating an opening for your ego to rear its unhelpful head.

A HIDDEN PRICE TAG

Actions require energy, but *not* acting also carries a price. Often we carry a low level of guilt for the things we haven't done. These avoidances rattle around at the back of our awareness, weighing us down. When we start acting consciously, we release ourselves from guilt and become energized and empowered.

Service is the rent we pay for being. It is the very purpose of life and not something you do in your spare time.

—MARIAN WRIGHT EDELMAN, activist and
founder of the Children's Defense Fund

This is not about showing how "good" you can be—to yourself or to anyone else. It's about creating a new muscle group that will serve you as you walk forward on this spiritual path of activism and power.

ACTION LOG

When we act kindly, it naturally boosts our self-esteem. Try keeping an action log of what you do each day to make a positive difference in the world.

Often we women minimize the good we do and compare it with the things we don't do. So notice and name your actions.

Then, if you're feeling bad about yourself or powerless, you'll be able to see in black and white the power you have through the choices you make. You'll see that you've done plenty to feel good about.

....

Don't tell anyone about your actions. Anonymity ensures that we stay humble and prevents them from becoming ego driven. Obviously, with some actions (paying a compliment or signing a petition), you can't hide your identity. But be anonymous whenever possible and watch how great it feels to feed your soul rather than your pride.

When I was about eight or nine, I offered to help an elderly woman carry her groceries down the road to her house. But afterward, I felt a huge amount of shame, and for years I couldn't figure out why. Then I realized that the pride I had felt in myself was disproportionate to my action—and that even though I hadn't told anyone about it at the time, deep down I was embarrassed. But in retrospect, how cool that at that age it even occurred to me to do a good deed! Unfortunately, it may have been the last time until my twenties, and I don't doubt it was the shame that put me off doing it again.

—GA

....

MAKE YOURSELF HAPPY

Scientific research shows that a sure way to be happier is to be kind to others. According to a study at the University of California, performing five random acts of kindness in a week increased happiness levels for up to a month.[5] In addition, various studies have found that giving to others can increase well-being and longevity,[6] and inspire others to do the same.

....

Acts of kindness will change your default setting to one of affinity and compassion for others. That's not to say you'll always feel like being kind, especially if you're hurting. There'll be plenty of times when you feel like retaliating, complaining, ignoring, or avoiding. You're human, after all! But acting kindly every day, no matter how mean you feel, will readjust your outlook, attitudes, and responses.

With each act of kindness, you'll cut the cords that bind you to feeling depressed and create new pathways and mental connections. And, of course, *WE*'s magic multiplier will kick in. The more love and kindness you give, the more you'll start to receive. It's a win-win situation. You gain an increased sense of fulfillment, and the world gets more love.

As I've said before, I don't have the sunniest of dispositions. My natural state is grumpy, and I have to work really hard at joviality. For most of my life, people, even strangers, have said "Smile!" because my resting face is depressed. When the winds are right, or I've run out of things to complain about, or I've managed to force myself out of this status quo, I can come across as giddy and childish and endlessly silly—until I'm not. But I'm telling you it takes work. And that work is usually climbing out of my head and my self-obsession and doing something for someone else—even if that something else is just being in a better mood. If I appear happy, it's because I'm choosing it! But funnily enough, it pays off. When I do it for someone else, lo and behold, I start to feel better, more in tune with those around me, and, yes, even giddy.

—GA

A Workout for the Soul

With the disappearance of God, the Ego moves forward to become the sole divinity.

—DOROTHEE SOLLE

The full power of *WE*'s Principles are felt when we apply them all simultaneously. Kindness comes last because the preceding Principles are entirely necessary to ensure that we don't use others' pain or drama to deflect attention away from our own.

Kindness is not self-abandonment or self-denial. It's a form of wholehearted giving that nourishes our soul. If we try to practice kindness without also practicing self-care, meditation, affirmation, and gratitude, we're at risk of people-pleasing, codependency, or ego-tripping.

True kindness comes from a spiritually aligned place. It involves standing in our own shoes and affording others the same dignity. If you find yourself obsessing about another's suffering, gently remind yourself to step back into your own life. You do not need to play God or feel that person's feelings. Do what you can and then let go of the results. Remember the Serenity Prayer. (See page 85.)

No matter how huge your heart and how broad your shoulders, you can give only what you've actually got. Giving more than you have—whether in time, money, or emotional resources—isn't giving, it's going into debt. When you're in debt in this way, you slide out of alignment and onto the slippery slope that leads back to self-obsession and ego-driven action and thought.

Practicing kindness requires you to keep spiritually fit. When we're aligned with the greater good (or God, or whatever you choose to call him/her/it), we're able to work miracles in the world around us.

....

WHO'S IN CHARGE?

Check your motivation regularly to ensure you're acting from a place of genuine compassion rather than ego.

Ask yourself who is running your show. Is it the little girl who was starved of attention except when she was being especially good and helpful? Or is it the woman whose heart is moved by the pain of another? Has your ego and its need to be right climbed into the driver's seat, or have you chosen not to tolerate abuses that you see around you? Look for telltale signs of ego and compulsivity: Are you getting frantic? Is your life getting out of balance? Are you feeling important or indispensable?

When you're not sure, pause and return to center. The more frantic you feel, the more time you need to set aside to meditate. Only when you detach from a situation will you gain clarity. If you return yourself to your still, centered core, the answers will be there waiting. Just make sure you create the space to hear them.

....

Giving

If I can stop one heart from breaking, I shall not live in vain.
                                        —EMILY DICKINSON (1830–1886), poet

Often we feel too far away and too powerless to believe we can make a difference in another's suffering. But it's not true. Kindness isn't limited by geography, kinship, or any other constraint.

Picture yourself in a street or park in your hometown.

Right in front of you, a young girl falls facedown into a small pond. There's nobody else around. She's going to drown if you don't act. What do you do?[7]

You run and pull her out, of course. Wrap her in your coat or find her a blanket and look after her until her parents or guardian can come get her.

How about if you've got an expensive dress on that will get ruined? "Who cares?" you'd say. "She's drowning."

The answer is clear for all of us. Who cares about a dress when someone's life is at stake? But what if the child were on the other side of the world? How does that affect your answer?

Across the world, one child dies of preventable causes every three seconds.[8] Do those children matter less? Of course not.

But the way we live has encouraged us to think either there's nothing we can do or that it's not our problem.

Giving what we can is a solution that has been practiced for centuries in many cultures, but which in our secular times many of us have lost touch with. It involves setting aside a percentage of our income—however small—to give to others who are in greater need.

It creates a shift within us that leads to a sense of freedom and empowerment.

Most of us carry guilt for the suffering we know is happening around the world. Even if we think we don't care or it's not our responsibility, it's impossible not to be affected. We see it in the news and on our streets.

In the long term, global political solutions are the answer, but while we're waiting for our leaders to act, avoidable deaths are happening all around us.

Whether it's 10 cents, $10, or $10,000, setting aside a portion of your income will also stop you from feeling powerless and guilty. There is something you can do, and now you're doing it.

If this isn't something you've done before, be prepared for internal objections to come flooding in. But giving what we can afford brings us a sense of agency, and it does so because it saves lives.

Exercise 3: Money Matters

This exercise is to help you empower yourself by getting honest about your spending.

No matter how much or how little money we have, most people get stressed about finances. You may not have enough to meet your own needs, or you may have plenty right now but still worry about what will happen in the future. Wherever you are on that spectrum, now is the time to empower yourself. So get curious. Download a spending app or keep a small notebook in your purse. Without judging yourself, notice and name every penny you spend and record it. At the end of a month, take a look at where your money went.

Knowledge gives you the power to make conscious choices.

Your spending patterns and priorities may already have shifted as you've been reading this book. Noticing and naming where your money goes will enable you to make new choices, so . . . empower yourself.

....

....

LUCKIER THAN YOU THINK

If you have a refrigerator, a bed to sleep in, and a roof over your head, you are richer than 75 percent of the world's population. And if you are reading this book, you are luckier than the estimated three billion people in the world who can't read at all. Rather than comparing your life with those who have more, turn your focus in the other direction and acknowledge how fortunate you are.

....

We're often encouraged to be skeptical about giving: "Charity does more harm than good, and doesn't it encourage dependency?" "What about all the money that goes into administrative costs or is lost to corruption?" "And what's the point anyway if my donation is only going to be a fraction of what's needed?" Except we wouldn't be skeptical, of course, if it were our daughter who was starving. Then we'd take every penny a stranger across the globe could afford to send.

....

THE LIFE YOU CAN SAVE

Some charities are a thousand times more effective than others. The same tools that are used to measure the efficacy of health treatments can be used to measure the effectiveness of charities. You can use an online calculator to check how much good a range of charities would do with what you donate. It's even possible to work out how many lives you can save over the course of your own life by giving a regular amount. Visit The Life You Can Save (www.thelifeyoucansave.org) in the United States or Giving What We Can (www.givingwhatwecan. org) in the United Kingdom.

....

WE encourages you to come out of denial. The choices you make affect others across the world. The money you spend on a coffee that you buy out of habit but don't actually enjoy could save the life of someone somewhere on the globe. Find whatever slack you can in your system and redirect it.

Once you start giving, you'll feel like a citizen of the world. It's another win-win: you'll be doing something to help another person who is in trouble, and in return you get to feel great. Start small and watch how your priorities start to shift. Before long, you'll find yourself wanting to increase what you give and discovering that you can.

Joining

Just imagine your daughter was standing there. What would you do, how would you fight?

—ANURADHA KOIRALA, Nepalese social activist

When you become an active member of your community, you create connections that bring healing both to yourself and to those around you. So while you're giving globally, try to find a way of acting locally. Many people are isolated, far from home and cut off from those they love. Local action dispels the alienation and loneliness that has become a familiar feature of modern living.

Most of us have a multitude of issues that we care about, and it can be hard to know which to pick or where to start. Use your heart as your guide and the exercise that follows.

Exercise 4: Finding Your Cause

This exercise will help you identify your cause. Have your journal beside you to write down what you discover. Close your eyes and picture the world in which you live. Think about the suffering that exists—both locally and globally. Make a list of the issues that upset you the most—those which really move you. We're not looking for the injustices that make you the most angry or outraged (those are often signs that the ego is engaged), but the suffering that makes your heart feel as if it might break when you think about it.

If it's difficult to find any issues that you really connect with, look through a newspaper or watch the news. Which stories provoke a visceral response (not an intellectual one)? Your body will know what you cannot stomach. Try not to judge what you choose. There are no right or wrong answers. Your list doesn't need to be long or worthy.

This is not about your intellect; it's about your inner knowing. There is only what you know in your heart. You may care about children, nature or animals, trafficking or poverty. Maybe it's the thought of the homeless being cold and alone at Christmas or children in a refugee camp. Maybe it's animals being killed for their fur or female genital mutilation or the vulnerability of asylum-seekers far from those they hold dear.

Now examine your list and ask which one moves you the most. There may already be one that leaps out at you. If you're not sure take it into your morning meditation. Look into your heart and ask which is the one that touches it the most deeply. Trust your first response. Once you've identified your biggest sorrow, make a commitment. Agree with yourself to find a way of doing something locally about the issue you've chosen.

Let the change you want to see begin with you right where you are. Maybe you find a dog rescue center and volunteer on weekends, or deliver meals to the elderly, or start writing to a prisoner who has no one. If you're in a twelve-step fellowship, you can

sponsor and do service. Or perhaps you'll find a local organization that works on the international issue you care most about.

As we work to create light for others, we naturally light our own way.

—MARY ANNE RADMACHER, author and artist

Spread your roots where you are planted. Becoming an active member of your community creates connections and a sense of belonging where you live, while bringing healing both to yourself and to the wider world of which you are a vital part. Even if you are already time restricted, trust that the space will emerge for your new commitment.

Remember that small is beautiful. Do only what you can. You will find that as you do, your capacity grows, and you will discover that you gain far more than you give.[9] It takes only a couple of minutes to get other mothers to sign a petition at the school gates or to make a phone call for a local charity or to drop some flowers at a sick neighbor's house.

....

PROGRESS, NOT PERFECTION

It's often easy to think there's no point in taking action, political or otherwise, unless we can do it perfectly. But baby steps are better than no steps at all. The global campaign for a Meat-Free Monday is a perfect example. If everyone went meat free for just one meal a week, in the United States alone it would have the same environmental benefit as taking 1.5 million cars off the roads and save 1.4 billion animals from being factory farmed. Plus, it would have a dramatic effect on world hunger, as the cereal needed to raise one cow could feed three people.[10]

....

I've often felt reluctant to take political action because I've felt so hypocritical. How can I campaign on climate change if I still fly and drive? How can I be against animal cruelty if I still wear leather? But then in the run-up to the 2009 climate change talks in Copenhagen, Denmark, I discovered that my flawed life could still be useful. Together with a group of other mothers and children, we lobbied the government and held protests at Parliament. Our message to MPs (members of Parliament) was loud and clear: we'll vote for the party that puts protection for the planet ahead of our individual right to fly. We were able to show politicians and the media that the demands for action on climate change didn't just come from the environmentally pure but also from those whose lifestyles would be adversely affected by the measures needed to tackle climate change.

—JN

The results are not up to you. It is your job only to plant the seeds by taking action. Once you start moving toward your higher purpose, the universe always responds in kind.

Seek out others who are on this path and care about active change. Use *WE*'s Principles to start new conversations: in your neighborhood, your local coffee shop, at the departmental water cooler—wherever you find yourself. Support one another. Set goals that relate to the issues that really matter to you rather than the temporal and the material. If you stay open, you will always find sister-travellers to join you on your way.

> *Love costs all we are, and will ever be. Yet it is only love which sets us free.*
> —MAYA ANGELOU (1928–2014), poet, writer, and civil rights activist

As a result of applying *WE*'s spiritual Principles to our lives, we come to see the extent to which we've been blown off course—by life itself, by our conditioning, by our choices—away from what we know really matters. This journey returns us to ourselves: our real values, our true nature.

Kindness gives us power in the face of suffering. It gives us the power to choose differently, act kindly, give what we can, and join with others. When we do, we find we have a sense of purpose and no longer feel alone. We experience the magic that is generated when all our powerful *ME*s are joined together as *WE*.

Kindness in the Wider World

> *If you think you're too small to have an impact, try going to bed with a mosquito in the room.*
> —ANITA RODDICK, British-born founder of the Body Shop cosmetic company, activist for political rights and protecting the environment

This is a path of love, and kindness is the tool by which we give expression to it in the world.

Gratitude has taught us that we're lucky. Through an accident of birth, we are lucky. Lucky to be here reading this book. Lucky that it is not our child who is begging on the corner or dying for want of a bowl of rice.

You may not be able on your own to topple an oppressive regime, change a polluting transportation system, or stop a much-needed women's refuge from closing, but when you stand together with others, with kindness in your heart, extraordinary things come to pass.

As you continue to practice kindness on a daily basis, you will see opportunities to effect bigger changes in your family, community, and the world at large.

Your sensitivity to the suffering of others will increase. Kindness will push you into action. You won't be able to stand on the sidelines doing nothing because, you know now that when you are spiritually aligned, you are more powerful than you could ever have imagined.

Reflection

Politics is about everything we do, from the moment we get up in the morning to the minute we go to bed at night. It's something everybody and anybody can be involved in.

—CAROLINE LUCAS, British politician

When I take action—no matter how small—I have the power to make the world a better place. Using kindness to align myself with the greater good gives me a sense of purpose and reminds me that I'm not alone. I'm part of a wonderful and growing movement of women who are walking into the light, guided by what we know to be right and true.

Action. Today I will choose to act kindly.

Affirmation. When I take action, the world is a better place.

We started this journey searching. We knew there was a better, more fulfilling way of living. Now the Principles have given us a direction and a focus for our lives.

Let's pause for a moment at the threshold of our new lives and allow that focus to zoom right out across our fragile Earth to the 7.3 billion people we share our planet with.

Imagine how it would look if it were truly governed by spiritual Principles.

How different things could be if, across the world, a desire to be fair rather than to have more became our primary motivation.

How would things change if compassion replaced judgement and if being kind became the new cool? If we all sought to abide by *WE*'s manifesto and put spiritual Principles at the center of our lives.

Just as each of our individual lives has been blown off course by thinking that externals could heal internal pain, so many of our institutions and governments have been governed by doctrines that exacerbate rather than solve the challenges the world faces.

Suffering is an inevitable part of being human. But what about suffering that is avoidable, caused by inaction, neglect, or greed?

We want to see the changes that have started within us translate into external shifts—not just for us but also for all those who suffer across the globe.

PART 3

The Manifesto

Never believe that a few caring people can't change the world.
For, indeed, that's all who ever have.
—MARGARET MEAD (1901–1978), cultural anthropologist and author

This is not a manifesto in the traditional sense of the word. It's a rallying cry to commit to a new way of life: one that is based on spiritual Principles.

It's a call to apply the tools we've now learned to every aspect of our lives: at home, at work, in the polling booth. To let them govern how we live, how we do business, how we raise our families, how we deal with our neighbors.

It's a call to a values-led existence that puts love at its center. One that refuses to discriminate on the basis of race, class, creed, or gender.

It's a call for love to become a way of life. To let it dictate our choices, our actions, and our interactions.

This manifesto will take commitment on your part. It will mean practicing these Principles on a daily basis. Like swimmers in deep water, we have to keep moving in order to stay afloat. Any time we stop using them, we'll start to slip back into old patterns of criticism, competition, and judgement. But if you continue walking this path and practicing the Principles in your daily life, they will keep you resilient and focused, and build your compassion and connection.

Practice is key. We are practicing. None of us gets to be perfect.

Perhaps you will want to work through the chapters again, maybe even with someone else to share what you've learned. At the very least, continue to meditate, practice gratitude, and take action. Put kindness to yourself and others at the center of your life.

This journey has no end—we'll be working on ourselves, our attitudes, and our actions for the rest of our days—but if we walk forward together, one woman at a time, amazing things will come to pass both for us individually and for the world in which we live.

A WORLD IN NEED
OF LOVE

It doesn't matter how strong your opinions are. If you don't use your power for positive change, you are, indeed part of the problem.

—CORETTA SCOTT KING (1927–2006), civil rights leader

The challenges that the world faces are, in many ways, analogous to the challenges each one of us faces internally.

Fear and resentment cause the global equivalent of synthetic pain. Just think how different our world would look if the West's response to the tragedy of 9/11 had come from a place of concern and compassion rather than fear and judgement.

And how different would our world look if economic goals were focused on sustainability rather than harnessed to a model built on "more," with its thirst for ever-increasing levels of consumption and debt?

The quick fixes we reach for when we're emotionally out of kilter are similar to the short-termism that drives much of today's politics. Just as many of us may battle with greed and pride, our governments, too, fail to end the arms trade for fear that someone else will get the profits or risk unpopularity at the polls by tackling the oil lobby.

Our collective preoccupation with the self has legitimized greed and prioritized individual advancement over the greater good. In place of the value systems that religions once provided for most of us—is a gaping spiritual void, which we've attempted to fill through the pursuit of material well-being. As a result, the richest have grown wealthier, and the rest have been left behind.

....

A WORLD APART

In the United States, the gulf between rich and poor is now wider than at any time since the 1920s, leaving the richest 0.1 percent owning as much as the bottom 90 percent. More than one in five American children now live in poverty[1]—the highest rate in any developing nation.

Globally, the wealthiest sixty-two *individuals* now own as much as the poorest half of the world's population.[2] Fuelling this extreme inequality is a global network of tax havens. As a result, poorer countries lose at least $170 billion a year—money that is desperately needed for vital services such as health care and education.[3]

....

None of this is inevitable. It's about choices.

Our current system leaves us polarized. It's a binary system where some of us are winners and, as a result, all of us are losers. Where those of us with jobs often work insane hours, while those who are out of work languish at the perimeter of society. Where the opportunities that the computer age promised for shorter working weeks and a fairer division of labor have been ignored in favor of a deregulated labor market, resulting in zero-hour contracts and round-the-clock working. Where wealthy nations battle with rocketing scales of obesity, and yet 800 million people go to bed hungry each night.

....

HUNGER AT HOME

Hunger is not just a problem in the global south. In the United Kingdom, as a result of austerity policies, there's been a massive rise in the numbers turning to food banks to survive.[4] In the United States, 48.1 million Americans now live in food-insecure households, with African Americans twice as likely to be food insecure as their white non-Hispanic counterparts.[5]

....

Those of us who are okay for now and have managed to achieve a degree of security find that it's increasingly accompanied by a nagging sense of unease. Deep down, we know our current system isn't fair and that while we're winning, someone else is losing. While our child rips open a mountain of presents on his or her birthday, elsewhere someone else's child has none. While we scrape edible but uneaten food into the trash can, others are starving. Increasingly, we're unable to square the lie that we're not all connected; that our actions don't have an impact on each other.

If we made kindness the governing Principle of our own lives, how much better could lives be across the globe, and how much happier would we, as individuals, be?

Study after study shows that it's not how much we have absolutely that governs our levels of happiness, but the levels of equality—including income equality—within a community. On an international level, global inequality causes wars and mass migration. Domestically, it contributes to higher crime and societal divisions.

....

HAPPINESS VERSUS WEALTH

Bhutan, a small land-locked kingdom nestled at the foot of the Himalayas, has pioneered another way of doing things. Instead of using gross domestic product (GDP) as a measurement of success, it uses a gross national *happiness* index, and its policies prioritize individual well-being and spiritual values over consumerism. Although it is one of the poorest nations on the planet, it regularly ranks in the top ten happiest nations.

The United Nations is now investigating how Bhutan's model could be used across the globe.

....

The voice of conscience is so delicate that it is easy to stifle it; but it is also so clear that it is impossible to mistake it.
—MADAME DE STAËL, 1766–1817, French intellectual

Our current economic system has a twisted set of values. All the money that changes hands to drill and sell oil counts as a positive, irrespective of the cost to the environment. And when there's an environmental disaster, the money spent clearing it up gets counted as positive economic activity and added to the GDP as well.

We count as positive the money the arms trade adds to our balance of trade but fail to set against it the catastrophic human and financial cost of the wars that result. Across the world, we now have cities in which children, asthmatics, and the elderly can't breathe, but the cost of treating them isn't taken into account when factoring in the value to the economy of private cars—let alone the cost in terms of human suffering.

WE's 9 Principles provide a new way of calibrating what matters most to us and our planet.

Equal Means Equal

The world is awakening to a powerful truth: Women and girls aren't the problem; they're the solution.
    —CHRISTIANE NORTHRUP, obstetrician, gynecologist, and author

As women, of course, we have additional battles.

Our fight for equality is far from won. And now America has elected a presidential team that threatens to turn the clock back still further.

The United Nations enshrines equal rights in its charter. But out of its 191 heads of state, only 12 are women.

In the British Parliament, fewer than 3 out of 10 MPs are female. In the United States, there are more CEOs of leading companies who are named John than there are women CEOs. And less than 1 percent of statewide elected executives are female and black.[6]

Across the globe, the work of women is consistently undervalued. Worldwide, when unpaid work such as housework and family care is included, women do 75 percent of the work, receive 10 percent of the pay, and own 1 percent of property.[7]

We are told business backs equality, but the movement toward equal pay has stalled across Europe, leaving women's pay lagging behind men by roughly 26 percent.[8] And in the States, if you're a black woman, the pay gap is 32.4 percent, rising to a scandalous 44.1 percent for Hispanic women.[9]

The United States is alone among developed nations in not providing paid maternity or parental leave across all its states—the other two in the world are Papua New Guinea and Oman. That leaves nearly one in four American women returning to work within two weeks or less of having a baby. About half of those women were back to work in under a week.[10,11]

Caring professions such as teaching and nursing, traditionally dominated by women, pay far lower salaries than careers that contribute far less to society but are dominated by men. And although Western economies would collapse without it, the work of caregivers isn't factored into the GDP at all. In the United Kingdom, caregivers (mainly women) would cost the country £119 billion if they had to be paid for—that's three times the defense budget.[12] The Canadian government has estimated the value of unpaid caring contributes over 30 percent to the country's GDP. Imagine what would happen if we all went on strike!

....

TOGETHER WE CAN!

In 1975 Iceland's women went on strike, as 90 percent of them walked out of their homes and jobs. The country ground to a halt. The following year, a law was passed that guaranteed equal pay. Five years after that, Iceland became the first country to elect a woman president, and it now has the highest gender equality in the world. Despite the landmark legislation, in 2016 female pay still lagged behind male pay by 18 percent. So there was another strike. At 2:38 p.m. promptly, women left their places of work—giving themselves the 18 percent of the day they weren't paid for.

....

We are living in the modern age, and we believe that nothing is impossible.

—MALALA YOUSAFZAI, Pakistani activist, Nobel Prize laureate

In the West, men's contributions in the home are increasing, but women still do the bulk of household tasks—which amounts to an extra nine hours' work per week for women living in the developed world.[13]

Further afield, economic reform has similarly failed to deliver women what it promised. In China, capitalism has created greater gender inequality rather than less. While pay was roughly equal under Communism, by 1988 women earned 87 percent of men's pay, and now they're down to 67 percent.[14]

In India, growing economic prosperity has actually resulted in an increase in honor and dowry killings among the middle classes.[15]

Across Asia over the last three decades, 163 million female fetuses have been aborted or killed at birth on the grounds of their gender.[16] That's more than the entire female population of the United States, and the resulting spike in surplus males has resulted in an increase in trafficking and bride purchasing from poorer countries.[17]

Around the world, 603 million women live in countries where domestic violence isn't considered to be a crime. And a staggering 200 million women have undergone female genital mutilation.

Nearer home, one woman is sexually assaulted in the States every two minutes, while in the United Kingdom women are murdered by their partners each week, yet rape convictions are falling. A British woman who has reported being raped has only a 5.7 percent chance of her attacker being convicted,[18] and in the United States, only 2 percent of rapists spend more than a day in prison.[19] The vast majority of rapes are never reported.

While genuine equality eludes us, warring ideologies seek to contain and define us. One requires our bodies to be waxed, tucked, and sliced, the other that we be hidden behind veils.

Our current way of living has failed catastrophically to provide freedom from exploitation and violence.

....

AN ALTERNATIVE APPROACH

Not all cultures prize youth and physical perfection in the same way as the West. For example, in Japan, the aesthetic of *wabi-sabi* places a higher value on age and imperfection than it does on youth. Wrinkles and signs of aging are treasured as unique and precious and viewed as adding to a woman's beauty. How great would it be if we could choose a different attitude that saw our life experience as beautiful rather than something that made us increasingly culturally and sexually invisible?

....

Equality: A New Paradigm

We've begun to raise daughters more like sons . . . but few have the courage to raise our sons more like our daughters.
—GLORIA STEINEM, women's rights activist, magazine publisher, and author

As women, we want equality, but we also want to live in a society that reflects our real values and the truth of who we really are.

We want fifty-fifty, but we have to ask, fifty-fifty of what?

Too often we've found ourselves fighting for our fair share of systems and institutions that leave us obliged to choose between our career and our family. They were designed around a workforce that didn't give birth to children and wasn't expected to nurture them. They don't work for us as women or for men, or for the generations that will come after us.

We don't want an economic system that puts profits ahead of people and limitless growth ahead of what's sustainable. That model fails to place any value on caring.

We don't want to lean in to win our share of systems that don't work for us.

We want a new model, one that is based on the reality of who we are and what we need. One that gives us the opportunity to be real and messy and whole. That recognizes the value of our unpaid labor as well as conventional measures of financial gain. That enables us to be honest about who we are and to build systems that are fairer and meet all our needs—of whatever gender, creed, or generation, and wherever we live in the world.

WE Together

You just need to be a flea against injustice. Enough committed fleas biting strategically can make even the biggest dog uncomfortable and transform even the biggest nation.

—MARIAN WRIGHT EDELMAN, activist and
founder of the Children's Defense Fund

Before walking this path, many of us have felt powerless and insignificant. We've often been told there was nothing we could do to make a difference, and we believed it. At some level, it may have let us off the hook. But now we know—from our own personal journeys—that action really can change things. We're no longer prepared to tolerate the knowledge that others are suffering due to problems that have solutions.

Think again about what would happen if we really did each decide to subject government policies to the same spiritual test we're starting to apply to ourselves. If we collectively made kindness our guiding value in every aspect of our lives.

Our economic priorities would shift. Protecting the planet would be put ahead of maximizing short-term profits. Refugees wouldn't be left to drown at sea. Caring responsibilities and child rearing would be accorded their real worth, and we'd share work more evenly so that we could all work to live rather than live to work.

The solutions that already exist to tackle poverty, inequality, and the threat of runaway climate change would be implemented.

We'd elect wise, spiritually whole politicians with a mandate to end world hunger rather than perpetuate it. There is enough food to feed the world's starving. The problem isn't a lack of resources, it's a lack of will.

Blueprints exist for how it can happen: 193 countries have agreed to the United Nations' Global Goals, designed to end world hunger, inequality, and climate change. But they won't be implemented unless we start speaking up and saying we're willing to have less so that others can have enough. And vitally, our voices will need to be heard above the hum of those whose vested interests our current systems reflect and serve.

Into Action

I am a dreamer, and having a dream is sometimes challenging,
but I never look at a situation as too difficult.
—SISTER ROSEMARY NYIRUMBE, Ugandan nun and humanitarian

Now that we've placed our lives on a spiritual foundation, we can take our values out into the world. We can take action to become fully congruent and to close the gap between what we believe and what we do.

If we ignore the obstacles our ego throws up and follow the nudging of our soul, we will each find our own path and our own way of being useful. The gentle revolution is already happening.

Across the world, women are changing the paradigm.

A Pakistani schoolgirl won the Nobel Prize and is changing the face of education.

In Utah, a young mother's account of being poor in the United States went viral and is shifting attitudes about low wages.

In London, a mother's post on Facebook led to thousands marching for Syrian refugees.

In Iran, a student's hunger strike turned the world's attention to the continued oppression of women.

In Uganda, a nun turned her convent into a safe haven for trafficked women and girls.

Women all over the world are taking actions, big and small, and one by one creating change.

As a woman, my country is the whole world.
—VIRGINIA WOOLF (1882–1941), British writer

Each of us has our own part to play. Nothing is asked of us that we don't already have to give. We all bring different qualities and different gifts. We are all needed. The internet gives us ways of reaching one another and getting organized that have never existed before.

Every one of us has our own calling, dictated by our heart.

Some of us will lead, some of us will support. Some of us will march, some of us will make tea, some of us will sew banners, some of us will write research papers. Others of us will sit with someone who is lonely and feels broken, as we have each felt in our own way.

But what we won't do is be indifferent to suffering. We won't tolerate discrimination and unfairness, and we will no longer believe that our voices and our actions won't change anything, because together they can, they will, and they already are.

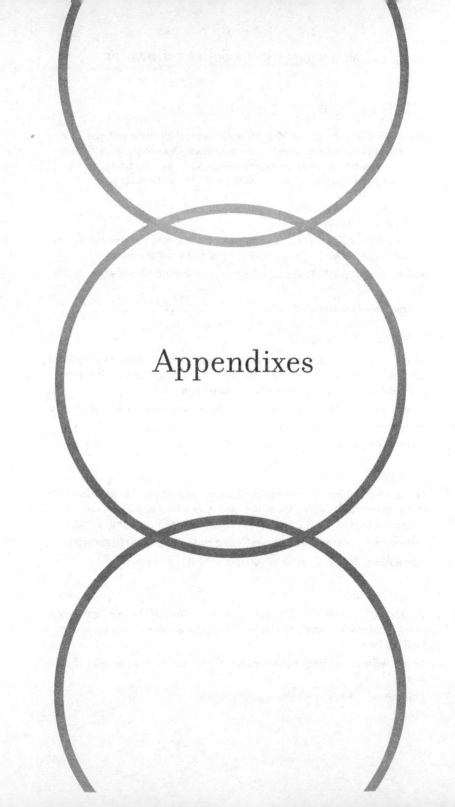

Appendixes

The 9 Principles at a Glance

The 9 Principles are a path of love, for ourselves and for the world. You might like to take a photo or write out the following summary. Place the list somewhere prominent—on your computer desktop, by your bedside table, or in your purse—to remind you to allow the Principles to guide you.

Principle 1: Honesty

Honesty is the guide that leads us home. It returns us to our true selves and enables us to live authentically, courageously, and congruently.

Action. Today I will have the courage to be me, irrespective of what others think.

Affirmation. I am true to myself.

Principle 2: Acceptance

Acceptance gives us the ability to handle whatever life throws our way. It asks that we sit with what is—even when it's painful. In return, it transforms our relationship with reality and enables us to find peace.

Action. Today I will embrace life as it is and feel whatever emotions need to be felt.

Affirmation. My feelings guide me home.

Principle 3: Courage

Courage is the Principle that frees us from our past. It enables us to live fully in the present by shedding the stories and unresolved anger that keep us trapped. It puts us firmly on the path to wholehearted, authentic living.

Action. I will take responsibility for feeling and releasing my anger safely.

Affirmation. Today I let go of being right so that I can be happy.

Principle 4: Trust

Trust is our antidote to fear. It aligns us with the flow of life—a magnificent energy that guides and directs us so that we live expansive, happy, and fulfilling lives.

Action. When I feel fear, I will ask myself what I would do if I weren't afraid and then do it.

Affirmation. Today I am safe, and I am happy.

Principle 5: Humility

Humility allows us to be one of many, to know that we are wondrous and enough just as we are. When we practice humility, we have a strong sense of our own intrinsic worth that isn't dependent on anything we do, have, or own.

Action. I treat every woman I meet as a friend.

Affirmation. My worth comes from within.

Principle 6: Peace

Peace resides in the stillness beneath the chatter of our thinking minds. In that state of serenity, we experience freedom from inner conflict and a sense of wholeness. We feel connected to the world in which we live, and loneliness begins to evaporate.

Action. Today, if I feel overwhelmed, I will pause and remind myself that underneath the surface, my true self resides.

Affirmation. Whatever else is happening, deep down I know I am absolutely okay.

Principle 7: Love

Love knows no bounds. It wants the best for everyone and doesn't discriminate or judge. Love is our authentic nature and is always present but, like the sun, it can be obscured temporarily.

Action. Today I will meet the gaze of all those I encounter with love.

Affirmation. I am love.

Principle 8: Joy

Joy feels like happiness, only better. It's generated from within and doesn't depend on what we have or haven't got. It's vital for our well-being and arises in the moment. Joy connects us with a sense of the divine.

Action. Today I will seek out joy and let it fill my heart.

Affirmation. I am resilient and filled with joy.

Principle 9: Kindness

Kindness is what love looks like when we take it out into the world. It pierces our hearts as keenly as any arrow, and in doing so, it allows love to flow in and out. Through gentle, loving actions, kindness transforms us into spiritual activists.

Action. Today I will choose to act kindly.

Affirmation. When I take action, the world is a better place.

Resources

Asking for help does not mean that we are weak or incompetent. It
usually indicates an advanced level of honesty and intelligence.
—ANNE WILSON SCHAEF, author

Sometimes the *WE* journey awakens us to issues that go beyond
the scope of this book. Perhaps it's an addiction to something or
someone, a trauma you can't move beyond, a need for therapy, a
new interest in women's organizations or world issues, a desire
to learn more about yoga, meditation, or faith. Read more about
these topics here, or visit our website, at www.WeWomenEvery
where.org.

Abuse

National Coalition Against Domestic Violence (NCADV)
(they list resources in all states): http://ncadv.org
/stay-connected/state-coalitions.

The National Domestic Violence Hotline: http://www
.thehotline.org/.

Safe Horizon (the nation's leading victim assistance
organization): https://www.safehorizon.org/.

Addictions

If you feel your life centers around a substance, person, relationship, or pattern of behavior that's making you unhappy and yet
you can't seem to shake it, then the following fellowships may be
useful:

Adult Children of Alcoholics (ACOA): www.adultchildren.org.

Al-Anon Family Groups (for families and friends of
alcoholics): www.al-anon.org.

Alateen (part of Al-Anon): www.al-anon.alateen.org.

Alcoholics Anonymous (AA): www.aa.org.

Chemically Dependent Anonymous (CDA):
www.cdawebsitedev.com.

Co-Dependents Anonymous (CoDA): www.coda.org.

Debtors Anonymous (DA): www.debtorsanonymous.org.

Emotions Anonymous (EA): www.emotionsanonymous.org.

Food Addicts Anonymous (FAA):
www.foodaddictsanonymous.org.

Gamblers Anonymous (GA): www.gamblersanonymous.org.

Love Addicts Anonymous (LAA): www.loveaddicts.org.

Narcotics Anonymous World Services (NA): www.na.org.

Nicotine Anonymous (NicA): www.nicotine-anonymous.org.

Overeaters Anonymous (OA): www.oa.org.

Sex Addicts Anonymous (SAA): www.saa-recovery.org.

Sex and Love Addicts Anonymous (SLAA): www.slaafws.org.

Underearners Anonymous (UA):
www.underearnersanonymous.org.

These are anonymous, mutually supportive groups offering
help for recovery from addictive, compulsive, or mental-health

patterns. They are free to attend and open to anyone who has a desire to change their relationship to a substance or behavior.

Their sites are full of information, support, and ways to connect online or via a meeting in your area.

Other Useful Resources

In the US

- National Institute on Drug Abuse (NIDA): www.drugabuse.gov.
- HelpGuide.org will help you select treatment programs: www.helpguide.org.
- National Institute on Alcohol Abuse and Alcoholism (NIAAA): www.niaaa.nih.gov.

In Canada

- Canadian Centre on Substance Abuse (CCSA): www.ccsa.ca, offers addiction information centers and help lines.
- Canadian Drug Rehab Centres: www.canadiandrugrehabcentres.com, offers a directory of treatment programs.

In Australia

- Government website, "Drug and Alcohol Use:" www.alcohol.gov.au, offers drug and alcohol information services.
- Lifeline: www.lifeline.org.au, offers addiction information and help lines.

Further Reading

Alcoholics Anonymous, *Alcoholics Anonymous* (New York: Alcoholics Anonymous World Services, Inc., 2001).

Augustine Fellowship, *Sex and Love Addicts Anonymous* (Boston: Augustine Fellowship, 1986).

Carnes, P., *A Gentle Path Through the Twelve Principles* (Minnesota: Hazelden, 2012).

Co-dependents Anonymous, *Co-dependents Anonymous* (Dallas: Co-Dependents Anonymous, Inc., 1995).

Mellody, P., Miller, A., and Miller, K., *Facing Love Addiction* (San Francisco: HarperOne, 1992).

Trauma

PTSD is a whole-body tragedy, an integral human event of enormous proportions with massive repercussions.

—SUSAN PEASE BANITT, therapist and author

In the aftermath of a traumatic event (a death, childhood neglect, sexual or physical abuse, disaster or war) it's natural to feel frightened, depressed, anxious, panicked, and disconnected. But if these feelings don't fade with time and you feel stuck with thoughts and memories that won't go away, you may be suffering from posttraumatic stress disorder (PTSD). Here are some questions to ask yourself:

- Do you re-experience the event via repeated upsetting memories or dreams?
- Do you feel intense physical and/or emotional distress when exposed to things that remind you of the event?

- Do you try to avoid talking or thinking about it?
- Do you now have a more limited sense of your future options (for example, getting a job you love, getting married, having children, or a normal lifespan)?
- Do you have problems sleeping or concentrating?
- Do you feel irrationally angry?
- Have you experienced changes in eating habits?
- More often than not do you feel sad, depressed, disinterested in life, worthless, or guilty?
- Have you relied on drugs or alcohol in an attempt to alleviate your pain?

Sometimes we can have a similar response to persistent childhood events that may seem smaller but which can haunt our adult lives. This could be witnessing domestic violence or living with an addicted parent. Either way, you may feel you'll never get over what happened, but there are support systems and approaches that can help:

Therapy
Talking things over with a qualified therapist is the first thing you can do for yourself. There are different therapists with different approaches. Here are some that have worked for us:

- Counselling. Talking to a trained empathetic professional in a safe and private environment on a short-term basis.
- Cognitive Behavioral Therapy (CBT). Based on the idea that negative thoughts and feelings can trap you in a vicious cycle, affecting your mind, body, and actions. CBT

is a way to talk through your current issues by breaking overwhelming problems down into smaller parts and examining negative patterns to find practical ways to improve the way you feel.

- Psychotherapy. A deeper, more long-term look at your issues, searching for root causes.
- Psychoanalysis. An examination of early childhood experiences and the unconscious.
- Group Therapy. A group that meets regularly to interact, support, and heal.

Eye Movement Desensitization and Reprocessing (EMDR)

A very practical, physical technique for dislodging memories that seem frozen.

Rewind Technique

Working with a trained practitioner to replay disturbing memories as if on rewind or fast-forward modes until the scenes evoke no emotion.

Emotional Freedom Therapy (EFT, Known as "Tapping")

Treatment involves tapping specific parts of the body while recalling the event and then experiencing and identifying the nature of the feelings that come up, verbalizing them, and accepting or reframing them.

Body Work

Exploring the many techniques that involve working with the whole body to shake trauma. These can include breath work, yoga nidra, Reiki, and singing.

Finding the Right Therapist or Practitioner

The internet is a great resource, but there are many ways to find someone to help. Ask family and friends. Talk to your medical practitioner. Make a shortlist of potential therapists and call them to chat to see first if you connect over the phone. Research their background. Not all therapists are good, and not all will be the right one for you. Don't just take the first option that becomes available to you, and assess your progress to make sure it really is working for you.

If you are working on a tight budget or even an extremely tight budget, it does not mean there is no hope for you to get professional help. Plenty of therapists and counselling centers work on a sliding scale, and some even do pro-bono work. Talking to a therapist can be incredibly helpful when one has a complex past or just needs help getting through a tough period of life. It can become one of the most meaningful, rewarding, and even life-changing relationships.

Women's Organizations

Feminism is an entire worldview or gestalt, not just a laundry list of women's issues.

—CHARLOTTE BUNCH, feminist author

In the US, the UK, Australia, New Zealand, and Scandinavia, mass-organized women's movements emerged in the midnineteenth century, although there have been feminist campaigns, literature, and heroines throughout recorded history. These nineteenth-century campaigning nations had certain things in common: Protestant culture, comparatively liberal political systems, and early mass moral reform movements (against slavery and alcohol, for international peace) often organized by more marginal Christian groups that encouraged women's activity (Quakers, Unitarians).

The first organizations were largely made up of middle-class women working closely with men (philosophers, radical liberals, and socialist members of parliament). The first country to give some women the vote was New Zealand in 1893, followed by Australia in 1902, and the United Kingdom by 1918. In the United States, all states complied by 1919.

Other countries took much longer and women are still unable to vote in Saudi Arabia and Vatican City to this day. The power to vote is only one step in our ongoing struggle for equal power, equal pay, and equal rights.

If you want to get more involved, there are plenty of groups. These range from support groups to political movements to development associations, charities, museums, NGOs, online magazines, and mentorship schemes. We've arranged them by country and what we outline below are just highlights. Use the internet or local networks to find more in your area, visit our website (www.WeWomen Everywhere.org) to find more recommendations, or create your own group.

US

Big Brothers Big Sisters of America: www.bbbs.org.

Emily's List: www.emilyslist.org.

Equal Rights Advocates: www.equalrights.org.

National Organization for Women: www.now.org.

National Women's History Museum: www.nwhm.org.

International

Nobel Women's Initiative: www.nobelwomensinitiative.org.

Raging Grannies International: www.raginggrannies.org.

UN Women: www.unwomen.org.

Women's Refugee Commission:
www.womensrefugeecommission.org.

Women's WorldWide Web (W4): www.w4.org.

UK

Fawcett Society: www.fawcettsociety.org.uk.

Mumsnet: www.mumsnet.com.

National Federation of Women's Institutes: www.thewi.org.uk.

Southall Black Sisters: www.southallblacksisters.org.uk.

Women's Aid: www.womensaid.org.uk.

Canada

Girls Action Foundation: www.girlsactionfoundation.ca.

National Council of Women of Canada (NCWC): www.ncwc.ca.

Australia

Australian Women's Health Network (AWHN): www.awhn.org.au.

Emily's List: www.emilyslist.org.au.

National Council of Women of Australia: www.ncwa.org.au.

World Issues

There comes a time when humanity is called to shift to a new
level of consciousness . . . that time is now.

—WANGARI MAATHAI (1940–2011), Kenyan-

born environmentalist and activist

Our world is in trouble. It would have been impossible to mention
all its myriad issues, but if while reading this book one or two struck
a chord with you, here is a shortlist of just some of the many organizations and societies that you may want to get in contact with:

International

Afghan Connection: www.afghanconnection.org.

Amnesty International: www.amnesty.org.

Fund for Global Human Rights: www.globalhumanrights.org.

GIVING What We Can: www.givingwhatwecan.org/trust.

Global Fund for Women: www.globalfundforwomen.org.

Greenpeace: www.greenpeace.org.

HelpAge International: www.helpage.org.

Human Rights Watch (HRW): www.hrw.org.

International Planned Parenthood Federation (IPPF):
    www.ippf.org.

Liberty: www.liberty-human-rights.org.uk.

Rainbow Centre: www.rainbowcentresrilanka.com.

Save the Children: www.savethechildren.net.

The Global Fund for Human Rights:
    www.globalhumanrights.org.

The Life You Can Save: www.thelifeyoucansave.org.

World Wildlife Fund (WWF): www.wwf.panda.org.

US

American Civil Liberties Union (ACLU): www.aclu.org.

Earthjustice (formerly the Sierra Club Legal Defense Fund): www.earthjustice.org.

Environmental Defense Fund (EDF): www.edf.org.

National Association for the Advancement of Colored People (NAACP): www.naacp.org.

National Audubon Society: www.audubon.org.

Natural Resources Defense Council (NRDC): www.nrdc.org.

PovertyUSA: www.povertyusa.org.

Southern Poverty Law Center (SPLC): www.splcenter.org.

US Human Rights Network (USHR): www.ushrnetwork.org.

Canada

Dalit Freedom Network Canada: www.dalitfreedom.ca.

Food for the Hungry: www.fhcanada.org.

UK

Child Poverty Action Group (CPAG): www.cpag.org.uk.

INQUEST: www.inquest.org.uk.

Show Racism the Red Card: www.srtrc.org.

The Forgiveness Project: www.theforgivenessproject.com.

Australia

Anti-Poverty Week: www.antipovertyweek.org.au.

Eco-shout (grassroots and environmental groups directory): www.ecoshout.org.au.

Gecko—Gold Coast and Hinterland Environment Council Association: www.gecko.org.au.

GetUp!: www.getup.org.au.

Giving

There are many valuable causes and charities wanting your support and donations—far too many to include in this book—but if you are looking for inspiration for daily acts of kindness then the following websites might be helpful:

Action for Happiness: www.actionforhappiness.org.

Helping Network: https://helping.network.

Love This City: www.lovethiscity.org.

Random Acts of Kindness Foundation:
www.randomactsofkindness.org.

For ideas on ways to ensure that you give to the most cost-effective charities, check out these two websites: www.thelifeyoucansave.org in the US or www.givingwhatyoucan.org in the UK.

Menopause

National Women's Health Resource Center: http://www
.healthywomen.org.

The North American Menopause Society: http://www
.menopause.org/for-women.

Office on Women's Health: https://www.womenshealth.gov
/menopause.

Yoga

*You cannot do yoga. Yoga is your natural state. What you can
do are yoga exercises, which may reveal to you where you are
resisting your natural state.*

—SHARON GANNON, cofounder of Jivamukti

Yoga is a whole-body exercise with the power to improve physical, mental, and emotional health. Flexibility increases, stress reduces, breath work teaches physical techniques to soothe worry and bring you back to a point of calm. It can help you to release the difficult emotions that get trapped in your body. The more you do, the more you learn to connect with what's happening right now. You'll find you sleep more deeply and feel generally better. For us, it has led to a more balanced life and a way to access deep peace and harmony.

There are many types of yoga. What we outline below is just a start. Ask people you know, research online, try different options, see what works best for you. You may find initial "taster" classes are free, and many places offer low-cost classes. Cost-effective ways to practice include shopping around for studio offers. You can also learn by yourself at home, via a book or DVD or internet video, although it's good to take a few lessons with a teacher at first.

Hatha
Gentle, often slower, focusing on the most traditional poses.

Iyengar
Focuses on precision positions and alignments, with use of props (belts, blocks, bolsters) to ensure correct posture.

Ashtanga
Vigorous, quick moving, athletic. The whole class is one succession of moves flowing into another.

Mysore Style
Ashtanga yoga taught one-on-one in a group setting where you set your own pace.

Vinyasa Flow
Another fast-paced workout style with minimal talk from the teacher.

Bikram
Set poses (twenty-six of them) done in special heated rooms; lots of sweating and flushing out of toxins.

Kirtan Chanting
A form of yoga that uses sound.

Kundalini
Designed to increase spinal energy. Classes involve breathing, chanting, and meditation as well as physical exercises. Kundalini yoga can fuse with meditation to create an all-body practice, tailored to help with specific issues (stress, anxiety, depression, addiction, and so on), and is best done with a teacher.

Yin
Quieter, seated poses held for up to ten minutes. A way to increase flexibility, release tension, and learn the basics of meditation.

Restorative
Like yin yoga, but with less focus on flexibility and more on healing and relaxing.

Meditation

Quiet the mind, and the soul will speak.

—MA JAYA SATI BHAGAVATI

All you need to meditate is a time and place to sit quietly by yourself. Even five minutes in the bathroom is good. If you're looking for a more structured practice, we list a few major traditions below. You'll find plenty more online or by asking around.

In essence, there are two types of meditation: structured and open. Structured meditation is built around a single thing for your mind to focus on while you meditate. This could be one word (often called a mantra), or a prayer or spiritual text. Open meditation simply invites you to sit (or lie or stand) quietly, relax, and observe what your body and mind are up to. The following may employ either approach:

Mindfulness
This Western, nonreligious technique can employ breath awareness (focusing your attention on inhaling and exhaling) and body scanning (focusing your attention on your physical body, starting from your toes and heading up).

Zen (also known as Zazen)
This technique comes from Buddhism but can be useful to non-Buddhists. The focus is on sitting still in one position, observing your breath and mind. It sometimes involves ruminating on Buddhist teachings and is often practiced with a teacher.

Transcendental Meditation (TM)

Practitioners are given a mantra (a word or sound) by a teacher to focus on during their meditation. You can also find mantras online.

Faith

Religion is for people who are scared to go to hell. Spirituality is for people who have already been there.

—BONNIE RAITT, Grammy Award–winning singer-musician

Some of us find a faith through conventional religion; others, through less formal faith-based paths and even secular or atheist groups that remove divinity but retain a sense of connection to an underlying truth.

Buddhism

More of a philosophy than a conventional religion, Buddhism focuses on personal spiritual development and uncovering deep truths about the nature of reality.

Christianity

Based on the teachings of Jesus, Christianity teaches we should follow his life story, believe in his divinity, and emulate his self-sacrifice and service to humanity. It's split into three major traditions: Orthodox, Catholic, and Protestant.

Islam

Islam means "submission to the will of God." Believers are called Muslims and follow the teachings of the Koran as revealed to the prophet Muḥammad, who also venerated Abraham, Moses, and Jesus as prophets. It has three major traditions: Sunni, Shi'ite, and Sufism.

Judaism
One of the oldest monotheistic religions in the world. Jews believe they must follow a wide range of laws set for them by God governing almost every aspect of life.

Hinduism
A group of faiths based around many different Indian beliefs and scriptures, which may be the oldest religion in the world.

Taoism
An ancient Chinese religious and philosophical tradition with worldwide popularity due to its manifestations in the Tao Te Ching, Tai Chi, I Ching, and Qigong.

Unitarianism
An open, inclusive, and tolerant approach to religion, developing out of Protestantism and incorporating teachings from many different faiths. Individuals are asked to create their own practice and answers.

Humanism
Religion without a god: an approach to life centered on human action and behavior and looking to science rather than religion.

Paganism
Recognizes the rich diversity of spiritual traditions and is typically a polytheistic or pantheistic, nature-worshipping religion.

Atheism

Lack, or an absence, of belief in deities.

Contemporary Female Spiritual Teachers

The Living Spiritual Teachers Project is an ongoing charitable project that provides biographical details of some of the most eminent spiritual teachers alive today. Here you can find biographical details, contact information, and useful links, as well as a list of their publications: www.spiritualityandpractice.com.

Starting *WE* Communities

WE's symbol is a circle, and our hope is that women will start to create their own circles to talk the book through together. Since the first edition of this book was published this has already started happening, with women either meeting face-to-face or using social media to connect.

The more support you can gather around you, the easier you will find it to do the work, grow, heal, and stay on the path. Look for others who are making the same journey or are keen to talk about the things that really matter. Gather them around you. Try working through the chapters together; share your experiences, your challenges, and your insights. Together you will have support when you need it and have maximum impact when you take action. So reach out to one another and become an active part of the movement away from *me* and toward *WE*.

- Let us know how you get on by using the #wewomen hashtag on social media or by writing into us: circles@ wewomeneverywhere.org. And check out our Facebook page. We can't wait to hear what happens!

Guidelines

If you're setting up a Circle, either online or in person, set yourself some guidelines early. Here are some you can use or adapt to ensure you create a safe and nonjudgmental space:

- **Confidentiality:** Everything that gets said between you remains private and stays in the circle.
- **Talk in the "I":** Share your own experience rather than give advice or direct feedback, or speaking on behalf of or about anyone else.
- **Consider rotating roles:** So no one person dominates or becomes overly responsible.
- **Equal time:** Consider dividing the time you allocate for talking by the number of people present so that everyone can talk.
- **Each person's time is sacred:** Don't interrupt!

Why not start and end meetings with a minute's meditation to get everyone centered? If you're meeting up in person with people you only know online, please take all sensible precautions. *WE* can stir up issues and past trauma. If it does, please seek professional help.

Further Reading

The wisdom in this book comes from many teachers, texts, and sources. If you want to go deeper and further into the wisdom and ideas behind *WE*'s Principles, these are some of the books we've found helpful along the way:

Principle 1, Honesty: Getting Real

Brown, B. *The Gifts of Imperfection*. Center City, MN: Hazelden, 2010.

Ferrucci, P. *What We May Be*. New York: J. P. Tarcher, 1982.

Hay, L. *You Can Heal Your Life*. San Diego: Hay House, 1984.

Lamott, A., and S. Lamott. *Some Assembly Required*. New York: Penguin, 2014.

Rosen, T. *Recovery 2.0*. London: Hay House, 2014.

Wolf, N. *The Beauty Myth*. New York: Harper Perennial, 2002.

Principle 2, Acceptance: Making Friends with What Is

Fruehwirth, G. *Words for Silence*. Massachusetts: Parachute Press, 2008.

Harris, T. *I'm OK—You're OK*. New York: Harper Perennial, 2004.

Kipp, M. *Daily Love*. London: Hay House, 2014.

Kurtz, E., and K. Ketcham. *The Spirituality of Imperfection*. New York: Bantam Books, 1992.

Linn, D. *Four Acts of Personal Power*. London: Hay House, 2007.

Moore, T. *Care of the Soul*. New York: Harper Perennial, 1995.

Sogyal, R., P. Gaffney, and A. Harvey. *The Tibetan Book of Living and Dying*. New York: HarperSanFrancisco, 2012.

Principle 3, Courage: Ending the Victim Trap

Bernstein, G. *May Cause Miracles*. New York: Harmony, 2014.

Cantacuzino, M. *The Forgiveness Project*. London: Jessica Kingsley Publishers, 2015.

Myss, C. *Anatomy of the Spirit*. New York: Three Rivers Press, 1996.

Penny, L. *Unspeakable Things*. New York: Bloomsbury, 2014.

Principle 4, Trust: Living Without Fear

Carlson, R. *Don't Sweat the Small Stuff . . . and It's All Small Stuff*. New York: Hachette Books, 1996.

Jeffers, S. *Feel the Fear and Do It Anyway*. New York: Ballentine Books, 2006.

Lerner, R. *Living in the Comfort Zone*. Deerfield Beach, FL: Health Communications, Inc., 1995.

Principle 5, Humility: Unmasking Our Ego

Bill, P., and W. Todd. *Drop the Rock*. Center City, MN: Hazelden, 2005.

Epstein, M. *Going to Pieces Without Falling Apart*. New York: Broadway Books, 1998.

Scott Peck, M. *Further Along the Road Less Traveled*. New York: Simon & Schuster, 1993.

Silverton, S. *The Mindfulness Breakthrough*. London: Watkins Publishing, 2012.

Principle 6, Peace: Ending the Conflict Within

Barks, C., trans. *The Essential Rumi*. London: Penguin, 1995.

De Mello, A. *Sadhana, A Way to God*. New York: Bantam Doubleday Dell, 1978.

Hawkins, D. *Transcending the Levels of Consciousness*. West Sedona, AZ: Veritas, 2006.

Holden, M. *Boundless Love*. London: Rider, 2002.

Hyde, L. *The Gift*. New York: Vintage Books, 2007.

Idliby, R., S. Oliver, and P. Warner. *The Faith Club*. New York: Atria, 2006.

Johnston, W. *The Cloud of Unknowing and the Book of Privy Counseling*. New York: Doubleday Image, 1973.

Keating, T. *Intimacy with God*. New York: Crossroad Publishing, 1996.

Myss, C. *Entering the Castle*. New York: Atria Books, 2008.

Nhất Hạnh, T. *Happiness*. Berkeley, CA: Parallax Press, 2009.

———. *Peace Is Every Step*. New York: Bantam, 1991.

Tolle, E. *The Power of Now*. Novato, CA: New World Library, 1999.

Principle 7, Love: Transforming Relationships

Augustine Fellowship. *Sex and Love Addicts Anonymous* (San Antonio: Augustine Fellowship, 1986.

Co-Dependents Anonymous. *Co-dependents Anonymous*. Dallas: Co-Dependents Anonymous, 1995.

Hendrix, H. *Getting the Love You Want*. London: Simon & Schuster, 2005.

Jackson, L. *The Light Between Us*. New York: Spiegel and Grau, 2016.

Mellody, P., A. Miller, and K. Miller. *Facing Love Addiction*. San Francisco: HarperOne, 1992.

Norwood, R. *Women Who Love Too Much*. New York: Pocket
  Books, 2008.
Olds, S. *Stag's Leap*. New York: Knopf, 2012.
Richo, D. *How to Be an Adult in Relationships*. Boston:
  Shambhala, 2002.
Yalom, I. *Love's Executioner*. New York: Basic Books, 2012.

Principle 8, Joy: Living Fully

Cameron, J. *The Artist's Way*. New York: J. P. Tarcher, 1992.
Campbell, R. *Light Is the New Black*. London: Hay House, 2015.
Csikszentmihalyi, M. *Flow: The Psychology of Happiness*.
  New York: Harper Perennial Modern Classics, 2008.
De Mello, A., and G. Galache, *Walking on Water*. Dublin:
  Columba Press, 1998.
Donius, W. *Thought Revolution*. New York: Atria Books, 2014.
Ferrucci, P. *Inevitable Grace*. New York: J. P. Tarcher, 1990.
Huffington, A. *Thrive*. New York: Harmony, 2015.
Kingston, K. *Clear Your Clutter with Feng Shui*. New York:
  Harmony, 2016.
Lamott, A. *Plan B*. New York: Riverhead Books, 2006.
Muzyka, Z. *Life by the Cup*. New York: Atria Books, 2015.
Olds, S. *One Secret Thing*. New York: Alfred A. Knopf, 2008.

Principle 9, Kindness: Love in Action

Armstrong, K. *Twelve Steps to a Compassionate Life*. London:
  The Bodley Head, 2011.
Harvey, A. *The Hope: A Guide to Sacred Activism*. London: Hay
  House, 2009.
Post, S., *The Hidden Gifts of Helping*. San Francisco: Jossey-Bass,
  2011.

Tolle, E. *A New Earth*. New York: Penguin, 2008.

Williamson, M. *A Return to Love*. San Francisco: HarperOne, 1996.

———. *The Age of Miracles*. London: Hay House, 2008.

Part 3: *WE*'s Manifesto

Benn, M. *What Should We Tell Our Daughters?* London: Hodder & Stoughton, 2013.

Campbell, B. *End of Equality*. London: Seagull Books, 2013.

Cobble, D., L. Gordon, and A. Henry. *Feminism Unfinished*. New York: Liveright, 2014.

Hooks, B. *All About Love*. New York: Harper Perennial, 2001.

Klein, N. *This Changes Everything*. New York: Simon & Schuster, 2015.

Neuwirth, J., and G. Steinem. *Equal Means Equal*. New York: New Press, 2015.

Ngozi Adichie, C. *We Should All Be Feminists*. New York: Vintage Books, 2014.

Orenstein, P. *Girls & Sex*. New York: HarperCollins, 2016.

Orr, J. *Marxism and Women's Liberation*. London: Bookmarks, 2015.

Sandberg, S., and N. Scovell. *Lean In*. New York: Knopf, 2013.

Walter, N. *Living Dolls*. New York: Little, Brown, 2011.

Wilkinson, R., and K. Pickett. *The Spirit Level*. New York: Penguin Books, 2010.

Endnotes

Why Now?

1. "Silent Epidemic of Violence Against Women," *The Guardian*, January 12, 2016.
2. Richard Wilkinson and Kate Pickett, *The Spirit Level: Why Greater Equality Makes Societies Stronger* (New York: Penguin Books, 2010).

Part 1, The Essentials: Preparing for the Journey

Essential Practice 2, Thinking Kindly: Changing the Messages We Give Ourselves

1. Lissa Rankin, "The Nocebo Effect: Negative Thoughts Can Harm Your Health," *Owning Pink* (blog), on the website of *Psychology Today*, last modified August 6, 2013, www.psychologytoday.com/blog/owning-pink/201308 /the -nocebo-effect-negative-thoughts-can-harm-your-health.

Essential Practice 3, Responsibility: Taking Care of Ourselves

1. "Moods & Hormones: Emotional Health and Well-being Throughout the Lifecycle," *Connections*, February 2012, on

the website of Women's International Pharmacy, www
.womensinternational.com/connections/moods.html.

Part 2, The 9 Principles

Principle 1, Honesty: Getting Real

1. Denis Campbell and Haroon Siddique, "Mental Illness
   Soars Among Young Women in England," *The Guardian*,
   last modified September 29, 2016, www.theguardian.com
   /lifeandstyle/2016/sep/29/self-harm-ptsd-and-mental
   -illness-soaring-among-young-women-in-england
   -survey.
2. Ibid.
3. Virginia Hughes, "Mice Inherit Specific Memories,
   Because Epigenetics?," *Only Human* (blog), on the
   website of *National Geographic*, last modified December
   13, 2013, phenomena.nationalgeographic.com/2013
   /12/01d/mice-inherit-specific-memories-because
   -epigenetics.
4. "Licking Rat Pups: The Genetics of Nurture," *The Nerve
   Blog*, on the website of Boston University, last modified
   November 11, 2010, sites.bu.edu/ombs/2010/11/11
   /licking-rat-pups-the-genetics-of-nurture.
5. Thanks to Rokelle Lerner for this: website of Rokelle
   Lerner Associates, www.rokellelerner.com.

Principle 2, Acceptance: Making Friends with What Is

1. Exercise inspired by Julia Cameron's "God Jar," *The Vein
   of Gold: A Journey to Your Creative Heart* (New York:
   G. P. Putnam's Sons, 1997).

2. Elisabeth Kübler-Ross and David Kessler, *On Grief and Grieving: Finding the Meaning of Grief Through the Five Stages of Loss* (New York: Scribner, 2005).
3. Thanks to Eckhart Tolle for this idea.

Principle 4, Trust: Living Without Fear

1. Sharon Horesh Bergquist, "How Stress Affects Your Body," TEDEd, ed.ted.com/lessons/how-stress-affects-your-body-sharon-horesh-bergquist.
2. Thanks to Jennifer's sister, Alison Nadle, for coming up with this acronym.
3. Phillippa Lally, Cornelia H. M. van Jaarsveld, Henry W. W. Potts, and Jane Wardle, "How Are Habits Formed: Modelling Habit Formation in the Real World," *European Journal of Social Psychology* 40, no. 6 (October 2010): 998–1009; also see James Clear, "How Long Does It Actually Take to Form a New Habit? (Backed by Science)," *The Blog, The Huffington Post,* last modified June 10, 2014, www.huffingtonpost.com/james-clear/forming-new-habits_b_5104807.html.
4. Susan Jeffers, *Feel the Fear and Do It Anyway: How to Turn Your Fear and Indecision into Confidence and Action* (London: Vermilion, 2007).
5. Ibid.

Principle 5, Humility: Unmasking Our Ego

1. Sue Dumais, "The Power of Positive Thinking," *Team Northrup Blog,* on the website of Team Northrup, last modified June 29, 2011, www.teamnorthrup.com/2011/06/29/the-power-of-positive-thinking.

2. This list is used by some twelve-step fellowships.

3. Julie Borowski, "18 Facts You Need to Know About U.S. Prisons," on the website of *Newsweek*, last modified February 23, 2015, europe.newsweek.com/eighteen-facts -you-need-know-about-us-prisons-308860.

4. Prison: The Facts," Prison Reform Trust, on the website of Apprentice Supermarket, summer 2014, fbclientprisoners.s3.amazonaws.com/Resources /Prison%20the%20facts%20May%202014.pdf.

5. Ibid.

6. "How Many Species Are We Losing?," on the website of the World Wildlife Federation, wwf.panda.org/about _our_earth/biodiversity/biodiversity.

Principle 6, Peace: Ending the Conflict Within

1. Paul Grossman et al., "Mindfulness-Based Stress Reduction and Health Benefits: A Meta-analysis," *Journal of Psychosomatic Research* 57, no. 1 (July 2004): 35–43.

2. Michael D. Mrazek et al., "Mindfulness Training Improves Working Memory Capacity and GRE Performance While Reducing Mind Wandering," *Psychological Science*, published online March 28, 2013, doi:10.1177/0956797612459659.

3. Rachel Moss, "How Much Time Do We Spend on Our Devices?" *The Huffington Post* (UK), September 10, 2014, www.huffingtonpost.co.uk/2014/09/10/digital-detox -technology-addiction-facts_n_5795982.html.

4. Thanks to Jack Kornfield for this analogy.

5. Neither of us can remember who first told us this story, but thank you, whoever it was!

Principle 7, Love: Transforming Relationships
1. Sex and Love Addicts Anonymous (SLAA), Love Addicts Anonymous (LAA), and Sex Addicts Anonymous (SAA).
2. Dr. Sharon Stills, "Health Benefits of Masturbation," on the website of the Women's Health Network, www.womenshealthnetwork.com/sexandfertility/health-benefits-of-masturbation.aspx.
3. "Domestic Violence—The Facts," on the website of Refuge, www.refuge.org.uk/get-help-now/what-is-domestic-violence/domestic-violence-the-facts.
4. According to a 2011 UN report.

Principle 8, Joy: Living Fully
1. Mihaly Csikszentmihalyi, *Finding Flow: The Psychology of Engagement with Everyday Life* (New York: Basic Books, 1998).

Principle 9, Kindness: Love in Action
1. Jen Green, *The Impact of Environmentalism: Food and Farming* (Chicago: Raintree, 2013).
2. Sarah Callard, "Is It Worth It? Refillable Packaging," on the website of *The Telegraph* (UK), last modified June 23, 2007, www.telegraph.co.uk/culture/3666069/Is-it-worth-it-Refillable-packaging.html.
3. Nicholas Cecil, "Packaging Adds 20% to Cost of Fruit," on the website This is Money, April 18, 2007, www.thisismoney.co.uk/money/bills/article-1609196/Packaging-adds-20-to-cost-of-fruit.html.
4. Paul Delaney, "How Long It Takes for Some Everyday Items to Decompose," on the website Down2Earth Materials, last

modified February 14, 2013, www.down2earthmaterials.ie
/decompose.

5. Sonja Lyubomirsky and Matthew D. Della Porta, "Boosting
   Happiness, Buttressing Resilience: Results from Cognitive
   and Behavioral Interventions" (in press) University of
   California, Riverside, 2008, sonjalyubomirsky.com
   /wp-content/themes/sonjalyubomirsky/papers
   /LDinpressb.pdf.

6. Jason Marsh and Jill Suttie, "5 Ways Giving Is Good for
   You," on the website of the Greater Good Science Center,
   University of California, Berkeley, last modified
   December 13, 2010, greatergood.berkeley.edu/article
   /item/5_ways_giving_is_good_for_you.

7. This metaphor comes from Peter Singer's short film *The
   Life You Can Save in 3 Minutes*, YouTube video, uploaded on
   June 6, 2010, www.youtube.com/watch?v=onsIdBanynY.

8. "Every 3 Seconds a Child Needlessly Dies," on the
   website of Save the Children, www.savethechildren.org
   /site/c.8rKLIXMGIpI4E/b.7892381/k.F0A6/Every_3_
   Seconds_a_Child_Needlessly_Dies.htm.

9. "One Day a Week Can Make a World of Difference," on
   the website of Meat Free Monday, www.meatfreemondays
   .com/about.

10. Inspired by a lecture given by Andrew Harvey in the Open
    Center, New York City, in 2006.

Part 3: The Manifesto

1. "Hunger and Poverty Facts and Statistics," on the website of Feeding America, www.feedingamerica.org/hunger -in-america/impact-of-hunger/hunger-and-poverty /hunger-and-poverty-fact-sheet.html.
2. "Richest 1% Will Own More Than All the Rest by 2016," Oxfam International press release, January 19, 2015, www .oxfam.org/en/pressroom/pressreleases/2015-01-19 /richest-1-will-own-more-all-rest-2016.
3. "Even It Up," antipoverty petition on the website of Oxfam International, act.oxfam.org/great-britain /cameron-inequality-petition-even-it-up.
4. Jenny Hope, "Hunger in Britain Is Becoming 'Public Health Emergency' as Number of People Turning to Food Banks to Feed Families Soars," on the website of the *Daily Mail* (UK), last modified December 4, 2013, www .dailymail.co.uk/news/article-2517898/Hunger-Britain -public-health-emergency-number-people-turning -food-banks-feed-families-soars.html.

    In 2008, 26,000 Britons were fed by food banks. By 2012, that number had risen to 347,000.
5. "African American Poverty: African American Hunger Fact Sheet," on the website of Feeding America, www .feedingamerica.org/hunger-in-america/impact-of -hunger/african-american-hunger/african-american -hunger-fact-sheet.html.
6. Amber Phillips, "The Sad State of Black Women in Statewide Political Office," *The Washington Post*, December 5, 2015, www.washingtonpost.com/news/the-fix

/wp/2015/12/05/the-sad-state-of-black-women-in
-statewide-political-office.

7. "Economics: Paid and Unpaid Work," on the website of
the Sexual Assault Support Center of Waterloo (SASCWR),
www.sascwr.org/files/www/resources_pdfs/anti_
oppression/Economics.Paid_and_Unpaid_Labor.pdf.

8. Beatrix Campbell, *End of Equality* (London: Seagull Books,
2013).

9. US Current Population Survey and the National Committee
on Pay Equity; also Bureau of Labor Statistics: Weekly and
Hourly Earnings Data from the Current Population Survey.

10. According to a 2012 survey conducted by the US Labor
Department.

11. *Family and Medical Leave in 2012: Technical Report*
(Washington, DC: US Department of Labor, September 7,
2012; revised April 18, 2014), ww.dol.gov/asp/evaluation
/fmla/fmla-2012-technical-report.pdf.

12. David Brindle, "Carers Save the Country ,£119bn a Year,"
The Guardian, last modified May 12, 2011, www.theguardian
.com/society/2011/may/12/carers-save-uk-119bn-a-year.

13. Bryce Covert, "Putting a Price Tag on Unpaid Housework,"
on the website of *Forbes*, last modified May 30, 2012, www
.forbes.com/sites/brycecovert/2012/05/30/putting-a
-price-tag-on-unpaid-housework/#1ef1685a544f.

14. Beatrix Campbell, "Why We Need a New Women's
Revolution," *The Guardian,* last modified May 25, 2014,
www.theguardian.com/commentisfree/2014/may/25
/we-need-new-womens-revolution.

15. Ibid.

16. Ibid.

17. Eleanor Clift, "Asia's 163 Million Missing Girls," on the website of The Daily Beast, June 21, 2011, www .thedailybeast.com/articles/2011/06/21/gender-selection -abortion-crisis-in-asia-india-u-s.html.

18. "Statistics," on the website of Rape Crisis England & Wales, rapecrisis.org.uk/statistics.php.

19. "The Criminal Justice System: Statistics," on the website of Rape, Abuse & Incest National Network (RAINN), rainn .org/get-information/statistics/reporting-rates.

Acknowledgments

This book owes its existence to many women. First among them is Claire Conrad, who was present from the moment *WE* was conceived and who has midwifed it into being.

Grateful thanks also to Lynn Nesbit and Rebecca Folland at Janklow & Nesbit, and Caroline Wood and all at Felicity Bryan. To our publishers on both sides of the Atlantic: at HarperCollins, Kate Elton, Carolyn Thorne, Polly Osborn, Isabel Hayman-Brown, Holly Kyte, Dean Russell, and Ellie Crisp; at Atria, Judith Curr, who believed in it before it existed, Leslie Meredith, and Jonathan Evans. And to Sandy Draper for her amazing editing of the early drafts.

Thanks also to: Mel Agace, Edward Anderson, Piper Anderson-Klotz, Rosemary Anderson, Helen Backhouse, Sam Bescelli, Alicja Brown, Olivia Buckland, Saskia Burke, Jamie Byng, Sydney Davis, Denzyl Feigelson, Connie Frieberg, Daisy Garnett, Elizabeth Gordon, Zoe Hunter Gordon, Mark Griffiths, Oscar and Felix Griffiths, Reverend Bill Hague, Katie Harris, Leon Hawthorne, Zara Hayes, Emma Hewitt, Jenny Howard and Gemma Knox at Sunshine, Susanna Kleeman, Clyde Klotz, Cynthia Lewis, Dr. Genevieve von Lob, Delphi Lythgoe, Sandra MacDonald, Professor Tessa McWatt, Peter Morgan, Deborah Nadel, Alison Nagle, Northeast Harbor

Library, Paul Olsewski, Julian Ozanne, Ciara Parks, Ruth Reid, Andrew Ruhemann, Arlo Nadel Ruhemann, Dr. Sadeghi, Estralita Serano, Anne Shamash, Chloe Smith, Ardu Vakil, Felix Velarde, Darren Waterston, Sara Watkins at KW Interactive, Jack Wilson, Meghan Wilson, and Theo Wilson.

And, of course, the women who've gone before us and those who will come after.

About the Authors

Jennifer Nadel

Jennifer Nadel trained as a barrister before becoming a writer, award-winning journalist, and campaigner. She was one of the UK's most senior female television correspondents and has broadcast for the BBC, ITV, and Channel 4 News. Her book on domestic violence was made into a BBC film and a Channel 4 documentary, and her report from Bosnia on the use of rape as a weapon of war was broadcast around the world. Her first novel, *Pretty Thing*, was published by Little, Brown in 2015. She is a trustee of the charity INQUEST and has a long history of activism. She has stood as a candidate for the UK parliament twice for the Green Party. A mother of three boys, she was born in Princeton, New Jersey, and is a dual US/UK national who lives in London.

Gillian Anderson

Gillian Anderson gained worldwide recognition in *The X-Files*, garnering awards and critical acclaim for her role as FBI Special Agent Dana Scully over the show's nine-year run. Some of her many screen credits include *The House of Mirth, The Last King of Scotland,* and the acclaimed BBC miniseries *Bleak House* and *Great Expectations.* She was nominated for an Olivier Award for her stage performance as Nora in *A Doll's House* and won the *Evening Standard* Theatre Award for her portrayal of Blanche DuBois in *A Streetcar Named Desire.* Gillian is on the BBC and Netflix's *The Fall* as DSI Stella Gibson, on NBC's *Hannibal* as Dr. Bedelia Du Maurier, and Starz's *American Gods* as Media. She is an activist, speaking out regularly on issues ranging from feminism to climate change and human trafficking. Born in Chicago, she lives in London with her three children.

Index

A

A21 Campaign, 180
abuse, 214, 237–39
  resources for, 313
acceptance, 83–108, 121
  Acceptance Cup exercise, 86–88
  and changing what we can, 103–6
  of emotions, 83–86, 92–102
  honesty and, 91
  of the past, people, places, and things, 88–89
  of reality, 91–92
  of responsibility, 90–91
  Serenity Prayer and, 85, 103
  Step into Your Light exercise, 89–90
  surrender, 84–88
  in wider world, 106–7
ACT (Action Changes Things), 51–52, 198, 262, 274
action(s), 51–52, 198, 306–8
  acceptance, 108
  anger release, 133
  anonymity and, 276
  choices, see choices
  fear release, 156
  gentleness, 20
  giving, 270, 278–84
  gratitude, 11
  humility, 180
  joining, 270, 284–88
  joy, 265
  keeping log of, 275–76
  kindness, 270, 274–77, 290
  love, 242
  love as feeling vs., 209
  meditation, 45
  peace, 206
  and price of not acting, 275
  self-care, 37
  self-honesty, 82
activism, 106, 264, 275, 307–8

finding your cause, 284–85
  progress vs. perfection in, 286–87
Acumen, 271
addiction, 46, 174, 211, 215, 258
  codependency, 210–11
  resources for, 314–16
Adichie, Chimamanda Ngozi, 20
Afghan Connection, 79
affirmations, 4, 17, 43
  acceptance, 108
  being right vs. happy, 133
  fear release, 156
  gentleness, 20
  gratitude, 11
  humility, 180
  joy, 265
  kindness, 290
  love, 242
  meditation, 45
  peace, 206
  self-care, 37
  self-honesty, 82
  stories and, 113–14, 115
alcoholism, 174
Alcott, Louisa May, 40
Allende, Isabel, 208
Amritanandamayi, Mata (Amma), 206
Angelou, Maya, 288
anger, 123, 132, 133, 205
  bucket exercise, 118–19
  forgiveness and, 172
  releasing safely, 116–19
  resentment and, 121, 123
Anne of Green Gables (Montgomery), 260
Appell, Elizabeth, 217
appreciation:
  of others, 235
  of your body, 30–31, 178
  see also gratitude
Arendt, Hannah, 170
Armstrong, Karen, 50

INDEX

Armstrong, Kristin, 5
artistic creativity, 246–48
artist's life exercise, 250–51
Artist's Way, The (Cameron), 246
attack thoughts, 160–61, 200
    self-blame, 160, 161, 213
Aung San Suu Kyi, 267
Austen, Jane, 70
avoidance, 92–94, 97, 186, 214–15, 277
    fear as, 149

B

Backhouse, Helen, 244
bad and good, fable about, 193–94
Baez, Joan, 51
Baker, Ella, 240
Ball, Lucille, 252
Banitt, Susan Pease, 316
Bates, Daisy, 174
Beattie, Melody, 8
beauty:
    in nature, 249–50
    in personal appearance, 26, 32–33, 63, 304–5
behaviors, in circle exercise, 190–91
Bhutan, 300
blood sugar, 25
body, 24–26, 60
    appreciation of, 30–31, 178
    beauty and cultural norms, 26, 32–33, 63, 304–5
    exercise and, 28–29, 177
    food and, 26–28, 177
    gratitude for, 32
    HALT and, 25–26
    hormones and, 33–36
    menopause and, *see* menopause
    menstruation and, 33–34
    rest and, 29–30
    weight and, 26, 27, 29
Body Shop, 288
body-mind connection, 140–41
boundaries, 255
brain, neural pathways in, 146–47, 150
Bron, Mila, 143
Brown, Brené, 6
Buck, Pearl S., 186
Bunch, Charlotte, 319

C

Cain, Susan, 182
Caine, Christine, 180
camel, tying up, 148–49
Cameron, David, 117
Cameron, Julia, 246
Campbell, Rebecca, 264
Cantacuzino, Marina, 171
cause, finding, 284–85
changes, making, 73, 103–6

charities, 282–83
child, inner, *see* inner girl
Child, Lydia M., 207
childhood, 75–76, 117, 161
    abuse in, 214, 237
    relationship patterns and, 214–16, 231
Children's Defense Fund, 275, 306
Chödron, Pema, 183
choices, 270, 271–72, 282, 283, 298
    daily, 273
Clinton, Hillary, 117
codependency, 210–11
Codependent No More (Beattie), 8
coincidences, 201, 263
Colette, 250
comforting yourself, 21, 23
community(ies), 284, 286
    WE, 330–31
comparison, 154–55, 158, 162–65, 180, 282
    social media and, 162–63
compassion, 155, 164–65, 179, 214, 218, 277, 291, 297
    acting from ego vs., 279–80
    "enemy's shoes" exercise, 218–20
competition, 154–55, 158, 162, 163–64, 179, 180, 225
complaining, 163–64, 277
connection, 164–65, 260–61, 284
conscious living, 194–96
Conscious Uncoupling: 5 Steps to Living Happily Even After (Thomas), 233
Constructive *C*s, 164–65, 177
consumer purchases, 271
control, 158, 163–64
    illusion of, 140
cooperation, 155, 164–65, 179
cortisol, 140
courage, 109–33
    releasing anger, 116–19
    releasing resentment, 121–31
    and seeking help, 120
    stories and, 110–16, 122
    in wider world, 131–32
Cox, Laverne, 222
creativity, 246–48
    artist's life exercise, 250–51
crime, 173–75
criticizing, 163–65
Curie, Marie, 156
C words:
    Constructive, 164–65, 177
    Toxic, 163–65, 177

D

daily miracles, 6–8, 196
dating, 222–25
    drawing up a partner spec, 223–24
    Golden Rule for, 225

INDEX

historical baggage and, 222–23
De Angelis, Barbara, 109
de Beauvoir, Simone, 67
decisions, 199
    see also choices
DeGeneres, Ellen, 45
depression, 119, 120, 123, 211, 243, 277
    clinical, 120
de Staël, Madame, 300
Dickinson, Emily, 280
Didion, Joan, 82
difficulty, transforming, 202
divine, 257–58
    see also spirituality
doing vs. thinking, 51–52
drama, 84, 93, 101, 107, 206

E

Earhart, Amelia, 136
Earth, 178–79, 291
Eat Pray Love (Gilbert), 64
economic inequality, 298
economic systems, 300–301, 303, 305
    GDP, 300, 302
Edelman, Marian Wright, 275, 306
ego, 50, 115, 157–80, 186, 264, 268
    acting from compassion vs., 279–80
    comparison and, 162–63
    as Edging Goodness Out, 158–59
    forgiveness and, 170–72
    intellectual stimulation and, 170
    kind actions and, 276, 278–80, 285
    love and, 209, 211–12
    rightsizing and, 176–78
    spiritual gym exercise, 166–69
    thinking and, 159–61
    Toxic Cs and, 163–65, 177
    uncertainty and, 200
Emma (Austen), 70
emotional archaeology, 172–73
emotions, 64, 74–75, 76, 97, 123, 131–32, 197,
    202, 203
    acceptance of, 83–86, 92–102
    anger, see anger
    avoidance of, 92–94, 97, 149, 186
    fear, see fear
    feeling and releasing, 97–99, 197
    grief, 96
    HALT and, 25–26
    love as action vs., 209
    noticing and naming, 70–72, 74, 91–92, 97,
        99, 101, 117–18, 197
    overwhelming, instant relief from, 216–17
    releasing past hurts, 172–73
    resentment, see resentment
    shaking to release, 102
    synthetic pain, 94–96, 122, 297
    thoughts and, 101, 159–60

empathy, 234–35
endurance, 104
"enemy's shoes" exercise, 218–20
Ensler, Eve, 108
enthusiasm, 254
Ephron, Nora, 133
equality:
    economic, 298
    for women, 62, 301–6
Essential Practices, 1–47, 74, 177–78, 211
    about, 2–4
    Four Essentials to self-care, 26–31, 177–78
    gentleness, 13–20
    gratitude, see gratitude
    meditation, see meditation
    responsibility (self-care), see self-care
    exercise, physical, 28–29, 177
    yoga, 324–26
exercises, 3–4, 52
    Acceptance Cup, 86–88
    artist's life, 250–51
    befriending yourself, 22–23
    centering yourself before, 4
    daily choices, 273
    daily miracles, 6–8
    discarding ideas about yourself, 65–67
    drawing up a partner spec, 223–24
    emotional archaeology, 172–73
    enemy's shoes, 218–20
    feeling and releasing emotions, 98–99
    finding your cause, 284–85
    gaining perspective, 269
    identifying and rewriting stories, 111–14
    identifying buried truths, 73–74
    inner circle, 190–91
    internal landscape, 183
    joy in practice, 252–54
    living proof of positive outcomes, 137, 201
    magic listening, 233–34
    meditation, 41–43, 187–88; see also
        meditation
    money matters, 281–82
    moving from fear to trust, 151–53
    mundane tasks, 194–95
    new script, 16–18
    reconnecting with your authentic self, 57–59
    releasing toxicity, 125–29
    reprogramming fear-based response system,
        142–43
    spiritual gym, 166–69
expectations, 130

F

"faking" new behaviors, 150
Fane, Sarah, 79
fear, 14, 64, 65, 135–56, 158, 192, 297
    acronym for, 139, 145
    as avoidance, 149

355

fear *(continued)*
  biological function of, 139, 140
  body-mind connection and, 140–41
  choosing trust over, 136, 141, 143, 155
  inner girl and, 144
  mind map and, 142–43, 146
  moving from fear to trust, exercise for, 151–53
  new direction and, 143–44
  reprogramming exercise for, 142–43
  self-fulfilling, 141
  Three-Second Rule and, 144
  trusting in opposite of, 145–46
  uncertainty and, 200
  unmasking, 138–41
  what-ifs and, 148
feelings, *see* emotions
Feminine Mystique, The (Friedan), 60
fight-or-flight response, 140
flow, 247
focus, 141, 178
  living in the present, 174–76
food, 26–28, 177, 299, 307
Ford, Debbie, 85, 106
forgiveness, 170–72
Forgiveness Project, 171
Four Essentials, 26–31, 177–78
Frank, Anne, 270
Friedan, Betty, 60
friendships, 212, 221, 254
  ending, 239
  see also relationships
Furstenberg, Diane von, 37

G
gadgets, 186
Gannon, Sharon, 324
Gbower, Leymah, 135
GDP, 300, 302
genetic inheritance, 65
gentleness, 13–20
  new script, 16–18
Gilbert, Elizabeth, 64
giving, 270, 278–84
  to charities, 282–83
  resources for, 324
goal pursuit, 159, 165, 268
God, 257–58
  reaction against, 258
  see also spirituality
Golden Rule, xviii, 255
  for dating, 225
good and bad, fable about, 193–94
gossip, 213
government, *see* politics and government
gratitude, 5–11, 40, 195, 235, 262, 263, 289
  for body, 32
  daily miracles, 6–8, 196
grief, 96

gross domestic product (GDP), 300, 302
group solidarity, 240
guilt, 213, 275, 281

H
habits, 146–47
  "faking" a new behavior, 150
HALT, 25–26
happiness, 243, 263, 300
  flow and, 247
  kindness and, 277
  wealth vs., 300
  see also joy
Herbert, Anne, 274
Hillesum, Etty, 203
honesty, 122
  acceptance and, 91
  in relationships, 225–26
  about self, *see* self
  in wider world, 79–81
hormones, 33–36
  stress, 140
Huffington, Arianna, 202
Huffington Post, 202
hugging, 236
human, being, 203
humility, 157–80
  Constructive *C*s and, 164–65, 177
  forgiveness and, 170–72
  and living in the present, 174–76
  rightsizing and, 176–78
  spiritual gym exercise, 166–69
  in wider world, 178–79
hunger, 299, 307

I
Iceland, 302–3
imperfections, 227
indecision, 199
infatuation, 230–31
inner circle, 190–91
inner girl, 75–77, 216
  fear and, 144
inner knowing, 285
inner light, 244
inner voice, 199
inspiration, 254
intellectual stimulation, 170
internal landscape, 183
intimacy dance, 232

J
jails, 173–74
Japan, 304
Jeffers, Susan, 14
joining, 270, 284–88
Jong, Erica, 103
joy, 41, 243–65
  activism and, 264

artist's life exercise, 250–51
availability of, 245
boundaries and, 255
creating space for, 252–56
creativity and, 246–48
flow and, 247
in nature and beauty, 249–50
necessity of, 243, 244–45
in practice, 252–54
in wider world, 243, 264–65
judgement, 212, 240, 291, 297
"enemy's shoes" exercise, 218–20

K
Kacungira, Nancy, 161
Katie, Byron, 225
Keller, Helen, 242
Kidd, Sue Monk, 55
Kilpatrick, Martha, 157
kindness, 264, 267–90, 291, 299
acting, 270, 274–77
choosing, 270, 271–72, 282, 283
ego and, 276, 278–80, 285
finding your cause, 284–85
giving, see giving
happiness and, 277
joining, 270, 284–88
in wider world, 288–89
King, Coretta Scott, 297
Kingma, Daphne Rose, 116
Klein, Naomi, xv
knowing, 192
inner, 285
what's good and bad, 193–94
Koirala, Anuradha, 284
Kübler-Ross, Elisabeth, 181

L
Labdrön, Machig, 159
labiaplasty, 63
Lamott, Anne, 265
Landers, Ann, 123
Latifah, 21
*Law of Attraction Plain and Simple, The: Create the
    Extraordinary Life That You Deserve* (Ricotti),
    189
legal rights and protections, 62, 238
light, stepping into, 89–90
Linn, Denise, 154
listening, 233–34
living in the present, 174–76
Lorde, Audre, 24
love, 14, 24, 207–42
appreciation and, 235
and choosing to be single, 221
codependency and, 210–11
dating, see dating
ego and, 209, 211–12
as feeling vs. action, 209

Golden Rule and, xviii
how you view and treat others, 212–13
infatuation vs., 230–31
infinite supply of, 209, 239–40
key to, 208–10
kindness and, see kindness
listening and, 233–34
receiving too little or too much, in childhood,
    214–15
romantic, 208, 220
romantic, three stages of, 231–32
search for, 208–9, 220
self and, 210–12
sexual, 228–29
template for, 214–16, 231, 237
unconditional, 209
understanding and, 217–20
in wider world, 240–41
see also relationships
Lucas, Caroline, 290
luck, 282, 289

M
Maathai, Wangari, 322
Macpherson, Miranda, 158
magic listening, 233–34
magic multiplying effect, 9, 18, 129, 155, 209, 277
Ma Jaya Sati Bhagavati, 327
manifesto, 293–95
mantra meditation, 187–88
marriage, 222–23
legal protections and, 238
masturbation, 229–30
maternity leave, 302
Mead, Margaret, 294
meaning, 267–68
gaining perspective, 269
Meat-Free Monday, 286–87
meditation, 39–45, 77, 182, 184–85, 186–87,
    201–5, 285
benefits of, 183–84, 190
daily practice of, 41–43
deepening practice of, 185, 189–90, 203
mantra, 187–88
methods for, 186–87
place for, 43
prayer and, 262
resources for, 327–28
time for, 185, 189–90
menopause, 34
resources for, 324
menstruation, 33–34
messages we get from others, 60–61, 64
discarding ideas about yourself, 65–67
messages we give ourselves:
changing, 13–20
negative, 13–18, 31
new script exercise, 16–18
stories, 110–16, 122

Meyer, Joyce, 14
mind:
 detox for, 191–92
 as garden, 146
 internal landscape and, 183
 peace of, *see* peace
 see also thoughts, thinking
mindful living, 194–96
miracles, 136
 daily, 6–8, 196
money:
 giving, 281–84
 keeping track of spending, 281–82
monkey trap, 124
Montgomery, L. M., 260
Morrison, Toni, 121
Mother Teresa, 13
movement:
 exercise, 28–29, 177
 shaking, 102
 thoughts and, 198
 yoga, 324–26
multiplying effect, 9, 18, 129, 155, 209, 277
mundane tasks, 194–95
Murdoch, Iris, 249
Murphy, Carmel, 197

N

naming, *see* noticing and naming
nature and beauty, 249–50
neediness, 214–15, 221
needs, ignoring, 22
negative thoughts, 13–18
 about body, 13, 31
 new script exercise, 16–18
Nin, Anaïs, 110
9 Principles, *see* Principles
no and yes, saying, 255
nocebo effect, 16
No-Harm Rule, 228–29
Norman, Mildred Lisette, 39
Northrup, Christiane, 301
noticing and naming:
 of actions, 275
 of emotions, 70–72, 74, 91–92, 97, 99, 101,
  117–18, 197
Novogratz, Jacqueline, 271
Nyirumbe, Sister Rosemary, 307

O

Obama, Michelle, xix
obsessive thinking, 95–96
Oliver, Mary, vii
Ono, Yoko, 2

P

Palmo, Jetsunma Tenzin, 204
Pankhurst, Christabel, xiii

parental leave, 302
Parks, Rosa, 131
past, 88–89, 124, 131
 emotional archaeology exercise, 172–73
pausing, 197, 202, 205
 indecision and, 199
 uncertainty and, 200
peace, 40–41, 161, 181–206
 inner circle and, 190–91
 internal landscape and, 183
 and living consciously and mindfully, 194–96
 meditation and, *see* meditation
 pausing and, *see* pausing
 thinking and, 182–83
 in wider world, 204–5
Peace Pilgrim, 39
people-pleasing, 72, 82
perfectionism, 53, 166, 227
 action and, 286–87
persistence, 166
perspective, gaining, 269
physical activity, 28–29
 thoughts and, 198
placebo effect, 16
plastic water bottles, 272
politics and government, xvii, 297, 301, 306–7
 see also activism
pornography, 63
poverty, 298
practice, 166
prayer, 41, 261
 answering of, 261–62
 meditation and, 262
 for someone else, 171
present, living in, 174–76
Principles, xiii, xvii–xviii, xx, xxii, 2–4, 49–291,
  310–11
 about, 50–54
 commitment to, 53–54
 egoic traits and, 169
 manifesto and, 294
 order and process of following, 51
 see also acceptance; courage; honesty;
  humility; joy; kindness; love; peace; trust
prisons, 173–74
progress vs. perfection, 286–87

Q

Queen Latifah, 21
*Quiet: The Power of Introverts in a World That Can't
  Stop Talking* (Cain), 182
Quindlen, Anna, 164

R

Radmacher, Mary Anne, 286
Raitt, Bonnie, 328
realistic, being, 22
reality, accepting, 91–92

relationships, 203, 207–42
  appreciation in, 235
  childhood and, 214–16, 231, 237
  codependency and, 210–11
  dating, *see* dating
  ego and, 209
  empathy in, 234–35
  friendships, 212, 221, 254
  harmful, 211, 237–39; *see also* abuse
  honesty in, 225–26
  intimacy dance in, 232
  leaving, 238–39
  listening in, 233–34
  power struggle in, 231–32
  template for, 214–16, 231, 237
  see also love
religion, 257–59, 298, 328–30
  see also spirituality
resentment, 116, 117, 131, 132, 170, 211, 297
  anger and, 121, 123
  expectations and, 130
  releasing, 121–31
  spiritual surgery for, 125–30
resources, 313–31
responsibility:
  accepting, 90–91
  for mental well-being, 205
  for self-care, *see* self-care
  trust and, 148–49
rest, 29–30, 177
  day of, 191–92
Return to Love, A (Williamson), 11
Ricotti, Sonia, 189
right, being, 124, 132, 161, 170
rights, legal, 62
rightsizing, 176–78
risk assessment, 149
Robinson, Shivon, 248
Roddick, Anita, 288
Roosevelt, Eleanor, 268
Runbeck, Margaret Lee, 257

S
sacred, 39–40
safety, 39, 57, 58, 203
  ego and, 158
  worry and, 139
Salbi, Zainab, xxiii
Salzberg, Sharon, 41
Satrapi, Marjane, 138
Schaef, Anne Wilson, 313
Schlaffer, Edit, 50
Schutz, Susan Polis, 243
script, new, 16–18
Secret Life of Bees, The (Kidd), 55
self, 55–82
  authentic, reconnecting with, 57–59
  discarding ideas about yourself, 65–67

finding, 67–70
  identifying buried truths, 73–74
  inner girl, 75–77
  losing, 56–57
  loving and, 210–11
  noticing and naming and, 70–72, 74
  people-pleasing and, 72, 82
  physical, *see* body
  stories and, 110–16, 122
  subpersonalities in, 58–59
  trusting process of, 78–79
self-blame, 160, 161, 213
self-care, 2–3, 21–37, 74–75
  appreciation, 30–31, 178
  beauty and, 26, 32–33
  befriending yourself, 22–23
  exercise, 28–29, 177
  food, 26–28, 177
  Four Essentials to, 26–31, 177–78
  rest, 29–30, 177
self-esteem, 139, 177, 238, 275
selflessness, 211
Serenity Prayer, 85, 103, 279
Seventh-day Adventist Church, 232
sex, 228–29
  masturbation, 229–30
  No-Harm Rule and, 228–29
shaking, 102
shame, 213
singing, 248
single by choice, 221
sleep, 29–30
social media, 60–61, 162–63, 185, 186
Solle, Dorothee, 278
spending, keeping track of, 281–82
spiritual gym, 166–69
spiritual hunger, 255–56
spirituality, xvii, 257, 328–30
  open mind about, 262–63
spiritual surgery, 125–30
spiritual truth, 145, 165, 259
Steinem, Gloria, 305
stories, 110–16, 122, 170
  identifying and rewriting, 111–14
Strayer, Cheryl, 83
stress, 102, 140
Substitution Rule, 146–47
support, 75, 119, 120
surrender, 84–88
  see also acceptance
Suu Kyi, Aung San, 267
synchronicity, 201

T
Teresa of Ávila, Saint, 178
Teresa of Calcutta, Saint, 13
Tharpe, Sister Rosetta, 245
therapy, resources for, 317–19

Thomas, Katherine Woodward, 233
thoughts, thinking:
    attack, 160–61, 200
    doing vs., 51–52
    ego and, 159–61
    emotions and, 101, 159–60
    fearful, *see* fear
    intellectual stimulation and, 170
    internal landscape and, 183
    knowing and, 192
    meditation and, 40, 42
    movement and, 198
    negative, substituting with positive, 147
    negative bias in, 160
    obsessive, 95–96
    about past and future, 174–76
    peace and, 182–83
    self-blame, 160, 161, 213
    Three-Second Rule and, 144, 160–61, 176
    see also messages we give ourselves
Three-Second Rule, 144, 160–61, 176
time, how you spend, 185
Toxic Cs, 163–65, 177
toxicity, releasing, 125–29
Trafford, Kate, 238
trauma:
    inheritance of, 65
    resources for, 316–17
trust, 135–56, 263
    acronym for, 145, 165
    choosing, over fear, 136, 141, 143, 155
    inner girl and, 144
    living proof of positive outcomes, 137, 201
    mind map and, 142–43, 146
    moving from fear to trust, exercise for, 151–53
    new direction and, 143–44
    in opposite of what you fear, 145–46
    reprogramming exercise for, 142–43
    resistance to, 149–50
    responsibility and, 148–49
    uncertainty and, 200
    in wider world, 154–55
truth, 115, 233, 258
    buried, identifying, 73–74
    empathy and, 234–35
    spiritual, 145, 165, 259
    telling, 79–81
    see also honesty

U
uncertainty, 200
Underhill, Evelyn, 246
understanding, 217–20
    empathy, 234–35
United Nations, 300, 301, 307
University of California, 184, 277

V
Vagina Monologues, The (Ensler), 108
values, 165
Vangole⌐, Moni, 262
vengeance, 170, 171
victims, 84, 97, 106, 110, 121, 124, 127–29, 149, 211
Viorst, Judith, 56
von Furstenberg, Diane, 37

W
wabi-sabi, 304
Walker, Alice, 8
water bottles, 272
Watson, Emma, 271
wealth, 298, 300
WE communities, 330–31
weight, 26, 27, 29
Weil, Simone, xvii
what-ifs, 148
White, Ellen G., 232
Whitman, Joy, 239
Wild (Strayer), 83
Williams, Serena, 176
Williamson, Marianne, 11
Winfrey, Oprah, 184
Winterson, Jeanette, 92
wishing the best for someone, 171
Wolf, Naomi, 32
women:
    equality for, 62, 301–6
    new paradigm and, 305–6
    work of, 301–3, 305
women's organizations, 319–21
Women Without Borders, 50
Woolf, Virginia, 308
Work, The, 225
working women, 301–3, 305
world issues, 297–308
    resources for, 322–23
worry, 139
    see also fear

X
Xue Xinran, 92

Y
yes and no, saying, 255
yoga, 324–26
Yousafzai, Malala, 303